D1203370

To Margy, Carolyn, Fethi and Turkan

EXPECTATION

WINTHROP PUBLISHERS, INC. *Cambridge, Massachusetts*

STATES THEORY

A THEORETICAL
RESEARCH PROGRAM

EDITED BY

JOSEPH BERGER
Stanford University

THOMAS L. CONNER
Michigan State University

M. HAMIT FISEK
Hacettepe University
Ankara, Turkey

Library of Congress Cataloging in Publication Data

Berger, Joseph.
    Expectation states theory.

    Bibliography: p.
    1. Social psychology—Research. 2. Expectation (Psychology) I.
Conner, Thomas L. joint author. II. Fisek, M. Hamit. joint author. III.
Title.
HM251.B455   301.1′01′8   73–4667
ISBN 0–87626–253–1

Copyright © 1974 by Winthrop Publishers, Inc.
    17 Dunster Street, Cambridge, Massachusetts 02138

All rights reserved. No part of this book may be reproduced in any form or
by any means without permission in writing from the publisher. Printed in
the United States of America. Current printing (last number): 10 9 8 7 6
5 4 3 2 1.

Contents

PART ONE 1

THE RESEARCH PROGRAM

Chapter One 3

Expectation States Theory:
A Theoretical Research Program,
Joseph Berger

PART TWO 23

THE DEVELOPMENT OF POWER AND PRESTIGE
ORDERS IN TASK-ORIENTED GROUPS
INTRODUCTION 24

Chapter Two 27

Evaluations and the Formation and Maintenance of
Performance Expectations,
Joseph Berger, Thomas L. Conner, and William L. McKeown

Chapter Three 53

A Model for the Evolution of Status Structures
in Task-Oriented Discussion Groups,
M. Hamit Fisek

Chapter Four 85

Performance Expectations and Behavior in Small Groups:
A Revised Formulation,
Joseph Berger and Thomas L. Conner

PART THREE 111

SOURCES OF EVALUATION AND SOCIAL INTERACTION
INTRODUCTION 112

v

Chapter Five   115

Sources of Evaluations and Expectation States,
Murray Webster, Jr. and Barbara I. Sobieszek

PART FOUR   159

STATUS CHARACTERISTICS AND SOCIAL INTERACTION
INTRODUCTION   160

Chapter Six   163

A Generalization of the Status Characteristics
and Expectation States Theory,
Joseph Berger and M. Hamit Fisek

PART FIVE   207

APPLICATIONS OF EXPECTATION STATES THEORY
INTRODUCTION   208

Chapter Seven   211

Raising Children's Expectations for Their Own
Performance: A Classroom Application,
Murray Webster, Jr. and Doris R. Entwisle

Appendix: A Bibliography of Expectation States
Research   244

Preface

This book is a collection of seven papers that are all part of a single research program on Expectation States Theory. Research dealing with four of the principal problem areas in the program is represented here and the papers themselves range from reports of the results of experiments to extensive theoretical statements. Part one traces the history of the research, presents an overview of the kinds of problems that have been dealt with, and an analysis of the structure of the program. Parts two, three, and four contain theory and research relevant to particular problem areas while part five describes an application of Expectation States Theory to an important natural social situation—the classroom.

It is difficult in a book with such closely related papers from many different authors to eliminate overlap and repetition. We decided not to try. The result is that each paper can be read in isolation if the reader desires. However, we felt that some suggestions about use of the book for students and instructors would be helpful. Reading any of chapters two through seven will be greatly assisted by reading chapter one first. Chapter four contains detailed presentations of many of the concepts, ideas, and assertions that are assumed or only briefly mentioned in other chapters. So, at least a quick or cursory reading of chapter four may serve as background for the remaining chapters. Also, the applications research presented in chapter seven is closely tied to the theoretical formulation developed in chapter five; therefore, a reading of chapter five prior to the chapter on applications may be of value. Diagrammatically, then, we recommend the following order:

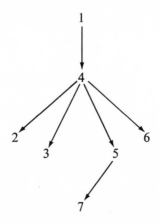

However, we reiterate that given a reading of chapter one, any of the remaining chapters may be read and used independently.

From the early 1960s the research on Expectation States Theory has been a collaborative effort. It has involved a large number of colleagues, professional associates, and students. Many of these students quickly assumed the role of colleagues and have gone on to make major contributions to this work. Among the colleagues and associates to whom we would particularly like to express our indebtedness, and whose own contributions are described in various places throughout this volume, are: Morris Zelditch, Jr., Bernard P. Cohen, S. Frank Camilleri, Robert Z. Norman, and Bo Anderson. We would also like to express a very particular indebtedness to J. Laurie Snell of Dartmouth College. Snell has been involved in different aspects of expectation states research from its very earliest days. He has been both a patient teacher and colleague, working with us especially on those aspects of expectation states research that have involved model-building activities.

Part One

THE RESEARCH PROGRAM

CHAPTER ONE

Expectation States Theory:
A Theoretical Research Program*

JOSEPH BERGER

I. INTRODUCTION

This book is a collection of papers by seven sociologists reporting on their research in Expectation States Theory. Expectation States Theory is a "theoretical research program."[1] As such it is a more complex theoretical structure than that typically designated by the phrase "a theory." As a theoretical research program it consists of a set of theories, bodies of empirical research, and a set of applied research activities.

*Research for this chapter was supported in part by a grant from the National Science Foundation (GS 34182). I would particularly like to acknowledge the comments and suggestions that were made on an earlier version of this paper by Murray Webster and Thomas L. Conner.

[1] The term "theoretical research program" has been adopted from Lakatos (1968, 1970). In addition, we have used a number of concepts that Lakatos introduced to analyze the structure of such programs. We have freely interpreted and adapted the use of these concepts in the analysis of the present program; therefore, we make no claim that our analysis corresponds in strict sense to the types of analysis Lakatos has made of such research programs.

Clearly not every combination of these elements constitutes a theoretical research program: more is required. First, the empirical research should be *relevant* to the specific theories in the set. "Relevant" is used in the obvious sense that the research is either the basis for a specific theory or it represents direct tests, refinements, or extensions of a theory. Second, the set of applied research activities should be *grounded* in the theories of the program. "Grounded" is to be understood in the sense that the applied research makes explicit use of the concepts, assertions, and techniques that are part of one or more of the specific theories in the program. And third, the specific theories in the program, in some fundamental manner, should be *interrelated*. Unfortunately, there is no obvious sense to this important requirement. On a descriptive level one can say that this refers to the fact that the theories in a particular research program are interrelated by the historical process of their development: that one can show that some later theory was "based upon" or "influenced by" an earlier theoretical formulation. In section II of this chapter, "On History," we shall briefly sketch how the research presented here (as well as some not presented) is interrelated in this "historical sense." But in the final analysis, such a demonstration of historical interrelation is rarely (if ever) fully satisfactory. This is particularly true given the difficulties in applying such terms as "based upon," and "influenced by." Again, more is required; and we claim that more is true. The specific theories in this program are interrelated in an "anatomical sense": the theoretical and applied research has, in general, been guided by a common set of meta-theoretical principles. The various parts of this research can also be shown to have commonalities as well as important differences with respect to the theoretical concepts and assertions they employ; and finally, it can be shown that the development of this research has involved, for the most part, although not exclusively, a common set of observational techniques and experimental settings. "Interrelation" in these terms will be discussed in the section "On Anatomy."

Studies in this volume are concerned with: The development of power and prestige orders in task-oriented groups (part two); the effect of status-characteristics in organizing social interaction (part four); the effect of sources of evaluations (significant others) in determining the individual's behavior in interpersonal situations (part three); and attempts to affect the modification of behavior in actual on-going social situations (part five). What are the substantive problems of this research? How are the parts of this research program interrelated in an "historical," and, more importantly, an "anatomical" sense?

II. ON HISTORY

To try to trace the development of this set of interrelated theoretical formulations, with their bodies of relevant research, is a difficult task, one that is subject to well-known pitfalls, as well as to a number of difficulties specific to this particular case. Such a history is invariably distorted because it is written from the perspective of the present. Theoretical "dead-ends" tend to be forgotten or minimized, while theoretical "payoffs" are overemphasized and often their original significance is lost sight of or distorted. A more rational picture of the evolution process emerges than reflects reality. This is particularly true with respect to the early stages of the process, where so much activity involved "groping" and "playing" with theoretical alternatives. This is probably less true of the later stages of the process, when existing formulations, concepts, techniques, and known empirical results facilitated the recognition of unsolved problems and provided guides to, as well as constraints upon, the next research moves. In tracing the development of the program, a special problem arises from the fact that, since the early 1960s, it has been a collaborative effort. Theoretical and experimental ideas appeared first as memos and draft manuscripts, and in this form they were circulated and served as a basis for discussions and the continual exchange of ideas among colleagues and students. Some of these papers were eventually "elevated" to technical reports. As technical reports they again served as the basis for further discussions and exchange of ideas. Often these reports underwent two or three revisions (sometimes over a period of several years) and some of them were eventually published. Thus many of the memos, draft manuscripts, and unpublished technical reports that are important to understanding the development of the program probably never will be published, having been superseded by more "fruitful" formulations and approaches. This situation probably is not unusual for this type of enterprise, but it complicates the task of tracing the various lines of development of the theoretical ideas.

The brief historical sketch presented here is subject to all the difficulties of reconstruction both general and specific to this type of enterprise. Thus, the term *sketch* is to be taken seriously. We neither attempt nor make any claim for completeness. We intend to list some of the major theoretical formulations that evolved, along with the "lines of influence" that can be traced from one formulation to a second formulation.

A. THE DEVELOPMENT OF POWER AND PRESTIGE ORDERS IN TASK-ORIENTED GROUPS

The original set of problems that led to an initial formulation of Expectation States Theories concerned itself with explaining the emergence of hierarchies in informal task-oriented groups. In particular, Bales had found that marked inequalities "emerged" in such groups in relatively short periods of time. What impressed this writer most about the results of Bales' research was that, in general, the various aspects of the group's hierarchical structure tended to be directly related to each other: rank positions on such "components" as rates of talking, rates of receiving, and rank positions on evaluations of best ideas and guidance. The initial theoretical problem, as it came to be formulated, was essentially the following: Given the members of newly formed task-oriented groups, who are alike with respect to major status characteristics (sex, age, educational position), how can we explain the emergence of a differentiated hierarchy, and, in particular, how can we explain the fact that the components of that hierarchy tended to be interrelated?[2] Briefly, the answer given was: Out of the interaction process in these groups, individuals developed high and low self-conceptions (of their performance capacities) at the same time that others developed high and low performance-conceptions for them. Furthermore, given the structure of an "idealized interaction process," these underlying conceptions normally tended to be congruent with each other. Thus as A's self-conceptions were raised (or lowered) the likelihood that he would perform would increase (or decrease), and since B's conception of A was changing in a consistent manner, the likelihood that he would give A chances to perform and would react to A's performance with positive and negative evaluations would also increase or decrease as a function of his changing conception of A. Thus it was reasoned that under the conditions of the "idealized interaction process," rank positions of received action opportunities and received rewards would each tend to coincide with rank positions on overall performance evaluations, and the latter would coincide with the ranked positions of initiated problem-solving behavior. Further, it was argued that the magnitude of the ordering interrelations would be greater in task groups that emphasized "task concerns" as compared to task groups that emphasized "process concerns" (Berger, 1958).[3] The gaps in this argument, and particularly those involved in making derivations from this argument were many indeed. However, what is of interest to us from the present perspective is that certain ideas and concepts that have been continually worked and reworked were already introduced in this initial formulation. First, the idea of explaining the characteristics of the group's hierarchy in terms of an *underlying* process (involving performance evaluations) by which stabilized performance expectations are formed; and second, the initial introduction of some of the concepts that have eventually become part of our conception of *the observable power and prestige order*: socially distributed

---

[2]It was assumed that, given a general theory that could account for the fact that the components of the group's hierarchy tended to be interrelated, one could use such a theory also to explain (in terms of special conditions) the fact that the magnitude of these interrelations would also differ in high- as compared to low-status consensus groups (a fact that Bales and his students had repeatedly observed [see Heinicke and Bales, 1953; Slater, 1955]). Further, it was believed that the fact that, under certain conditions, measures of popularity ("who do you like most") were not highly correlated with other aspects of the group's hierarchy (see Bales, 1953) was a distinct and separate theoretical problem, and no attempt was made to deal with it.

[3]In fact, the actual terminology used here in describing the answer to this initial theoretical problem underwent some changes during the period from 1958 to 1960.

chances to perform (action opportunities), problem-solving behavior (performance outputs), and communicated evaluations (positive and negative reactions).

The nature of the second theoretical formulation in this problem area was strongly influenced by the author's joint research with J. Laurie Snell. The formulation involved constructing a stochastic model that enabled the theorist to describe the action process by which the hierarchy in task-oriented two-man groups emerges and is maintained. The result was a finite-state, discrete-time Markov chain model (Berger, 1960). The states of this model were action cycles, which were sequences of behavior such as: A gives B an action opportunity, B makes a performance output to A, A positively (or negatively) evaluates this performance output. These cycles were distinguished in terms of whether or not they led to changes in the self-other performance expectations of the members of the group, and, if they did lead to changes, the cycles were distinguished according to the type of changes involved. Further, it was assumed that the transition probabilities (the probabilities of moving from one action cycle type to a second) were a function of the self-other performance expectations each of the members of the group held at the outset of their interaction. In the truest sense of that term, this was a representational model (see Berger et al., 1962).

As it turned out, the action cycle model was never subjected to empirical test.[4] Before research on this model could be undertaken, a second model was constructed that "simply seemed to be more promising" (Berger and Snell, 1961). The second formulation was also a finite-state, discrete-time model. However, its appeal rested on three substantive considerations. First, the *states* of the model were self-other performance expectation states: high self–low other; low self–high other; high self–high other; low self–low other. Second, the model enabled us to describe for the first time the way in which one of the components of observable interaction could be treated as a *probabilistic function* of the underlying expectation states. In so doing, expectation states became conceptualized, in a rigorous sense, as *theoretical constructs*. Therefore, once an interaction process evolved, inferences about the existence or change of expectation states could be made only on the basis of conditions or behavior that was postulated to lead to specific states, or behavior that was postulated to be consequences of these states.[5] Third, the model provided for

---

[4]However, the idea of action cycles, in considerably revised form, was incorporated in a general formulation of expectation states theory that was subsequently developed with respect to this problem area (see Berger and Conner, 1966, 1969, and chapter four of this volume).

[5]Although by experimental manipulation or assumption one might attempt to assign (as in fact we have done) an individual to a specific state at the *outset* of an interaction process, conceptualizing expectation states in these terms as theoretical constructs means two things: (1) that no theoretical assumptions are being made as to the relation of a specific expectation

the reintroduction of *unit evaluations* (more precisely, *differential* unit evaluations) as a mechanism in the study of expectation state processes. In short, this formulation involved constructing a rigorous theoretical and mathematical version of some of the basic ideas in our initial formulation.

On the most general level, the second model was concerned with the processes of expectation *changes* and expectation *maintenance*. From the present perspective, the detailed theoretical arguments embodied in this model are not of major interest. However, in terms of more general considerations, this particular model had, and still has, consequences of considerable importance to our theoretical research program. First, it involved the conceptualizing of an experimental setting that became the standardized experimental situation employed in much of the research in this program.[6] Second, it led to the construction of *variant* models, such as that developed by Berger and Zelditch (1962) to describe the relations of expectation states to formal authority structures.[7] And third, it led to developing models to describe, in similar terms, the *emergence* and *maintenance* of expectation states (see Conner, 1965; and Berger, Conner, and McKeown, chapter two, this volume).[8]

The research up to this point, aside from the initial general theoretical formulation, had consisted primarily of developing and testing different mathematical models dealing with the emergence, maintenance, and change of performance expectation states under specific interaction conditions. Sometime during the early 1960s the author, in collaboration with Thomas Conner, decided to pull together this theoretical and empirical research and construct a second *general* formulation of how expectations are formed and how they operate to determine behavior in task-oriented groups. This formulation was eventually issued as a technical report (Berger and Conner, 1966), and in time

---

state that emerges or changes *during* the interaction and the individual's cognitions about that state, and (2) therefore, an individual's verbalizable constructions about his cognitions cannot be used to infer what states may have emerged or changed during the course of the process. This mode of theorizing about expectation states, which was first developed in the Berger-Snell 1961 model, has also been employed in subsequent models (particularly Conner, 1965; Berger, Conner, and McKeown, chapter two; and Fisek, chapter three).

[6] On a practical level it led to the design and development of the Interaction-Control Machine (ICOM) (see Webster, 1967). The actual design and construction of the original ICOM was done by Robert Z. Muzzey.

[7] This particular research also drew upon long-standing research interests of Zelditch that were concerned with the conditions under which formalized authority relations are maintained or eroded. In effect, it involved constructing an expectation states change and maintenance model for the process described and investigated in the Evan-Zelditch experiment (see Evan and Zelditch, 1961). For a general and recent statement of this theoretical problem, see Zelditch (1972).

[8] This model has also served as a conceptual basis for the more recent development of an alternative set of theoretical formulations by Martha Foschi and her students (see Foschi, 1969, 1971) who are concerned with refining our understanding of the processes involved in expectation state changes.

was published in *Acta Sociologica* (Berger and Conner, 1969). Subsequent to this second general formulation, in fact, if not in publication chronology, came the two- and three-man group experiments by Conner (1965), and by Berger, Conner, and McKeown (1969); and the theoretical and empirical research by Fisek (1969) on the emergence of power and prestige orders in three-man groups. In part, as a result of this latter research and further theoretical work, a *revised* version of the second general formulation was developed by Berger and Conner. These most recent process formulations by Berger, Conner, and McKeown, and Fisek, and this revised general formulation by Berger and Conner, are presented in part two of this volume.

B. STATUS CHARACTERISTICS AND SOCIAL INTERACTION

It is an interesting feature of the development of theoretical research programs that they are marked, in relatively short periods of time, by the appearance of theoretical variants, both within single problem areas, and across problem areas.[9]

While theoretical and experimental work was taking place on the problem of power and prestige orders in small task-oriented groups, it became clear to us that a theory concerned with the formation and maintenance of expectation states could be applied to a wide range of "classical" sociological problems.

Early in the 1960s, B. P. Cohen, M. Zelditch, Jr., and the author started to work seriously on one of these problems: The effect of status characteristic differences on social interaction. Sociologists had long been concerned with the effect of status characteristics upon the behavior of individuals in face-to-face interaction situations. Further, an extensive body of literature existed on this problem that demonstrated that such status characteristics as age, sex, race, occupational class, had marked effects in determining the behavior of individuals in a wide variety of small group situations. Research on this problem drew on prior work by Cohen on reference group theory (see Cohen, 1962), on research interests that Zelditch and the author had in the general problem of status crystallization, and on research interests that we all, by this time, shared in the problem of how expectation states are formed and maintained. Our original theoretical work on the problem started in 1963, but went through a long series of formulations involving continual revisions, subsequent elaborations, and, eventually, extensive simplifications. Our theoretical results were originally issued as a technical report (Berger, Cohen, and Zelditch, 1965) and published as the theory of "Status Characteristics and Expectation States" (Berger, Cohen, and Zelditch, 1966). The experimental

---

[9]Consider, for example, the proliferation of Balance Theory formulations during the 1950s, given Heider's initial work: Newcomb (1953); Cartwright and Harary (1956); Festinger (1957); revised Heider (1958); Abelson and Rosenberg (1958).

research that it generated has been relatively extensive. Aside from other considerations, this was undoubtedly due to the fact that the theory dealt with a problem that was defined as "socially relevant" in the late 1960s.

One of the most interesting features of the experimental research generated by the Status Characteristics and Expectation States Theory is that much of it was immediately addressed to theoretical problems that went beyond the original formulation (see Berger, Cohen, and Zelditch, 1972). As a consequence, it soon became clear that the theory could be reformulated (see Berger and Fisek, 1969) so as to extend its scope and refine its structure. The history of the research on this problem and our present generalization of the original Status Characteristics Theory is presented in chapter six of this volume.

C. SOURCES OF EVALUATION AND SOCIAL INTERACTION

The history of expectation states research in this third problem area, dealt with in part two of this volume, requires only a few comments. A good deal of the work that has been done on "Source" theory (although by no means all of it) has already been published or is in the process of being prepared for publication.

As is the case of the Status Characteristic Theory, the basic premise in the work on Source Theory was that a theory concerned with the formation and maintenance of expectation states could be applied to one of the classical problems in sociology: What are the conditions and processes by which significant others and multiple significant others (*sources of evaluation*) determine the behavior of individuals in specific interpersonal situations?

Among the sources that led to Webster's initial formulation of this problem (Webster, 1968) was an unpublished theoretical paper by Berger, Zelditch, Anderson, and Cohen (see Berger et al., 1967) concerned with the *source conditions* under which an individual's self-evaluations are determined and stabilized. Interestingly enough, considering the authors involved, this theory, in a strict sense, was neither a process nor an expectation states formulation. Taking off both from this work on the conditions of stable self-evaluations, and the expectation states research in Conner (1965), Berger and Conner (1966 and 1969), and Berger, Conner, and McKeown (1969), Webster constructed a relevant expectation states formulation (see Webster, 1968, 1969). His initial version of Source Theory restricted itself to the case of a *single evaluator*. Following his empirical research, Sobieszek extended Webster's original theory to deal with the problem of *multiple evaluators*. Her research was built upon and extended the theoretical ideas and assertions of the initial formulation. And in a very conscious manner she introduced just those theoretical additions and changes that would increase the scope of the original theory. Subsequent research by Webster, Sobieszek, Roberts, and Savage have contributed to the refinement and extension of this work. The history, development, and present status of this quickly evolving body of research are presented by Webster and Sobieszek in chapter five of this volume, "Sources of Evaluation and Expectation States."

D. APPLIED RESEARCH

It was to be expected that at some stage in the emergence of our program, interest would develop in applying the theoretical ideas and formulations to on-going social situations. No attempt will be made here to describe the history of the applied research, since it merits a separate treatment in its own right.

From the standpoint of our interest in backgrounds, it suffices to say that there have emerged two separate bodies of applied work. Not surprisingly the first of these has as its theoretical basis the original theory of Status Characteristics and Expectation States (Berger et al., 1966). This research, undertaken and organized by Elizabeth G. Cohen and her students, was initiated in 1968. One of its principal concerns has been to develop techniques by which the effects of status characteristic differences can be modified or eliminated in on-going interpersonal situations (see E. G. Cohen, 1968).

The second line of applied research was initiated in 1970 by Doris R. Entwisle and Murray Webster. Using some of the basic ideas and assertions of expectation states theories, a primary concern of their work has been to develop techniques by which the expectation states of individuals can be changed in natural social situations. A brief summary and major example of the work by Entwisle and Webster is presented in chapter seven of this volume, "Raising Children's Expectations for Performance: A Classroom Application of Expectation States Theory."

The amount of research in both of these applied branches is already, from a comparative standpoint, extensive; and they continue to be areas of active concern. The most significant feature of the applied research is the extent to which it has been both guided and informed by the theoretical ideas of various expectation states formulations. Further, most of the applied research has been based upon the results and findings of experimental studies of expectation state processes, initially conducted under highly controlled conditions. In addition, the process of information input has not been unidirectional. Thus, although the work is still in an early stage of development, the interchange that has evolved between theoretical, experimental, and applied research activities is one of the most promising developments of our program.

III. ON ANATOMY

Expectation States Theory is a theoretical research program. From one perspective the program can be said to consist of a set of related specific theoretical formulations, bodies of relevant research, and a set of applied research activities. But from a second perspective, Expectation States Theory, as is true of research programs generally, can be viewed as consisting of a number of different types of theoretical elements. On this level we can analyze the program in terms of: (a) a set of "core" as well as a set of "auxiliary" theoretical concepts and relations; (b) a set of meta-theoretical ideas and principles that has guided the theory-building strategy; and (c) a common set of observational techniques and experimental situations that has been used in the research.[10]

A. THE THEORETICAL CORE AND THE AUXILIARY SET

In examining the research in this program one can distinguish, to begin with, a core set of theoretical terms and assertions. The elements of this set include such concepts as: *unit-evaluations, self-other expectation states and structures,* and the *observable power and prestige order*. They also include theoretical assertions that describe the determination of the power and prestige order through the operation of underlying expectation states and structures, and theoretical assertions that describe, given specified social conditions, the maintenance of an established order. As will be seen, these concepts and theoretical assertions are employed in each of the specific formulations included in this volume (as is also true of many of the specific formulations that are not included here). In this sense, these theoretical elements constitute a *common theoretical core* for much of the research in Expectation States Theory.

In addition to the core set of theoretical concepts and relations, we can also distinguish a second class of concepts and assertions that are elements in the research program. Using a term introduced by Lakatos we shall refer to this as the "auxiliary set" of theoretical elements.[11] Included in the auxiliary set are such concepts as: *diffuse* and *specific status characteristics, single* and *multiple sources of evaluations,* and theoretical relations such as the *salience* and *burden of proof* assumptions. The auxiliary concepts were introduced to deal with the substantive issues that are involved in applying or extending the

[10]The issue of what kinds of concepts and techniques are most adequate for the analysis of research programs generally has received, up to now, relatively little attention by social scientists. The particular concepts and distinctions we employ here have been selected because they provide a simple way to describe some of the ways in which the elements of the program are interrelated. In using these terms and distinctions, however, we do not commit ourselves to the position that they represent the most fruitful ways that can be devised to analyze the anatomy of theoretical research programs (see Berger, Anderson, and Zelditch, forthcoming). Again our indebtedness to Lakatos with respect to this problem is clear (see Lakatos, 1968, 1970); and again we make no claim that we have, in a strict sense, applied his ideas.

[11]See previous footnote.

core concepts and relations of Expectation States Theory to specific problem areas. Thus, to deal with the effect on social interaction of broadly defined socially valued categories such as age, sex, occupational class, or race, the theoretical notion of a *diffuse status characteristic* was developed. And the concepts, definitions, and assumptions that constitute the Status Characteristics and Expectation States Theory describe the processes by which such status characteristics determine the expectation states and structures that develop in a specific interpersonal situation. Thus the new concepts and relations introduced in this specific formulation *tie into* the core concepts and relations. For once the formation of expectation states and structures has been accounted for within the special conditions in which diffuse status characteristics are operating, the organization of social interaction in the situation can then be explained by using the basic expectation states concepts and assumptions. In a similar manner, in order to deal with the effect of significant others and conflicting significant others on the behavior of individuals in an interpersonal situation, the theoretical concepts of *single* and *multiple sources of evaluations* were developed by Webster and Sobieszek. And the additional concepts and relations that they introduced in their specific formulations of Source Theory provide theoretical elements that describe the processes by which sources of evaluations determine expectation states and structures. And once again, by employing the basic concepts and assumptions that relate behaviors in specific ways to expectation states, the effects of sources of evaluations on the individual's behavior is explained.

In general, it is in this manner that specific expectation states formulations have used and built on the core concepts and relations of Expectation States Theory. And on the basis of previous experience, it is reasonable to expect that the auxiliary set of concepts and relations will increase. It will increase as new specific expectation states formulations are developed to deal with the substantive issues involved in different problem areas.

B. SOME COMMON META-THEORETICAL PRINCIPLES

Any analysis of the anatomy of a research program must include some description of the meta-theoretical ideas that have guided the theory-building strategy of its practitioners. Such a strategy clearly has evolved in this work. Its two most obvious features have been: (1) an emphasis on developing structurally explicit theoretical formulations; and (2) an emphasis on developing scope-defined constructions.

Structurally Explicit Formulations

As will be quickly apparent to the reader, there is a very conscious effort made in these papers, and in most expectation states research, to present in explicit form the structure of specific theoretical formulations. The definitions of major theoretical terms and concepts are explicitly formulated. Substantive assumptions are clearly distinguished from definitions and, where possible, are designated as the type of theoretical elements they are: substantive assumptions. In short, the effort is made to delineate, as clearly as possible, the conjunctive set of definitions and assumptions that constitute a specific theory. The principal functions of such an approach are to enable us to determine what are and what are not the consequences of a specific theoretical structure, and what theoretical elements (definitions and/or assumptions) are involved in any particular derivation. Thus we are often in a position to determine whether or not a specific structure (a) is, in general, *adequate*, that is, whether or not it will yield derivations that are relevant to some phenomenon of interest to us; or (b) requires *reformulation*, that is, it does provide us with derivations relevant to the phenomenon of interest, but in fact, these are not corroborated by experimental tests; or (c) is *limited*, that is, it yields one set of corroborated derivations but also entails a second set of derivations that are not corroborated. Therefore, this strategy enables us to determine the general nature of the confirmation problem posed by a specific theory: whether the theory is simply inadequate, whether it requires reformulation, or whether its problem is one of limited empirical support. As a consequence, this strategy often enables us to pinpoint those definitions and theoretical assertions that require redefinition and reformulation.

It is in this context that we consider formalization as an aspect of our theory-building strategy. I think it is fair to say that we do not consider model building to be a panacea for the many problems that confront sociologists in the area of social theory. A theory that, in terms of conceptual and empirical considerations, is inadequate will normally *not* be transformed into a useful or empirically significant formulation by simply interpreting it within a formal structure. However, it should be added that the attempt to formalize such a theory may well highlight its inadequacies and motivate efforts to reformulate it. Further, we do not believe (nor in our own research have we followed) the dictum that *any* substantively promising theory can be formalized. In fact, there may not exist an appropriate mathematical theory with a well developed theorem structure that can be profitably used for the particular problem. Or, if an appropriate mathematical theory exists, it may entail measurement conditions that the sociologist, given the present state of his art, is unable to meet. In either case, no matter how skillful or sophisticated the mathematical exercise involved, the resulting formalization is not likely to yield a significant development in our theoretical knowledge. However, we do believe that if we have a theory that is at least conceptually adequate (if not refined and elaborated) and is empirically acceptable (if not well established), then we have a *candidate* for formalization. If it should also be the case that there exists an appropriate mathematical system (entailing measurement requirements that can be met), then the formalization of this theory is likely to yield a more *powerful* theoretical structure. At the very least, formalization in this case enables us to make more precise the deductive implications of our original formulation. Insofar as this increases our capacities to test our original formulation, it enhances our ability to refine and develop our theoretical knowledge. In the final analysis, this, as we see it, is the fundamental rationale for formalization as a theory-building activity.[12]

Scope-Defined Formulations

Throughout much of the work presented in this volume and also much that is part of this research program generally, a conscious effort has been made to employ a strategy of developing scope-defined theoretical formulations. The basic idea is simple enough—although it is impressive how seldom it has been employed as a theory-building strategy. In effect, what we have continually sought to do, in a very conscious manner, is to formulate and state in as explicit a form as possible the set of social conditions within which a particular theoretical formulation is assumed to hold. These are the social conditions that are taken to be *initially given*; and unless processes that are part of the particular theory specifically describe changes and transformations of some of these initial conditions, they are assumed to be fixed conditions. Thus, our theoretical formulations always presuppose a specific social situation whose particular features are described in terms as abstract as is both possible and appropriate to the formulation. In the first instance, this forces us to be fully aware of the scope of a particular formulation; and if it had no other function, it would have the important virtue of enabling us to define the *generality* of a particular process. But in fact it has other consequences that are significant in developing successive theoretical formulations. By making the formulation of scope conditions part of his theoretical task, the researcher is forced to be aware of, as well as provided with, the opportunity to make a decision on the major restrictions and simplifications he is introducing into his system. The theory-building rationale for such an approach is clear: If we know the conditions, particularly the simplifying conditions, under which a

---

[12]In claiming that constructing theoretical formulations in terms of explicit structural forms is a meta-theoretical principal that has guided our research, we are not making any claims as to how these theoretical ideas did, in fact, evolve. The sources and processes by which theoretical ideas evolve are multiple. At one end of the "inductive-deductive" continuum are theoretical formulations that evolve out of an attempt to simplify and codify a body of empirical research (as presumably was the case of Homans' work in the *Human Group* [1950]); while at the other end of the continuum are formulations that evolve out of an attempt to explicate some familiar and often used theoretical notion (as presumably was true in Heider's work on the theory of balanced cognitive structures [see Heider, 1946]). The "logic of discovery" (to use an old fashioned expression), unfortunately, is still not a well-understood process. However, what we do claim is this: given a set of theoretical ideas, however they have been generated, constructing them (or more accurately, reconstructing them) in terms of an explicit logical or mathematical structure can facilitate the testing, refining, and generalizing of these theoretical ideas.

formulation is assumed to hold, and if indeed it is found to hold under these conditions, we also know what restrictions and simplifications have to be changed in order to increase the scope of the theory.

The operation of the strategy will be clear in reading the papers in this volume. In the work of Webster and Sobieszek, for example, their initial formulation dealt with the effect of a single significant other (a *single* source of evaluations) in determining the behavior of individuals in a specific situation. Empirical tests provided evidence that their formulation could, in fact, adequately describe processes operating in this situation, and subsequent theoretical work was then addressed to the more complex situation in which there were *multiple* sources of evaluations and the question of how such sources affect the individual's behavior. Similarly, the original Status Characteristics Theory by Berger, Cohen, and Zelditch (1966) restricted itself to describing the process by which differences on a *single* diffuse status characteristic determine the behavior of group members in a task situation. Experimental tests of the Status Characteristic Theory led us to believe that we can, indeed, describe how status characteristics organize the behavior of individuals under certain conditions. As a consequence, work was undertaken, which is presented in this volume, that was addressed to the problem of extending the original theory to deal with situations in which *multiple* status characteristics operate simultaneously to affect the individual's behavior.

With all this said, however, it should also be noted that there are some scope conditions, which are in fact common to all our formulations, that up to now have not been modified or changed. Among these conditions, for example, are the conditions that in the interpersonal situations of interest to us there exists a "collective" and a "unitary task," and that the individuals in such situations are "task oriented." How the processes of interest to us operate in situations where the task structure is more complex, or where no "task" exists in the traditional sense (a "purely expressive" situation, for example) are questions of concern to us, but at present they represent problems still to be solved in our research program.

There is nothing in this strategy of developing scope-defined formulations that dictates what the next theoretical moves are, in the sense of determining which conditions are to be modified, or how a particular situation should be further complicated. However, given the success of some initial formulation whose scope conditions have been explicitly defined, this strategy both forces and enables the theorist to focus on those restrictions and simplifications that have to be dealt with in order to increase the generality of his formulation.

C. COMMON OBSERVATIONAL TECHNIQUES AND EXPERIMENTAL SETTING

A considerable amount of the experimental research in the program has been carried out within a specific experimental situation. Historically, the construction of the experimental situation grew out of repeated attempts that began in the late 1950s to develop an experimental setting in which the "critical components" of interaction could be investigated under highly controlled conditions. By this time, on the basis of theoretical considerations, the critical components had been conceptualized as being certain task-relevant behaviors: chances to perform (action opportunities); problem-solving attempts (performance outputs); changes in the unit evaluations of problem-solving attempts (exercised influence); and communicated evaluations (specific positive and negative reactions). It was assumed that differences in these task-relevant behaviors, separately or in various combinations, led to the formation of expectation states under specified task conditions; and once formed, these task-relevant behaviors could all be regarded as functions of expectation states. Thus an experimental situation was sought in which we could study, in a highly controlled manner, the process by which these task-relevant behaviors, separately and/or in various combinations, led to expectation states and were in turn determined by expectation states.

The specific experimental situation that was eventually constructed within these general theoretical requirements was developed to enable us to investigate the "expectation states maintenance and change" process model formulated by Berger and Snell (1961). This model stipulated in abstract terms the task conditions under which the process of maintenance and change would take place (and thus defined the scope of the process), and focused on changes in unit evaluations (exercised influence) as the critical task behavior that was determined by and presumably would lead to changes in expectation states. Thus, to meet the specific requirements of this model, and working within the more general theoretical requirements that had been developed, our standardized experimental situation was created.[13]

We shall not go into the detailed features of our experimental situation because they are amply described in a number of the reports in this volume. However, two aspects of the standardized situation are worth noting. First, its relative success as an instrument for research in our program is in all likelihood related to the fact that the process observed, using the experimental situation, has proved to be highly *stable*. Experimental results, using the experimental situation, have been replicated, and have also been replicated under conditions where there has been considerable variation of theoretical

[13]It is interesting to note that, up to now, relatively little research has been done that has involved using other features of this standardized experimental situation in studying the emergence and effects of expectation states on behavior. Thus, it is possible, using the standardized experimental situation, to experimentally manipulate a component such as *initiated performance outputs* (while controlling the other components) and study the process by which this component affects and is dependent on expectation states. In addition, to the author's knowledge, no research has yet been carried out, which can be done in this situation, in which the effect and dependence of specified action combinations (see action-cycles model [Berger, 1960]) on expectation states is investigated.

nonrelevant variables. Second, the situation has proven to be highly *adaptable*. That is, it has proven to be possible, given appropriate experimental ingenuity, to study a wide range of expectation states problems using the experimental situation.

The advantages of having a large number of researchers employing a single standardized experimental situation are obvious. Research results build on previous research results. The theorist is not forced continually to start over again. Furthermore, differences in results cannot easily be attributed to differences in observational techniques and procedures. Such differences must be accounted for in terms of variations in experimental manipulations and in terms of substantive theoretical considerations. Clearly, the use of such a standardized experimental situation contributes to the rapid accumulation and growth of knowledge in a research program. But just as clearly, there are pitfalls that one must be alerted to when relying upon such a situation. By its very nature, a standardized experimental situation is a highly controlled, simplified, and focused observational setting. In part, its research advantages stem from these features. However, these same features of the standardized experimental situation can easily operate to close out theoretically relevant information. Partly because of our sensitivity to this problem, other experimental settings have been used in order to test and to apply our theoretical conceptions. Thus, for example, Fisek (see chapter three) developed an expectation states model that was based on a process that originally had been investigated in the standardized experimental situation (see chapter two). Fisek's model, in turn, was tested in an open interaction situation (a Bales-type setting). In fact he found that his model could not fully account for the expectation formation processes that occurred in *all* of the groups he studied. His results, among others, have forced us to consider and conceptualize *other* conditions and processes by which expectations are formed (see chapter four). Similarly, the applied research by E. G. Cohen and her students and by Entwisle and Webster, by its very nature has required open interaction situations or actual on-going social settings. Their research has not only provided further tests for theoretical ideas originally tested in the standardized situation, but has also provided theoretical problems that had not emerged from research in the standardized setting.[14]

So, although it is true that there has been a commitment to and use of a common set of observational techniques and settings (the standardized experimental situation), it is also the case that other observational techniques and settings have been used to further this research. Nevertheless, the use of

---

[14]It has also been the case that other highly controlled experimental settings (other than the standardized settings being discussed here) have been constructed, as required, to empirically investigate specific expectation states formulations (see Lewis, 1966; and Foschi, 1969, 1971).

such a common set of observational techniques and settings has been one of the major factors that has served to interrelate the various parts of this research program.

IV. FINAL COMMENTS

In one sense, this book is an introduction to expectation states research for the advanced undergraduate, graduate student, and our professional colleagues. It is intended to provide an overview of our research and some of its substantive parts. However, in at least three other senses, this is not a traditional introductory book.

First, only some of the substantive areas to which expectation states formulations have been applied are explicitly dealt with. Other areas, in which promising formulations are still at an early stage of development, are not treated. These include, in particular, research on the expectation states conditions under which a formal set of authority relations are maintained or eroded (see M. Zelditch, Jr., 1972), and research on the relations of performance expectations to decision-making processes (see Camilleri and Berger, 1967, and Camilleri et al., 1972).

Second, within the substantive fields that are explicitly treated in this volume, no attempt is made to represent *all* the research that has been done or is presently being done. Where possible, summaries are presented of the major lines of expectation states research in a given area (as in parts three and four of this volume). In other areas, a major example of the type of research that is presently being carried out is presented (as in part five); and in still other areas, both examples and codifications that are possible at this stage are presented (as in part two). As a consequence, a number of research activities that are important to the development of expectation states theories in these areas are not presented. These include, among others, recent research by Martha Foschi on formal theories concerned with expectation state changes (see Foschi, 1970, 1971); mathematical models by Thomas Fararo concerned with status characteristic and expectation state processes (Fararo, 1968, 1970, 1971, 1972); and research by Elizabeth G. Cohen and her students on the effects of status characteristic differences in interpersonal situations (see Cohen et al., 1970, 1971, and Lohman, 1972). To compensate at least partially for the incompleteness necessitated primarily by space considerations, we have prepared a special bibliography of both published and unpublished expectation states research (see the appendix at the back of the book).

There is one final sense in which this book is not a traditional introductory text. No attempt is made, in the material that is presented, to ignore existing theoretical and empirical difficulties, or to "tidy up" conceptual edges, or to force an integration of the different parts. This book presents a picture of some parts of expectation states research as it appears at this time. A year or two from now this picture will undoubtedly be different. Existing ideas and assertions will have been challenged by new experimental tests, and new formulations will have appeared on the scene. In other words, this book is intended to present expectation states research as it presently is: a theoretical research program in progress.

REFERENCES

ABELSON, R. P., and M. J. ROSENBERG. 1958. Symbolic psycho-logic: a model of attitudinal cognition. *Behavioral science* 3: 1–13.

BALES, R. F. 1953. The equilibrium problem in small groups. In *Working papers in the theory of action*, eds. T. Parsons, R. F. Bales, and E. A. Shils, pp. 111–65. Glencoe, Ill.: The Free Press.

BERGER, J. 1958. Relations between performance, rewards, and action-opportunities in small groups. Unpublished Ph. D. dissertation, Harvard University.

―――. 1960. An investigation of processes of role-specialization in small problem-solving groups. Proposal funded by the National Science Foundation (July).

BERGER, J., and J. L. SNELL. 1961. A stochastic theory for self-other expectations. *Technical report no. 1*. Laboratory for Social Research, Stanford University.

BERGER, J., B. P. COHEN, J. L. SNELL, and M. ZELDITCH, JR. 1962. *Types of formalization*. Boston: Houghton Mifflin Company.

BERGER, J., and M. ZELDITCH, JR. 1962. Authority and performance expectations. Unpublished manuscript, Stanford University.

BERGER, J., B. P. COHEN, and M. ZELDITCH, JR. 1965. Status characteristics and expectation states. *Technical report no. 12*. Laboratory for Social Research, Stanford University.

―――. 1966. Status characteristics and expectation states. In *Sociological theories in progress*, vol. 1, eds. J. Berger, M. Zelditch, Jr., and B. Anderson, pp. 29–46. Boston: Houghton-Mifflin Company.

BERGER, J., and T. L. CONNER. 1966. Performance expectations and behavior in small groups. *Technical report no. 18*. Laboratory for Social Research, Stanford University.

BERGER, J., M. ZELDITCH, JR., B. ANDERSON, and B. P. COHEN. 1967. Status conditions of self-evaluation. *Technical report no. 24*. Laboratory for Social Research, Stanford University. (Revised version is *Technical report no. 27*, February, 1968.)

BERGER, J., and T. L. CONNER. 1969. Performance expectations and behavior in small groups. *Acta sociologica* 12, no. 4: 186–98.

BERGER, J., T. L. CONNER, and W. L. McKEOWN. 1969. Evaluations and the formation and maintenance of performance expectations. *Human relations* 22 (December): 481–502.

BERGER, J., and M. H. FISEK. 1969. An extended theory of status-characteristics and expectation-states. Unpublished manuscript, Stanford University.

BERGER, J., B. P. COHEN, and M. ZELDITCH, JR. 1972. Status characteristics and social interaction. *American sociological review* (June): 33–45.

BERGER, J., B. ANDERSON, and M. ZELDITCH, JR. The structure of social theories: the nature and development of sociological theories. Forthcoming.

CAMILLERI, S. F., and J. BERGER. 1967. Decision-making and social influence: a model and an experimental test. *Sociometry* 30 (December): 365–78.

CAMILLERI, S. F., J. BERGER, and T. L. CONNER. 1972. A formal theory of decision-making. In *Sociological theories in progress*, vol. 2, eds. J. Berger, M. Zelditch, Jr., and B. Anderson. Boston: Houghton Mifflin Company.

CARTWRIGHT, D., and F. HARARY. 1956. Structural balance: a generalization of Heider's theory. *Psychological review* 63: 277–93.

COHEN, B. P. 1962. The process of choosing a reference group. In *Mathematical methods in small group processes*, eds. J. M. Criswell, H. Soloman, P. Suppes, pp. 101–18. Stanford University Press.

COHEN, E. G. 1968. Interracial interaction disability. *Technical report no. 1* (October). School of Education, Stanford University.

COHEN, E. G., M. LOHMAN, K. HALL, D. LUCERO, and S. ROPER. 1970. Expectation training I: altering the effects of a racial status characteristic. *Technical report no. 2* (January). School of Education, Stanford University.

COHEN, E. G., S. ROPER, and D. LUCERO. 1971. Modification of interracial interaction disability through expectation training. Read at American Education Research Association meeting, New York (February).

CONNER, T. L. 1965. Continual disagreement and the assignment of self-other performance expectations. Unpublished Ph. D. dissertation, Stanford University.

EVAN, W. M., and M. ZELDITCH, JR. 1961. A laboratory experiment on bureaucratic authority. *American sociological review* 26: 883–93.

FARARO, T. J. 1968. Theory of status. *General systems* 13: 177–88.

———. 1970. Theoretical studies in status and stratification. *General systems* 15: 71–101.

———. 1971. Macro-status and micro-status. Paper presented at American Sociological Association meetings, Denver, Colo.

———. 1972. Status and situation: a formulation of the structure theory of status characteristics and expectation states. *Quality and quantity: the European journal of methodology* 6: 37–98.

FESTINGER, L. 1957. *A theory of cognitive dissonance*. Evanston, Ill.: Row, Peterson and Company.

FISEK, M. H. 1969. The evolution of status structures and interaction in task oriented discussion groups. Unpublished Ph. D. dissertation, Department of Sociology, Stanford University.

FOSCHI, M. 1969. Contradiction of specific performance expectations: an experimental study. Unpublished Ph. D. dissertation, Stanford University.

———. 1970. On the concept of "expectations." Paper presented at the Pacific Sociological Association meetings, Anaheim, Calif., April 1970.

———. 1971. Contradiction and change of performance expectations. *Canadian review of sociology and anthropology* 8: 205–22.

HEIDER, F. 1946. Attitudes and cognitive organization. *Journal of psychology* 21: 107–12.

———. 1958. *The psychology of interpersonal relations*. New York: John Wiley & Sons.

HEINICKE, C., and R. F. BALES. 1953. Developmental trends in the structure of small groups. *Sociometry* 16: 7–38.

HOMANS, G. C. 1950. *The human group.* New York: Harcourt Brace.

LAKATOS, I. 1968. Criticism and the methodology of scientific research programmes. In *Proceedings of the Aristotelian Society* 69: 149–86.

———. 1970. Falsification and the methodology of scientific research programmes. In *Criticism and the growth of knowledge*, eds. I. Lakatos and A. Musgrave, pp. 91–195. Cambridge, England: Cambridge University Press.

LEWIS, G. H. 1966. Performances, evaluations and expectations: an experimental study. Unpublished Ph. D. dissertation, Stanford University.

LOHMAN, M. R. 1972. Changing a racial status ordering—implications for desegregation. *Journal of education and urban society*, vol. 4, no. 4, August.

NEWCOMB, T. M. 1953. An approach to the study of communicative acts. *Psychological review* 60: 393–404.

SLATER, P. E. 1955. Role differentiation in small groups. *American sociological review* 20: 300–10.

SOBIESZEK, B. 1970. Multiple sources and the formation of performance expectations. Unpublished Ph. D. dissertation, Stanford University.

———. 1972. Multiple sources and the formation of performance expectations. *Pacific sociological review* 15 (January): 103–22.

WEBSTER, M. 1967. The interaction control machines at the Laboratory for Social Research. Unpublished paper presented at the Small Group Session, Pacific Sociological Association meetings (April).

———. 1968. Sources of evaluations and expectations for performance. Unpublished Ph. D. dissertation, Stanford University.

———. 1969. Sources of evaluations and expectations for performance. *Sociometry* 32: 143–259.

ZELDITCH, M., JR. 1972. Authority and performance expectations in bureaucratic organizations. In *Experimental social psychology*, ed. Charles G. McClintock, pp. 484–513. New York: Holt, Rinehart & Winston.

THE DEVELOPMENT OF POWER AND PRESTIGE ORDERS IN TASK-ORIENTED GROUPS

INTRODUCTION TO PART TWO

The primary substantive concern of this section is with the development of hierarchical orders in informal, task-oriented groups, whose members are initially status equals. Such orders are typically manifested, on the observable level, by the distribution of the different types of behaviors: the receipt of opportunities to perform, problem-solving attempts, the communication of evaluations of problem-solving attempts such as positive reactions, and the exercise of influence. Thus, explaining the development of hierarchical orders in such groups also entails accounting for the properties that the distributions of these observable behaviors come to exhibit: that these behaviors tend to be unequally distributed among group members; that they tend, under specific conditions, to be highly related to each other; and that they tend, within fixed conditions, to be stable. Explaining the development of these hierarchical orders and the properties of their behavioral manifestations in groups, whose members are initially status equals, has been a major concern of expectation states research. The history of earlier theoretical and mathematical formulations relevant to this problem is detailed in chapter one (see "On History") and, therefore, will not be reviewed here. In this section we present three papers that are among the most recent theoretical and experimental investigations of the development of hierarchical orders within the framework of Expectation States Theory.

Chapter two, "Evaluations and the Formation and Maintenance of Performance Expectations," is a reprinted paper (Berger, Conner, and McKeown, 1969). This paper deals with the formation of expectation states as a result of the evaluations and differential evaluations of performances individuals make within a very specific set of interaction conditions. A set of assumptions and definitions is developed to describe this process by which expectation states are formed and maintained. Following this, the assumptions and definitions are interpreted within a Markov chain model that enables the theorist to obtain precise and testable derivations. A three-man experiment, specifically designed to test the theory and model, is then described and the theory and model are evaluated in the light of the results of the experiment.

Chapter three, "A Model for the Evolution of Status Structures" by M. Hamit Fisek, is also concerned with the formation of expectation states, but in the context of three-man open interaction discussion groups similar to those studied by Bales and his students (see Bales, 1953). A formal model is constructed that describes a process by which expectation states

24

are developed under conditions similar to those of Bales' studies, and how they in turn determine differential rates of initiated performances in such groups. An experiment specifically designed to test this model is described; and the adequacies and limitations of the model are assessed on the basis of analysis of the results of data from fifty-nine such discussion groups.

Chapter four, "Performance Expectations and Behavior in Small Groups" by J. Berger and T. L. Conner, is a general theoretical paper. From the standpoint of research in the expectation states program, it consists of two different types of theoretical components. First, it contains terms, definitions, and assumptions that are used to analyze how behavioral inequalities are determined by established expectation states and structures, and how such behavioral inequalities and expectation states and structures are maintained. These ideas, or subsets of them in various forms, appear in all the papers in this volume as well as in much of the research of Expectation States Theory. These terms, definitions, and assumptions are part of the "core-theoretical set" of the expectation states program.[1] Second, the paper presents terms, definitions, and assumptions that are used to describe one of the processes by which expectation states are formed, in terms of differential rates of accepted performances. As such, it represents an attempt to elaborate and generalize the performance-evaluation process that is central to the theoretical and experimental research of the proceeding chapters in this section. Alternative processes by which expectation states are formed in groups operating within different social conditions are formulated in other sections of this volume (see, in particular, part four).

Work related to the problems considered in this section is continuing. The probability model presented in chapter four has been reformulated as a continuous-time discrete state Markov process by Conner (see Conner, 1972), and a program of experiments to test this formulation is presently under way. In addition, another formulation of the process involved in the change of expectation states has been developed by M. Foschi (1969, 1970, 1971) and is presently being subjected to empirical tests.

REFERENCES

BALES, R. F. 1953. The equilibrium problem in small groups. In *Working papers in the theory of action*, eds. T. Parsons, R. F. Bales, and E. A. Shils, pp. 111–65. Glencoe, Ill.: The Free Press.

[1] See Chapter 1.

BERGER, J., T. L. CONNER, and W. L. MCKEOWN. 1969. Evaluations and the formation and maintenance of performance expectations. *Human relations* 22 (December): 481–502.

CONNER, T. L. 1972. A continuous time, discrete state Markov model of performance expectations and behavior in small groups. *Technical report no. 8.* Department of Sociology, Michigan State University.

FOSCHI, M. 1969. Contradiction of specific performance expectations: an experimental study. Unpublished Ph. D. dissertation, Department of Sociology, Stanford University.

———. 1970. On the concept of "expectations." Paper presented at the Pacific Sociological Association meetings (To appear in *Acta sociologica*).

———. 1971. Contradiction and change of performance expectations. *Canadian review of sociology and anthropology* 8: 205–22.

CHAPTER TWO

Evaluations and the Formation and Maintenance of Performance Expectations*

JOSEPH BERGER

THOMAS L. CONNER

WILLIAM L. McKEOWN

Bales and his associates (Bales et al., 1951; Bales, 1953; Bales & Slater, 1955; Heinicke & Bales, 1953) have shown that task-performing groups whose members are the same in age, sex, race, education and occupation (that is, are initially status equals) tend to develop a stable power and prestige order. This power and prestige order is reflected in the inequalities which develop in activity initiated and received and in ratings members make of who had the best ideas, who guided the group discussion, and who demonstrated leadership. Others (Harvey, 1953; Sherif et al., 1955; Whyte, 1943) have found that an already established power and prestige order will deter-

*This paper was originally issued, under the same title, as *Technical Report No. 22* (1969), Laboratory of Social Research, Stanford University. It also appeared in *Human Relations* 22: 481–502. Reprinted by permission of the authors with minor changes. Research for this paper was supported in large part by grants from the National Science Foundation (NSF G-13314, G-23990, GS-1170). We would particularly like to acknowledge the assistance of J. Laurie Snell in developing the mathematical model presented in this paper. We would also like to acknowledge the help given us at various stages of this investigation by Bernard P. Cohen, Hamit Fisek, Murray Webster, Morris Zelditch, Jr.

mine the evaluations of performances, anticipations for future performances, and influence exercised.

Berger & Conner (1966) argue that such findings can be explained by assuming that the members of these groups come to develop, through time, stable conceptions of the performance capacities of each other. These conceptions, or performance expectations, are beliefs about the relative task abilities of individuals that the members of these groups come to hold. Typically these expectations are differentiated; that is, they represent conceptions of inequalities in the task abilities of group members. If differentiated, these performance expectations legitimate and determine inequalities in opportunities to perform, in performance rates, in evaluations of members' contributions, and in the relative influence of different members on the decisions of the group. Further, they argue that these inequalities in behavior, which are determined by performance expectations, operate to maintain these expectations. Thus once established, the power and prestige order of such groups tends to be stable.[1]

But the assumption of a structure of performance expectations, to account for the known features of the power and prestige order of these groups, itself gives rise to a basic question: how are such performance expectations formed? What are the processes by which differentiated performance conceptions emerge in groups whose members are initially status equals, and how do these conceptions become stable? This is the problem to which this paper is addressed. More specifically, we shall be concerned with isolating and conceptualizing *one* of the processes which we believe operates in the formation and maintenance of performance expectations. This is a process in which performance expectations are conceived of as emerging from, and being maintained by, the evaluations of performances individuals make in task-oriented situations. We shall refer to this as the *evaluation-expectation* process.

In the next section we shall present a set of assumptions to describe the operation of the evaluation-expectation process as it occurs within a specific set of interaction conditions. Following this, a mathematical model for our theory is developed. This model enables us to describe the features of the evaluation-expectation process in a highly precise manner. In the remainder of this paper, an experimental test of our theory and model is described, and the status of our formulation is evaluated in the light of our findings from this investigation.

---

[1] For an application and extension of this argument to the case of task-oriented groups whose members are initially differentiated in terms of socially valued status characteristics (sex, race, occupation, etc.) see Berger et al. (1966a).

I. THEORY

A. SCOPE CONDITIONS

The theory to be presented is seen to apply to small task-focused groups whose members are initially undifferentiated and who are collectively oriented to solving some problem. Implicit in this type of characterization of groups is the idea of a social situation in which there obtains a particular set of initial status and task conditions. Our first task is to specify these conditions.

We imagine a group containing two or more actors, $p, o_1, o_2 \ldots, o_n$. However, we view the group from the point of view of one actor, say p. Strictly speaking the other actors, $o_1, o_2 \ldots, o_n$, are objects of orientation to p. For purposes of developing and experimentally testing our theory we shall confine our attention to a group with three persons, say p, o and q.

We assume p, o and q are engaged in the solution of some task, T, which for simplicity we view as having only two outcomes—success or failure. T may be almost any kind of activity, but for the theory to apply it must involve a series of contributions or problem-solving attempts by one or more of the actors. Moreover, the members of the group are committed to the successful completion of the task, and it is both legitimate and crucial for them to take each other's behavior into account in order to achieve this goal. In this sense the group is "task-focused," and its members are "collectively oriented" in solving their problem.

One way in which we may think about performance expectations is in terms of the idea of task ability. If a person were believed to have a great deal of task ability, then he would be expected to perform well, and vice versa. So we require as a condition for our situation that there be some ability or skill associated with successfully completing T. We will speak of a specific performance characteristic, C, which has two states, high and low. Ordinarily a person who possessed the high state of C would be good at the task while a person with the low state would be poor at the task. For example, if the task were to decide jointly a series of moves in a chess game, then C would be chess playing ability and, as a theoretical simplification, we would think of there being only good players (those with the high state of C) and poor players (those with the low state of C).

Since we are concerned with the formation of beliefs about task ability we must insure that p, o and q initially have no such beliefs. Hence we require that two additional things be true of the actors and their situation. First, they must initially have no direct knowledge of their abilities—that is, no direct knowledge of the states of C they or the other members of the groups possess. Second, they must not differ on other characteristics which have status value for them (e.g., occupation, age, race and sex) from which they could infer task ability. In this sense the members of the group are "initially undifferentiated" and are presumed to be status equals.[2]

B. ASSUMPTIONS

The process with which we are concerned is one in which expectations are formed and maintained as a consequence of their relations to the evaluation of performances. We imagine that in an open interaction situation, as p and the others concern themselves with their task, they are continually providing each other with chances to perform and are continually making contributions directed at successfully completing the task. As this takes place, p and the others are also engaged in evaluating each other's problem-solving attempts. On the basis of these evaluations they are communicating positive and negative reactions, and accepting and rejecting specific contributions. During the early phases of this process certain crucial events are seen to take place in a random manner—particularly the way in which chances to perform are distributed to group members and whether or not these chances are utilized to make problem-solving contributions. However, as the process unfolds, the evaluations (and differential evaluations) of performances become significant, and under certain circumstances p will generalize from these evaluations to the assignment of states of C to himself and others. Such an assignment represents the formation of performance-expectations. Should such an assignment occur, we assume that it will markedly affect p's future behavior. Specifically, it will affect the likelihood that he will give specific others chances to perform, that he will positively or negatively evaluate their contributions, and that he will or will not be influenced by them. Further, we believe that these behaviors of p, because of the way in which they are dependent upon his assignment of states of C, will in general operate to maintain his assignment of states of C. Thus, under the assumption that the task conditions are unchanged, we reason that, once formed, the performance expectations of p will be maintained.

In order to *isolate* the evaluation-expectation process from other processes which may affect the formation of expectations, we shall concern ourselves with a situation in which certain events of the open interaction situation are controlled. The assertions which follow allow us to describe the formation and maintenance of performance expectations in a situation where actors are repeatedly evaluating each other's performances. At the same time, other behaviors such as the giving or denying of performance opportunities or the differential utilization of such opportunities—behaviors which might affect the formation of expectations—have been controlled.

[2]For a discussion of the nature of status characteristics and their effect upon performance expectations see Berger et al. (1966b).

The situation has the following structure: imagine that p, o and q are given a series of task problems and that they are to select the correct answer to each problem from the two alternative answers which are presented. Suppose further that their selection of an answer has several stages. First, each person makes a preliminary selection or initial choice between the alternatives. Next, after all have made their initial choices, each finds out what the others have selected. Last, each makes a private final selection. So for each task problem each person makes an initial choice of an answer, receives information about the initial choices of the others, and makes a private final choice of an answer.

From the standpoint of any one of our actors in this situation, say p, he is required to make an initial choice and communicate it to o and q. This is theoretically equivalent to his having been given a performance opportunity which he cannot decline. His initial choice is his performance output. No actor can receive more opportunities than another actor, and all must be responsible for the same number of performance outputs. Thus, inequalities in performance expectations cannot be inferred from inequalities in opportunities to perform or inequalities in performance rates.

If p happens to disagree with o and q about the correct answer (i.e., p initially selects a different alternative from o and q), then he must decide who is right. That is, he must decide whether to positively evaluate his own performance and negatively evaluate o's and q's performances, or vice versa. If he does the latter, that is, changes his mind, then he has been influenced by o and q; if he retains his original evaluations of the answers, he hasn't been influenced. We will assume that p disagrees with o and q on the answer to each task problem so that he must on repeated occasions decide either that "I'm right and they're wrong" or "They're right and I'm wrong." This can easily be arranged by appropriate experimental manipulation.

Let us look more carefully at each of the stages of p's selecting an answer to a task problem.[3] He must first select which of two possible answers (call them A and B) is the correct one. If he thinks A is correct, then we assume that he will actually choose A—that in this situation the alternative he selects and communicates to others will directly reflect his evaluation of that alternative. To put the principle more generally, any time p evaluates the alternative answers differentially, he will, if required to make a selection, choose that alternative he positively evaluates.

ASSUMPTION 1

At any stage of the process: if p positively evaluates one alternative and negatively evaluates the second, then p will select the first and reject the second.

---

[3]We assume, for reasons that will be clear later in the discussion, that it makes no difference for the purpose of formulating our assumptions which particular task problem in the process is being considered.

Once p has made an initial choice, he finds out that o and q have both chosen a different answer. We assume that p will suppose that o and q have both acted in accord with Assumption 1—that their behavior is neither random nor capricious but, in fact, reflects their evaluations.

Assumption 2

At any stage of the process: p associates a disagreement between himself and the others on choice of alternative answers with different evaluations of alternatives by himself and the others.

P is now forced to make a final decision. We believe that there are two activities going on simultaneously, or possibly alternating with each other at this stage. P probably is trying to decide which alternative is right, A or B; and also who is right, himself or the others. He might first decide who is correct and then what is correct, or he might first decide what is correct and then who is correct.

If p initially is *unable* to decide *who* is right, he is still required to choose between alternatives. Either he continues to view his preliminary choice as correct, or he changes his evaluations of the alternatives and makes a selection that accords with the preliminary decision of others. These responses provide an observable indication of whether p has been influenced or not on a given step of the process, and we define them accordingly:

P makes an s-response at any stage of the process if his final selection of an alternative is the same as his preliminary selection. P makes an o-response at any stage of the process if his final selection of an alternative is the same as the preliminary selection of the others.

We now assume that as a consequence of making a final decision, p will also assign unit evaluations to persons that are consistent with the final evaluations of alternatives that he has made. Unit evaluations of persons are positive or negative evaluations of himself or others that are relevant to a given step of the process. Thus, for example, if he makes an s-response, he will come to believe, "This time I was right and they were wrong"; or if he makes an o-response, "This is one they got, and I missed."

If p initially is *able* to decide *who* is right, then we claim he will evaluate the alternatives A or B in accord with these unit evaluations of persons, and by Assumption 1 his final decision is determined. Thus, during any step of the process, if p evaluates and chooses among alternatives, he will then evaluate persons. If he evaluates persons, he will then evaluate and choose among alternatives; and such evaluations of persons and alternatives will be consistent. These ideas are embodied in Assumption 3.

ASSUMPTION 3

At any stage of the process: if p assigns unit evaluations to alternatives then he will assign unit evaluations to persons, or if he assigns unit evaluations to persons then he will assign unit evaluations to alternatives; and such evaluations of persons and alternatives will be consistent.

Now consider the impact of p's having made unit evaluations of persons at a particular stage. On the basis of such unit evaluations, p may come to believe that he and the others differ with respect to the ability required for the task, and, more important, that they differ in a particular manner. Thus, for example, from "I am right and they were wrong in this case" p may be led to believe "I am better at this than they are," which is equivalent to assigning the positively evaluated state of C to himself and the negatively evaluated state of C to the others. However, we do not believe that p's having evaluated persons assures that he will, on any given stage of the process, actually assign states of C. The consequence of p's unit evaluations of persons, on any stage, is that the *possibility* then exists *which did not exist previously for* him to assign states of C. Moreover, if he does assign states of C, the positively evaluated state of C will always be assigned to the person who was given the positive unit evaluation, and the negatively evaluated state of C will be assigned to the negatively evaluated person.

ASSUMPTION 4

At any stage of the process: given p has not assigned states of C, if p assigns unit evaluations to persons then the possibility exists that p will also assign states of C to self and others and his assignment of states will be consistent with his unit evaluations.

Once p has assigned states of C to self and others, we believe that this assignment will be stable. The stability of the assignment of expectation states is not problematical if p believes himself to be more competent than the others and makes an s-response, or if he believes himself to be less competent and makes an o-response, because his unit evaluations of persons in these cases are consistent with his assignment of states of C. If, however, p believes himself more competent and makes an o-response, or believes himself less competent and makes an s-response—possibilities which we do not exclude in our formulation—his unit evaluations of persons are inconsistent with his assignment of states of C. Thus it is not self-evident that p's assignment of states will remain unchanged. We argue that this stability in the assignment of expectation states is a function of at least two important features of the evaluation-expectation process: (1) the way in which the assignment of states of C affects the *subsequent* assignment of unit evaluations of persons, and (2) a change in significance of unit evaluations of persons given an assignment of expectation states.

Given that p has already assigned states of C to self and others, he now has a basis other than the properties of the task for assigning unit evaluations to persons. In fact, we assume that the assignment of states of C, once it has occurred as a *consequence* of unit evaluations, will *in turn* affect the way in which p subsequently assigns unit evaluations to persons.

ASSUMPTION 5

At any stage of the process: if p has assigned positively and negatively evaluated states of C to self and others, then he will tend to assign positive and negative unit evaluations to self and others consistent with assignment of states of C.

Assumption 5 has several important implications which are relevant to the issue of the stability of expectation states. First, once p has assigned states of C to self and others, his process of making final decisions is *more likely* to be structured in the order *who* is right and then *what* is right than was true before he assigned states of C. Second, taken with earlier assumptions, 5 implies that if p believes he possesses the high state of C and others the low, he is more likely to make s-responses than a p who has not assigned states of C. Similarly, if p believes he possesses the low state of C and others the high, he is more likely to make o-responses than a p who has not assigned states of C. *Thus, once p has assigned states of C, he is expected to be more frequently making those very responses which are consistent with these assigned states.*

Aside from the process described by Assumption 5, stability of assignment is also seen to be related to a change in the significance of unit-evaluations of persons. Given an assignment of C, inconsistent unit evaluations are more likely to be subject by p to special interpretations. Thus, for example, if p believes himself more competent than others and makes an o-response, this behavior is more likely to be dismissed, minimized, or rationalized as a "special event" than the case where a p has not yet assigned states of C. As a consequence, after assignment of states of C, inconsistent evaluations tend to become irrelevant to changes in p's beliefs about task ability. Therefore, we argue:

ASSUMPTION 6

At any stage of the process: if p has assigned positively and negatively evaluated states of C, this assignment is maintained.

C. THE MATHEMATICAL MODEL

It is now possible on the basis of our assumptions and arguments to begin the construction of a mathematical model for describing more precisely the formation of p's expectations and the resultant changes in whether he is influenced by the others. Let us begin by labeling the three possibilities for p's assignment of states of C. First, p may believe he possesses the high state of C and o and q and the low state. We will designate this by the symbol $[+ -]$ where the first entry in the bracket denotes p's expectations for himself and the second entry his expectations for the others. If p believes he possesses the negatively evaluated state of C and the others the positively evaluated state then we will designate that by $[- +]$. Finally, p may not have assigned states of C and we will designate that by $[0\ 0]$.

In line with the definition, we shall continue to employ a short designation for whether p is influenced or not. If p is not influenced, we say that he made an s-response; if he is influenced, we say that he made an o-response.

Our substantive formulation says that if p begins the series of task problems in $[0\ 0]$, he may at some time change to $[+ -]$ or $[- +]$ as a result of his decisions about who is right. If he changes from $[0\ 0]$ to $[+ -]$ he will make more s-responses, and if he changes to $[- +]$ he will make more o-responses. The model we have formulated asserts in addition that in order to understand p's decision behavior for any particular task problem we need know only what his expectations were before he began to work on that problem (and not what his previous decisions about who is right were) and how his decision about who is right on the current problem will change his expectations before the next problem is presented.

Suppose that before he begins to solve a particular task problem p is in $[0\ 0]$. We know that when faced with making his final choice p will sometimes make an s-response and at other times make an o-response. We assert that there is a specifiable and stable probability (call it a_1) that he will make an s-response on that problem which does not depend on his past behavior but only on the fact that he is in $[0\ 0]$. Thus, no matter which problem p is attempting to solve and no matter how p has solved previous problems, the model asserts that he will make an s-response with a fixed probability if he is in state $[0\ 0]$. Similarly, we assert that if p is in $[+ -]$ he will make an s-response with probability a_2 and if he is in $[- +]$ with probability a_3. As a first approximation we assume that a's do not differ across individuals.

If p is in $[0\ 0]$ and makes an s-response, Assumption 4 in conjunction with Assumption 1 tells us that the possibility exists for him to assign states of C which are consistent with his decision. That is, the possibility exists for him to infer from his feeling that "This time, I was right and they were wrong," that he is better than the others. Hence, there is a possibility of his moving to the $[+ -]$ state following his s-response. We assert that there will be a specifiable and stable probability (call it r) that p will move to $[+ -]$ and that the value of the probability will not depend on his prior responses. By a similar line of reasoning we assert that if p is in $[0\ 0]$ and makes an o-response, then his will move to $[- +]$ with probability d.

Once p has moved to either $[+ -]$ or $[- +]$ Assumption 6 tells us that he will remain in that state for the remainder of the series of problems. Moreover, Assumption 5 taken in conjunction with earlier assumptions implies that the probability that p will make an s-response once he is in a new state will be different than previously. In particular, a_2 will be greater than a_1, and a_3 will be less than a_1.

The possibilities and their probabilities of occurrence for a particular task problem can be represented by a set of three tree diagrams, one for each kind of assignment of the states of C that are possible for p before he begins to solve a problem. Figure 2-1 shows the diagrams for this process. This formulation of the process means that we have a Markov Chain with the expectations that p holds for himself and the others as the states of the chain. The one-step transition matrix for the chain can be easily computed from Figure 2-1 and is given in Figure 2-2.

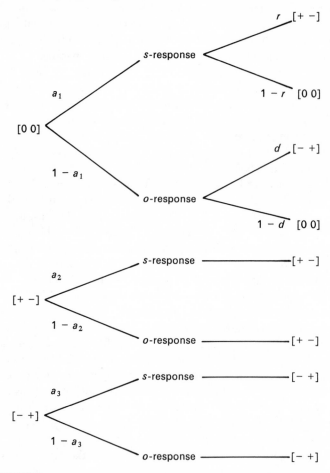

FIGURE 2-1

Tree diagrams showing probabilities of each kind of response given the expectation state and probabilities of state changes following responses.

$$
\begin{array}{c}
\begin{array}{cccc}
 & [0\ 0] & [+\ -] & [-\ +]
\end{array}\\
\begin{array}{c}
[0\ 0]\\[2em]
[+\ -]\\[2em]
[-\ +]
\end{array}
\left[
\begin{array}{ccc}
1 - a_1 r - (1 - a_1)d & a_1 r & (1 - a_1)d\\[2em]
0 & 1 & 0\\[2em]
0 & 0 & 1
\end{array}
\right]
\end{array}
$$

FIGURE 2-2

One-step transition matrix for change of expectation states.

The initial vector of the chain is also easily obtained. We assume that everyone begins the process in [0 0]. Thus the initial distribution vector contains a 1 for that state and zeros for the other states.

II. THE EXPERIMENT

Recall from our previous discussion that the theory applies to a situation in which three individuals, p and two others, are engaged in the solution of a task, T, which has two outcomes—success or failure. An ability is associated with the solution of T, and initially p and the others have no opinion of each other's ability and are not aware of any external status differences between themselves. Through time, as p and the others attempt to complete T, they evaluate the contributions which each is making toward the solution of T, and on the basis of those evaluations accept or reject these contributions. The theory asserted that each person would generalize from performance evaluations to beliefs about relative ability and that their beliefs about ability would then come to govern their evaluations of performances and the acceptance of influence.

The experiment which was carried out focused upon the evaluations of contributions and the acceptance of influence. Three subjects were confronted with an n-step decision process in which each made an initial choice between binary alternatives, received information about the other persons' initial choices, and, on the basis of evaluations of those choices, made a private final choice between the alternatives. Communicated initial choices were taken to be equivalent to performance outputs where the person was always given an opportunity to perform and always accepted that opportunity. Thus differences in opportunities to perform and in rates of performances, which might occur in the open interaction situation, were controlled. The communication of initial choices was further controlled by the experimenter so that each person would continually disagree with the others on initial choices, and, hence, would always have to *differentially* evaluate them. The private final choices of each person were taken to be equivalent to acceptance and rejection of influence from the others.

There were other restrictions placed upon the experimental situation. Each binary choice was required to be "nearly veridical," meaning that in each case there would exist a perceivable "correct" choice and sufficient ambiguity about the choice to create uncertainty. Each subject was to be task-focused; that is, motivated to make the correct final choice.

There were 42 trials in the experiment. For each trial the subjects were seated in booths with separate panels of lights and buttons so that none could see the movements of the others. To make his initial choice a subject pushed one of two labeled buttons. After having pressed his button, one of a set of two lights came on informing him which button the other subjects had pushed. To make his final choice, a subject pushed one of another set of two buttons. The buttons on each panel were connected to a master control panel so that choices could be monitored and recorded and so that which one of the pair of information lights came on could be controlled. As indicated above, it was arranged that on all trials, with the exception of two preliminary trials, a subject was led to believe that the other subjects' preliminary choices differed from his own.

Subjects were instructed to make what they felt to be the correct preliminary choice, and after having taken the information from the other subjects into consideration, to make what they felt was the correct final choice. To operationalize collective-orientation it was repeatedly emphasized to the subjects that it should be of no importance whether their initial and final choices coincided, that the utilization of advice and information from others was both legitimate and crucial, and that it was primarily important that they make a correct *final* choice.

To operationally define "success" and "failure" at the decision-making task, a set of "standards" with respect to number of correct final choices was presented to each set of subjects. A score of 31–40 correct final decisions was defined as "good" and a score of from 0–30 correct final decisions was defined as ranging from "poor" to only "fair."

The actual task used was a variant of a previously developed visual perception task (see Moore, 1965; and Conner, 1966). Subjects viewed a series of rectangles which were divided, checkerboard fashion, into smaller, equal sized rectangles, either black or white in color. Each larger rectangle was projected from a 35mm slide to a screen, and subjects were asked to choose whether there were more white or more black rectangles within the larger one. As already indicated, the decision with respect to any particular slide was a near veridical decision in the sense that a high proportion of the time it is expected that a subject would choose the correct alternative (i.e., the color which did in fact cover more of the area) although there is enough ambiguity about the decision for influence to be possible.

To operationalize the idea of a performance characteristic or ability which is instrumental to the successful completion of the task, subjects were told that the ability to choose the correct answers to the slides was a newly discovered ability called "spatial judgment" ability, and that the ability was unrelated to other skills that they might already possess. The latter instruction was given to ensure that a subject would not use knowledge of special skills he already had to infer his spatial judgment ability.

In order to control for any lack of homogeneity between task slides, and hence to control for possible spurious effects due to task properties, the order of presentation of the slides was specified by a two-stage randomization. First, the 40 slides were randomly assigned a number from 1 to 40 and ordered according to those numbers. The resulting *relative* order was *fixed* for all experiments. Second, for each experiment the slide which was presented first was randomly selected. Thus, if the initial slide was selected to be 23, the actual order of presentation in the experiment would be 23, 24, 25, . . . , 38, 39, 40, 1, 2, 3, . . . , 20, 21, 22.

The order of events as they occurred in the experiment began with the reading by the experimenter of the instructions for the experiment. The instructions explained the routine mechanics of the experiment, the nature of the task and of the decisions, and other special requirements or features such as scoring standards and emphasis on the final choice.

Following the reading of the instructions the experimenter presented 42 slides, although the subjects were told that there were only 40. The extra two slides were included in order to be able to arrange agreement trials at the beginning to allay suspicion of the manipulation of the information exchange. On the remaining 40 trials the subjects continually disagreed on preliminary choices. At the end of the slide series, a short questionnaire was administered which asked each subject to rate his and his partners' performances on the test and to predict future performance for himself and his partners on a similar test in which each worked separately. A post-session interview was then conducted in which the attempt was made to ascertain if experimental manipulations were successful, if the subject became suspicious of the manipulated disagreements, and if the subject's perception of and behavior in the situation coincided with the interpretation which the experimenter was making of it. The interviewer also fully explained to each subject the purpose of the study and made him aware of the aspects of the experiment which involved deception. Each subject was asked to not discuss the experiment with his friends.

III.   RESULTS

A.   SUBJECT POPULATION

Ninety-five subjects, each a male undergraduate from a local junior college, participated in the experiment. We eliminated 32 of these from the analysis because they became suspicious of one or more of the deceptions. We decided that a subject had become suspicious if:

1. He volunteered the information in the post-session interview that he thought the exchange of information was "rigged."
2. He had read previously about deception experiments (such as the Asch conformity experiments) and thought the present experiment was similar.
3. He had heard from others that there was deception in the present experiment.
4. He had participated previously in a deception experiment and thought the present experiment was similar.

Three subjects were eliminated from the analysis when post-session interview revealed that they had become confused by the experimental procedure and did not understand what kind of information was being furnished to them about the choice behavior of the other members of their groups. Another two subjects were eliminated from the analysis because they represented a violation of the initial condition of the theory requiring that each subject begin the process equal in status to the other subject. Data from any subject who had an obvious physical characteristic which would be interpreted as a status characteristic (such as being a Negro) or who participated with someone else who had such a characteristic was not included. This left 58 subjects whose response data could be examined to test the theory.

Models to be Examined

The most general form of our model is the 5-parameter version, which allows movement to either of the two differentiated expectation states. This is the form of the model we are most interested in and the one we believe will describe the process for this particular situation.

However, we will investigate two other versions of the model—a 1-parameter Bernoulli process model, and a 3-parameter model. The 1-parameter model is obtained when both r and d are zero. This model assumes the occurrence of a process in which there is no change of behavior as a function of the evaluational activities of the members of the group. Thus, although technically a special case of our general model, the substantive claims of the 1-parameter model are different from those developed in the assumptions of our evaluation-expectation theory. Therefore, we examine it as a baseline model from which to compare the predictions of our other models. Two different forms of 3-parameter models can be obtained from our general model, one by setting $d = 0$ and restricting movement only to the $[+ -]$ state, and the second by setting $r = 0$ thereby restricting movement only to the $[- +]$ state. Both of these forms do assume the occurrence of a process in which expectations emerge as a function of behavior and changes in behavior occur as a function of the formation of expectations. However, they differ in their characterization of the *particular form* of the evaluation-expectation process.

In an experiment reported by Conner (1966) which was identical to the present one except that each subject was confronted with a single other subject, it was found that change from the undefined expectation state was only to the [+ −] state. It is possible for that to have happened in the present experiment even though each subject was confronted by two other subjects. But it is also possible for the majority effect to have become of overriding importance restricting movement to only the [− +] state. Since at this stage we do not know the specific form of the evaluation-expectation process for the *particular case* involved in our experiment, we shall also consider these two 3-parameter versions of our general model in examining the results of this experiment.

Parameter Estimation

Our analysis of the response data will consist of a comparison of the empirically obtained values of a list of quantities with the values of those same quantities obtained from computer simulations of the process. The simulation values represent approximations of the values that would have been arrived at from analytic expressions for the quantities. As with many models like ours, however, these analytic expressions are difficult, and in some cases impossible, to obtain.

Before simulations could be conducted, estimates for each of the parameters of the model had to be obtained. In each case a series of expressions involving the parameters was obtained for the expected frequencies of certain response events. Because the expressions are complicated, values for the parameters could not be obtained by setting the expressions equal to empirical quantities and analytically solving the resulting system of equations. Rather, approximate values were arrived at by numerically solving the system of equations with the help of a computer. For the 5-parameter model it was found that $a_1 = .690$ (a_1 is the probability of an s-response in the [0 0] state), $a_2 = .846$ (a_2 is the probability of an s-response in the [+ −] state), $a_3 = .320$ (a_3 is the probability of an s-response in the [− +] state), $r = .030$ (r is the probability of moving on one trial from the [0 0] to the [+ −] state), and $d = .025$ (d is the probability of moving on one trial from the [0 0] to the [− +] state). Since the values obtained for r and d were so similar we decided to work with a simpler model that assumes $r = d$. We obtained new estimates for this 4-parameter model and they are given below:

$$a_1 = .698$$
$$a_2 = .846$$
$$a_3 = .332$$
$$r = d = .028$$

Notice that the estimates are in accord with our theoretical expectations that a_2 would be greater than a_1 which would in turn be greater than a_3.

For the simpler 3-parameter model we were also able to obtain estimates. The estimates for the three parameters are given below:

$$a_1 = .462$$
$$a_2 = .782$$
$$r = .186$$

Because the estimation procedure is independent of the content of the one state to which movement is allowed, and since $a_2 > a_1$, the only 3-parameter model that is possible is one which restricts movement to only the $[+ \, -]$ state. Therefore, we can already conclude that a model which allows movement to only the $[- \, +]$ state cannot describe the observed process.

In estimating the parameter in the Bernoulli model it was not necessary to use the complicated procedure above. Rather the simple maximum likelihood estimate based on the proportion of s-responses per trial for all trials and subjects was computed. It was found that:

$$a_1 = .696$$

B. PRINCIPAL RESULTS

Since there are no absolute rules for deciding on an adequate list of model testing quantities, there is a certain degree of arbitrariness in selecting empirical features of the data to examine. We did attempt to select (1) quantities that would characterize what we believe are substantively significant features of the data as well as (2) quantities which would allow us to discriminate between the three models. The second of these criteria is of special significance since the evaluation of any specific model is based in part on how adequate it is in comparison to some theoretically relevant second model.

Since changes in the rate of acceptance of influence are of particular substantive importance, the first quantity we will examine is the proportion of s-responses on successive trials. We will examine both the observed curve and simulation curves based on each of the models. The simulations were standard Monte-Carlo simulations in which a computer generated pseudorandom numbers whose values determined responses and state changes for a fixed number of "subjects." We generated 40 different sets of data, each set based on 58 subjects and 40 trials. From each set we calculated the value of the quantities being examined and then calculated the average of those values over the 40 sets of data.

Let us first consider the predictions that each of these models make for the curve of s-responses. The predictions of the 1-parameter model are straightforward. Since the process postulated here is one in which no change of behavior is assumed to have occurred, the curve for the mean proportion of s-responses should be *constant* through time. The predictions of the 3-parameter model for this quantity are also straightforward but markedly different. In the process postulated by this model, our subjects are initially in an undifferentiated state in which they are making s-responses at a rate of 46 percent. As the process unfolds, these subjects move into high-low states in which they are now making s-responses at a rate of 78 percent. Further, since the estimated change of state parameter is relatively large ($r = .186$) given the number of trials involved, almost all subjects will have moved to the high-low state by the end of the experiment. Therefore the 3-parameter model predicts a sharply *increasing* curve of s-responses. The situation for the 4-parameter model is considerably more subtle. In the process assumed to have occurred under this model, all subjects start out in an undifferentiated state where the rate of s-responses is near 70 percent. As the experiment continues, some move to $[+ -]$ where the s-response rate is 85 percent and some to the $[- +]$ where the rate is only 33 percent. Thus the decrease in the rate of s-responses for those moving into the low-high state is approximately 2.4 times the size of the increase in these responses for those moving to the high-low state. However, the relative likelihood of moving into one type of differentiated state as compared to a second is a function of the rate at which responses, consistent with these expectation states, are occurring in the undifferentiated state. The estimates for this model tell us that while the subject is in the undifferentiated state, s-responses, which are consistent with a high-low state, are occurring at approximately 2.3 times the rate of o-responses (70 percent vs. 30 percent). Therefore, we should expect to find roughly the same difference in the numbers who have moved into high-low states as compared to low-high states. Thus the effect of differences in the change of response rate is compensated for by the effect of differences in the change of state frequencies. As a consequence, while postulating the occurrence of a considerably more complex process than the 1-parameter model, the 4-parameter model makes essentially the same prediction for this quantity; namely, that the s-response curve will be *constant*.

Figure 2-3 shows the average proportion of s-responses for successive blocks of eight trials for both observed and simulated responses. The observed curve is based on the responses of 58 subjects, and each simulated curve is based on the average of 40 sets of the responses of 58 subjects—in effect 2,320 subjects.

The observed curve is clearly more consistent with the curves of the 1- and 4-parameter models and is within the limits of variation of those curves. The 3-parameter curve is definitely not an accurate description of the observed curve.

The second quantity we will examine is alternations. An alternation is a pair of adjacent responses where one is an s-response and the other an o-response. In particular we are interested in changes in alternating behavior through time. Such a quantity provides us with information on changes in

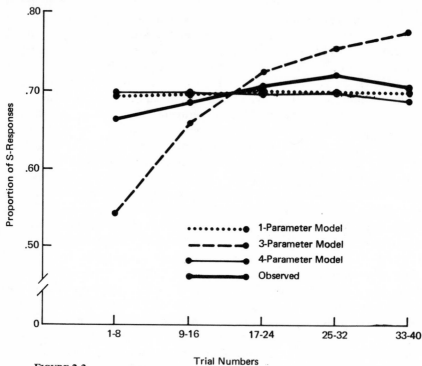

FIGURE 2-3

Proportion of s-responses per trial, computed for blocks of eight trials.

the relative stability and instability of the subject's response behavior as the process evolves. The predictions from the 1-parameter model are again straightforward. It predicts no change in the degree of consistency in s-responses; therefore, the curve for the mean proportion alternations through time should be *constant*. In the case of the 3-parameter model, however, a change is predicted. This follows only in part from the fact that this model assumes a process in which a change of state has occurred. What is relevant here is that in moving into a high-low state the subject is now making a particular type of response, for example s-responses, at a rate closer to 100 percent than was the case while he was in the undifferentiated state (78 percent vs. 48 percent). As a consequence, this model predicts a general *decrease* through time in the mean proportion of alternations. The predictions from the 4-parameter model are similar to those from the 3-parameter one, although the argument is slightly more complicated. For the subjects who have moved into the low-high state there should be no change in their rate of alternating behavior. The rate at which these subjects are making their most frequent responses in the low-high state (o-responses, 67 percent of the time)

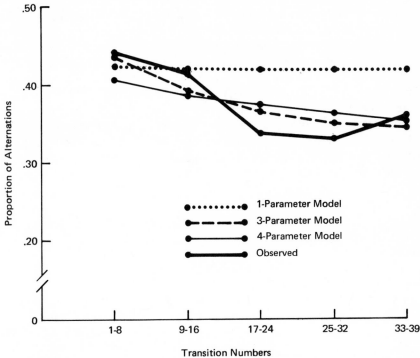

FIGURE 2-4
Proportion of alternations per transition, computed for blocks of 8, 8, 8, 8, and 7 transitions.

is not significantly closer to (or farther from) the 100 percent level than the rate of their most frequent response while in the undifferentiated state (*s*-responses, 70 percent of the time). Therefore, for these subjects the model claims that there was no increase in the degree of consistency in their behavior. On the other hand, for those subjects who have moved from the undifferentiated state into the high-low state, the rate of their most frequent response, *s*-responses, has shifted significantly close to the 100 percent level (70 percent vs. 85 percent). For these subjects change of state also involves increase in the consistency of their behavior. Consequently, the overall prediction of this model is that the mean proportion of alternations *decreases* through time.

Figure 2-4 shows the average proportion of alternations for successive blocks of transitions for both observed and simulated data.

The curves predicted by the 3-parameter and the 4-parameter model show the expected decrease of alternations through time and are in good agreement with the observed curve. The 1-parameter curve, as expected, is flat and is clearly not an adequate representation of the observed curve. So although the 1-parameter model could predict the *s*-response curve it does not predict the alternations curve, and while the 3-parameter model failed to predict the *s*-response curve it does predict the alternations curve. The 4-parameter model is consistent with both curves.

The third quantity we will examine is the variance among subjects at different times in the process in their likelihood of making *s*-responses. We examined blocks of eight trials and computed the variance of the number of *s*-responses per subject for each block. The predictions of the three models for this quantity are quite different. The 3-parameter model claims that during the earlier phases of the process there are subjects in the undifferentiated state, and because the value of *r* is so large, there are some subjects who have already moved into a high-low state. Thus, during these phases *s*-responses

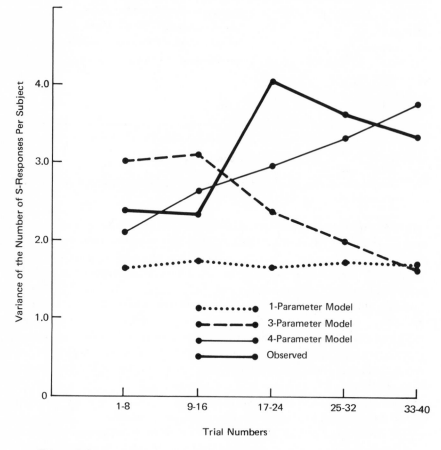

FIGURE 2-5

Variance of the number of *s*-responses per subject, computed for blocks of eight trials.

are being generated by two populations, one at a rate near 46 percent and the other at a rate near 78 percent. However, the large value of r also means that by the end of the process almost all subjects will have moved to the high-low state and thus will be making s-responses at the same general rate. Therefore, this model predicts that overall the variance among subjects should *decrease* through time. The 4-parameter model claims that during the earlier phases of the process most subjects are still in the undifferentiated state making s-responses at a rate near 70 percent. Further, since the values of the change of state parameters in this case are small, at the end of the process we should find three groups of subjects: those who have moved to high-low, those who have moved to low-high, and those still in the undifferentiated state. Subjects in each of these states will be making s-responses at different rates (70 percent, 85 percent and 33 percent). Hence this model predicts that overall the variance among subjects should *increase* with time. For the 1-parameter model since no change of state is assumed to occur, no change in the number of subpopulations producing s-responses at different rates is predicted. As a consequence, the variance of s-responses among subjects should be *constant* through time.

Figure 2-5 shows the observed and simulated curves. It is clear that neither the 3-parameter nor the 1-parameter curve is consistent with the observed curve. The 4-parameter curve is not an exact match to the observed curve but is certainly the most nearly consistent curve. It is not known whether the departures in this latter case are attributable to sampling variation or not.

Overall Assessment of Fit

The 4-parameter model seems to have provided a much better account of the three observed quantities we examined than did the 3-parameter model or the 1-parameter model. Table 2-1 presents in summary form the particular results of our analysis.

The only model which predicted all quantities was the 4-parameter model, although it was not as successful as we would like on the blocked variance curve. The 1-parameter model failed in predicting the alternations curve and the blocked variance curve. The 3-parameter model also failed in predicting two quantities—the s-response curve and the blocked variance curve.

The significance of these findings merits some further discussion. The finding that the 4-parameter model is in general more adequate than the 3-parameter model in accounting for our results is, in the first instance, of *factual* significance. It tells us that for this particular case of p interacting with two others—as contrasted with the cases, for example, in which he is interacting with one other or three others—the assumption of a process in which two differentiated states emerge in differing proportions is more tenable than that of a process in which only one differentiated state (either [− +] or

TABLE 2-1. Summary of Whether Each Model Was or Was Not Successful in Predicting the Process Trends of the Three Quantities That Were Examined

Quantities	Models		
	1-parameter	3-parameter	4-parameter
Proportion of *s*-responses per trial	yes	no	yes
Proportion of alternations per transition	no	yes	yes
Variance of number of *s*-responses per subject	no	no	yes

[+ −]) is formed. In what ways the evaluation-expectation process is affected by increases in the size of the group (as one possible variation on this experiment) can only be answered by further experimentation.

On the other hand, the superiority of the 4-parameter model to the 1-parameter model provides us with information of a different nature. It tells us that the assumption of a process in which there is no change of behavior as a consequence of the evaluational activities of the members of the group is inadequate (in a comparative sense) in accounting for these experimental results. Since changes of state and behavior are basic features of our evaluation-expectation theory, the inadequacy of the no-change model is a result of general *theoretical* significance.

IV. SUMMARY

We began our investigation with the general argument that the known features of power and prestige orders which emerge in task-performing groups can be accounted for by assuming that the members of these groups come to hold stable and typically differentiated conceptions of the performance capacities of each other. This argument in turn, poses the problem of: how do these stable differentiated conceptions, performance expectations, develop in task groups? We believe that *one* of the ways in which performance expectations are formed involves the generalization of evaluations made by group members of each other's problem-solving attempts. In order to isolate and investigate this process we have constructed a theory which describes its operation in a situation where actors are continually evaluating and accepting or rejecting each other's performances but where other behaviors, which might affect the formation of expectations, have been controlled. On the basis of the assertions of our theory, we reason that the occurrence of differential performance evaluations will lead the actor to form differentiated performance expectations. Once these expectations are formed, the actor's evaluations of subsequent performances will tend to be consistent with these expectations, and the rate at which he is influenced by others will be accordingly changed. Finally, since his behavior will tend to be in accord with his expectations the process becomes self-maintaining. Thus, under the given task conditions, his expectations, once formed, will remain unchanged.

An experiment was conducted in order to investigate the process described by our theory. The experiment consisted of a series of forty trials on each of which subjects made an initial choice between two alternative answers to a task problem presented, exchanged information with the other two subjects about initial choices, and made a private final choice. The exchange of information was controlled by the experimenter so that on each trial each subject believed that he had selected a different alternative from the one the other subjects selected. Each subject's initial choice was his performance output for that trial, his evaluation (or reevaluation) of the choice alternatives after exchanging information was his unit performance evaluation, and his final choice indicated his acceptance or rejection of influence on that trial. It was predicted that the evaluations each subject made of his own and the others' performances on each trial would lead him to form performance expectations for himself and for the others. Since he was always in disagreement with the others, we assumed that either he would come to believe himself better at the task than the others or worse. In the former case his rate of acceptance of influence would drop while in the latter case his rate would rise.

We constructed a Markov chain model which formalizes the process described by our theory. The states of the chain were the expectations p could hold for himself and the others. Either his expectations would be unformed, state [0 0]; or he would hold high expectations for himself and low for the others, state [+ −]; or he would hold low expectations for himself and high for the others, state [− +]. For each state we assigned a probability of not accepting influence (s-response) on any trial for any person in that state. Movement between states was hypothesized to be restricted to either moving with a fixed probability from [0 0] to [+ −] on any one trial after making an s-response, or moving with a fixed probability from [0 0] to [− +] on any one trial after making an o-response (accepting influence). This results in a model with five parameters which are restated below:

$$\text{P }(s\text{-response in } [0\ 0]) \qquad = a_1$$
$$\text{P }(s\text{-response in } [+\ -]) \qquad = a_2$$
$$\text{P }(s\text{-response in } [-\ +]) \qquad = a_3$$
$$\text{P (moving from } [0\ 0] \text{ to}$$
$$[+\ -] \text{ after an } s\text{-response}) = r$$
$$\text{P (moving from } [0\ 0] \text{ to}$$
$$[-\ +] \text{ after an } o\text{-response}) = d$$

We also considered two other models—a 3-parameter model in which movement either to $[+ \ -]$ is not allowed ($r = 0$) or in which movement to $[- \ +]$ is not allowed ($d = 0$), and a 1-parameter model which did not allow any change of state.

Estimates of the parameter values for each of the models was carried out and we were able to immediately reject the 3-parameter model with $r = 0$ because it was found that the probability of an s-response increases if movement is restricted to only one state. For the remaining version of the 3-parameter model, the 5-parameter model, and the 1-parameter model, reasonable estimates for all parameters were obtained. Additionally, it was found that for the 5-parameter model, $r \cong d$. Consequently we simplified it to a 4-parameter model with the same parameter governing movement to either $[+ \ -]$ or $[- \ +]$.

The evaluation of the fit of the three models was carried out by comparing the observed values of three empirical quantities with the values of those same quantities obtained by computer simulation of the response process specified by each model. We found that the predictions of the 4-parameter model were clearly in greater accord with the observed data than those of either the 3-parameter model or the 1-parameter model.

These findings enable us to conclude (1) that the assumption of a process in which there are no changes in behavior will not adequately describe the observed process; and (2) the assumption of an evaluation-expectation process in which *two* differentiated states are seen to emerge, in differing proportions, does provide a generally adequate basis for characterizing the observed behavior in this particular case.

REFERENCES

BALES, R. F. 1953. The equilibrium problem in small groups. In T. Parsons, R. F. Bales, & E. A. Shils, (eds.). *Working papers in the theory of action.* Glencoe: The Free Press, pp. 111–161.

BALES, R. F., and P. E. SLATER. 1955. Role differentiation in small decision-making groups. In T. Parsons, R. F. Bales et al., (eds.). *Family socialization and interaction process.* Glencoe: The Free Press, pp. 259–306.

BALES, R. F., F. L. STRODTBECK, T. M. MILLS, & MARY E. ROSEBOROUGH. 1951. Channels of communication in small groups. *American sociological review* 16: 461–8.

BERGER, J., B. P. COHEN, M. ZELDITCH, JR. 1966a. Status characteristics and expectation states. In J. Berger, M. Zelditch, Jr., & B. Anderson (eds.). *Sociological theories in progress.* Boston: Houghton Mifflin Company, pp. 29–46.

BERGER, J., B. P. COHEN, T. L. CONNER, M. ZELDITCH, JR. 1966b. Status characteristics and expectation states: a process model. In J. Berger, M. Zelditch, Jr., & B. Anderson (eds.). *Sociological theories in progress.* Boston: Houghton Mifflin Company, pp. 47–73.

BERGER, J., & T. L. CONNER. 1966. Performance expectations and behavior in small groups. Stanford: Laboratory for Social Research, Stanford University, *Technical report no. 18.*

CONNER, T. L. 1966. Continual disagreement and the assignment of self-other performance expectations. Unpublished Ph. D. dissertation, Department of Sociology, Stanford University, Stanford, California.

HARVEY, O. J. 1953. An experimental approach to the study of status relations in informal groups. *American sociological review* 18: 357–67.

HEINICKE, C., & R. F. BALES. 1953. Development trends in the structure of small groups. *Sociometry* 16: 7–38.

MOORE, J. C. 1965. Development of the spatial judgment experimental task. Stanford: Laboratory for Social Research, Stanford University, *Technical report no. 15.*

SHERIF, M., O. J. HARVEY & B. J. WHITE. 1955. Status in experimentally produced groups. *American journal of sociology* 60: 370–9.

WHYTE, W. F. 1943. *Street corner society: The social structure of an Italian slum.* Chicago: University of Chicago Press.

CHAPTER THREE

A Model for the Evolution of Status Structures in Task-Oriented Discussion Groups*

M. HAMIT FISEK

I. THE PROBLEM AND ITS BACKGROUND

Bales and his associates began two lines of research that until recently have progressed relatively independently. The first has been concerned with developing mathematical models to describe observed regularities in discussion groups, mainly the distribution of participation. Another line of research, of wider scope, has been concerned with developing a theoretical explanation for the emergence of status orders in task groups. The modeling work has suffered from lack of theoretical foundations; it has concentrated on rela-

*This paper is derived from the author's Ph. D. thesis written under Professor Joseph Berger and submitted to the Department of Sociology at Stanford University. He would like to thank Professor Joseph Berger and Professors Bernard P. Cohen and Francis Sim, who made up his advisory committee. The research was supported by NSF grants GS 1513 and GS 170 and a grant from the Stanford University Computation Center to cover the costs of computation.

tively unimportant issues, such as the exact mathematical shape of the total distribution of participation, and has ignored issues of greater substantive interest, such as the description of the changes in the distribution of participation over time, while the theoretical structure developed has lacked the means to provide a precise description of the observed regularities in discussion groups. This paper attempts to present an integrated theoretical formulation and mathematical model of interaction and the emergence of status orders in discussion groups. The results of a study designed to evaluate the empirical validity of the model will be presented.

The first models constructed to describe interaction were proposed by Bales (1953). They may be described as algorithmic-statistical, consisting of sets of rules that may be used to simulate interaction in conjunction with a random number device. These models have only recently been evaluated in terms of empirical evidence by Lewis (1970 *a*). His conclusion is that the goodness-of-fit to the available data is inadequate. Bales and his associates (Bales et al., 1951) have also investigated the harmonic function as a possible model for the distribution of overall participation rates. Their conclusion was that the fit obtained is not satisfactory.

Stephan and Mishler (1952) have proposed the exponential function as a model for the distribution of participation rates. Evaluating the goodness-of-fit of the model on data they themselves had gathered and also on the Bales data, they claim a reasonably satisfactory goodness-of-fit.

Kadane and Lewis (1969) reevaluated the evidence and the fit of both the exponential model and the harmonic model, and concluded that although a marginally better fit obtains for the exponential model, the evidence is not conclusive for preferring one model over the other. For particular cases, both models provide good descriptions of the data.

Kadane and Lewis also discussed the evidence for the models proposed by Coleman (1960) and Leik (1965, 1967). Coleman suggested that the observed regularity in participation rates may be due to the data being aggregated across groups after having been ordered. He claimed, in fact, that order statistics calculated on samples from a uniform distribution may be approximately exponentially distributed. Leik, on the other hand, suggested that every actor is characterized by a participation potential and that his output in a group will be a function of this potential as well as the potentials of the other group members. He also claimed that the distribution of participation potentials is skewed normal and order statistics on samples from such a population may be approximately exponentially distributed. Kadane and Lewis (1969) presented a convincing analytic argument that suggested that some of the basic assumptions of both models are untenable.

The exponential distribution stands out as the most interesting of the models of the distribution of participation rates, not only on the basis of goodness-of-fit but also because Horvath (1964) has provided a theoretical foundation for it. Horvath proposed two substantive assumptions about the nature of interaction: that each member of the group has the same constant probability of initiating an act; and that each member exercises this probability in turn, going down the hierarchical structure of the group. It is straightforward to derive the exponential distribution as a consequence of these assumptions.

The Horvath model has one fewer independent parameter than the Stephan-Mishler model although both are based on the exponential distribution. Kadane et al. (1969) has evaluated the goodness-of-fit of the Horvath model to the available data and concluded that the goodness-of-fit leaves something to be desired. However, the Horvath model does point out how one can construct models of the distribution of participation rates based on substantive assumptions and thus it can serve as a starting point for further model building.

Expectation States Theory as developed by Berger and his associates (Berger and Snell, 1961; Berger et al., 1966; Berger and Conner, 1969; Berger and Conner, chapter four, this volume) explains the development of status orders in task-performing groups and the effects of such orders on behavior. The development of task-performance expectations can occur through a number of different processes. A classic example is the activation of a status characteristic and the assignment of task-performance expectation states on the basis of expectations associated with the status characteristic. In general, processes based on the interaction in the group can be activated by inequalities *in any aspect of the interaction* among the group members. A process that is particularly relevant to ad hoc discussion groups is the "evaluation-expectation process" (see chapter two of this volume) and will be the basis of the analysis here. However, it should be noted that this process is *only one* of a number of different processes by which expectation states may be formed.

The evaluation-expectation process assumes that interaction consists of repetitions of sequences of behavior of the following kinds. An *action opportunity* is a socially distributed chance to perform; for instance, a question like "What do *you* think?" constitutes an action opportunity. A *performance output* is a task-oriented act, a problem-solving attempt. A *reward action* communicates the acceptance (positive reward action) or rejection (negative reward action) of performance outputs. We need the additional ideas of a *unit evaluation*, which is a specific and momentary evaluation of a person or the performance of a person, and a *performance expectation*, which is an anticipation by a group member of the quality of his own or some other's performance.

Berger and Conner define what they call the *full fundamental sequence* of behaviors (see chapter four of this volume). It consists of the following sequence of behaviors: action opportunity—performance output—action opportunity—reward action. The reward action element of this cycle implies an unobservable element—the unit evaluation. That is, an action opportunity is given to an actor; he produces a performance output and gives an action opportunity to the others so that the others can communicate the results of their evaluations of his output. The action opportunity is then given to another actor. In every such sequence of behavior each person in the group may make a unit evaluation of the performing actor's output. If a person has not already assigned task-performance expectations to the performing actor, then he may do so based on the unit evaluation of his output. This is the central mechanism of the evaluation process; a person making a positive unit evaluation of an actor's performance may assign positive task performance expectations to him, if he has not already assigned such expectations, and similarly for negative evaluations. Thus the output of each actor is evaluated and these evaluations lead to the development of expectations for each actor by the actors in the system. Once the assignment of performance expectations has occurred, it will determine patterns of inequality in observable behavior, which in turn will maintain the performance expectations.

II. THE FORMULATION

In attempting to formulate a theoretical model for a phenomenon that must of necessity exist in many different forms, it becomes necessary to be rather stringent in determining the scope and initial conditions under which the formulation is expected to be applicable. Precision can be achieved only at the expense of narrowly defined scope conditions. This theory is intended to apply to small task-oriented discussion groups whose members are initially undifferentiated either in terms of social characteristics or performance expectations. The scope of the theory is limited to only one observable aspect of group interaction, the initiation of verbal acts. The following initial conditions are assumed to obtain.

The group must be working on a common and valued task and must be collectively oriented. That is, the group members must be jointly working on a problem where it is both necessary and legitimate to take into account each other's behavior. They must be equally committed to the successful completion of the group task. Initially the members of the group must not hold task-performance expectations for each other. Furthermore, there must be no social or personal basis such as prior acquaintance or differentiating status characteristics that can serve as a basis for developing such expectations. In short, all members of the group must start out as status equals.

The group task must not involve any rules or norms that structure the interaction in the group in any specific way. Ideally, the group task must be intra-systemic—that is, it must be a problem such that the group has to develop the rules or norms for approaching the problem rather than acquire them from an external system. Neither should the task provide any particular type of group member with special advantages in problem solution.

All the basic concepts necessary to the formulation are taken from Expectation States Theory. Several need to be modified to fit the purpose at hand. The concept of action opportunity covers not only overtly distributed chances to perform. Silence is an action opportunity; in fact, it may be the most common kind of action opportunity: an actor who pauses during a speech, or simply remains silent, is offering the other actors in the group a chance to perform in the same way as though he had overtly passed the "conversational ball" to another actor.

The concept of performance output covers all meaningful verbal acts. For present purposes, identifying reward actions and non-task outputs serves no useful end. We can thus simplify the full fundamental sequence to what may be called the basic interaction cycle by ignoring the reward actions and the associated action opportunities. The basic interaction cycle consists of an action opportunity followed by a performance output, followed by a unit evaluation, the unit evaluation being unobservable. In fact, unit evaluations are not properly a part of the interaction process but rather the element linking the interaction process to the evaluation-expectation process. The observable interaction process consists of repetitions of the basic cycle— action opportunity followed by performance output.

We can conceptualize the interaction process more formally as a discrete-time stochastic process defined over a set of actors (A_i), each trial of which is an interaction cycle and which on every trial takes on a value symbolizing the actor who performs on that trial. This definition of the interaction process is, of course, strictly operational—it is equivalent to the sequence of performance outputs by the actors in the system. If we assign a number to every actor in the system and use their numbers to represent performance outputs, a realization of the interaction process for a three-actor system may look like 1232213131 . . . . One of the goals of this formulation is to describe accurately the stochastic properties of the process.

It is convenient to relativize the concept of expectation states and think of it as a *relation*. Differences in task-performance expectations between different actors can be represented as a set of high performance expectation relations between the actors. Since the "high performance expectation relation" is the basic conceptual element of the formulation, a formal definition is in order:

DEFINITION

The *high expectation relation, H,* is said to hold between two actors, A_i and A_j, that is, $A_i H A_j$, if and only if actor A_i has higher task-performance expectations for actor A_j *than he does for himself.* The H relation is asymmetric and transitive.

It follows from the definition of the H relation that it is irreflexive; an actor cannot have higher performance expectations for himself than he does for himself, so A_iHA_i is not a possible relation. Asymmetry means that if an actor (A_i) has high performance expectations for another actor (A_j), then actor A_j will *not* have high performance expectations for actor A_i. Transitivity means that if actor A_i has high performance expectations for actor A_j, and if actor A_j has high performance expectations for actor A_k, then actor A_i will have high performance expectations for actor A_k. The definition of the H relation describes the properties of status orders in the types of groups of concern here; that is, task-focused, ad hoc discussion groups. In fact, the properties of irreflexivity, asymmetry, and transitivity define H, and by that token they define the status hierarchy as a partial order (for a discussion of such orders see Harary et al., 1965).

It is convenient to represent the status structure of a group as a digraph, and the definition of the H relation satisfies the basic axiomatic system of digraphs. The set of points (the group members are conceptualized as points) is finite and not empty, the set of lines representing H relations is finite, and contains no distinct parallel lines or loops. In fact, the status structure is an acyclic digraph, because the definition of the H relation excludes the possibility of having any cycles in the digraph.

The definition of the H relation rules out structures that would be considered "unbalanced" (Heider, 1946, Cartwright and Harary, 1956) in the structural sense. That is, a situation in which one actor has high expectations for a second, the second actor has high expectations for a third, and in turn the third has high expectations for the first, would be recognized as an unstable structure, and on substantive grounds it would be ruled out by the transitivity and asymmetry properties of the H relation.

The fact that a high expectation relation rather than a low expectation relation is conceptualized as the basic building block of status structures reflects an implicit assumption about the nature of status orders in task groups. Status orders in such groups are assumed to be deference orders rather than dominance orders; high status is not exacted by the high status member, but rather is given by the low status members. What determines the status order is not so much that an actor may think another less able then himself, but that he may think another more able than himself.

By the initial conditions specified earlier, the digraph of a group at the beginning of a group session consists of a number of isolated points—there are no H relations. The actors are status equals; they have no task-performance expectations for each other. As the group interacts, H relations are formed and the status structure of the group—its digraph—changes. This is the *structure process*, the sequence of status structures the group forms over time.

There are three distinct processes that operate concurrently over the time the group is in session. The interaction process is the only process that has observable components and "drives" the other processes. The unit evaluation process mediates between the interaction process and the structure process. Driven by the interaction process, in turn, it provides the motive power for changes in the status structures; it drives the structure process. Of course, the structure process determines the features of the interaction process.

Each trial of the interaction process is an interaction cycle. An action opportunity is offered and taken, an actor performs and is evaluated by the other actors in the system. According to their evaluations of his performance, the actors in the system can form expectations for the performing actor. This is the unit evaluation process component of the interaction cycle. Every time an actor performs there is a probability that he is positively evaluated. Given that he is positively evaluated, there is a probability that a positively evaluating actor may assign to him higher performance expectations than he has for himself—if such an assignment does not violate any of the assumptions of the system. The simplest assumption that can be made is that the probability of H relation formation can be treated as a simple parameter for homogeneous populations, within the initial conditions of the formulation.

ASSUMPTION 1

Given that actor A_i makes one or more consecutive performance outputs, there is a probability (π), that actor A_j, $(i \neq j)$, will form a high expectation relation with regard to A_i, if the A_jHA_i relation does not already exist.

This assumption defines the structure process to be a "one-step change of state" process. The development of the expectation structure occurs in a series of discrete steps. Thinking of the "states" of the structure process as the possible different digraphs of the group, the system changes state as new H relations are formed and the digraph of the system changes.

There is no allowance made for the possible breaking of H relations once formed. Such a mechanism unduly complicates the basic model, and for single group sessions it is doubtful that it presents an improvement over the simpler model. Given that H relations, once formed, cannot be broken, if the value of the parameter (π) is not zero, then the structure process should reach one of a set of absorbing states, in other words, it should become stable or reach equilibrium. How quickly it does so, of course, depends on the value of the parameter and the performance probabilities of the actors in the different states of the system.

To specify the performance probabilities of actors it is necessary to identify actors or rather "positions" in the digraph of the system. A level assignment (see Harary et al., 1965) serves this purpose, associating a number with each point of the digraph. To obtain a descending level assignment an integer (called a level) is assigned to each point of the digraph such that if there is a line from A_i to A_j then the level of A_i is greater than the level of A_j. The notion of level corresponds pretty closely to the concept of rank in a status structure. To insure a unique level assignment so as to avoid confusion in identification of points the following conventions are adopted. The level assignment must be minimal (that is, it must have the smallest possible number of levels), the first level for each weak component of the digraph must be the integer 1, and all other points must be assigned the lowest possible level values. Such a level assignment determines levels so that any two actors, A_i and A_j, who are within the same weak component (that is, who are at least connected by a semipath) but are not connected by a path will have the same level if and only if they are equidistant from the nearest actor to whom they are both connected by a path. It is useful to compare level assignments within a single weak component; comparisons are meaningless for points in different weak components.

It is now possible to consider the mechanism for the allocation of action opportunities in the group. Such allocation follows the principles of distributive justice among status equals; resources are allocated equally. Among actors who have no expectations for each other, that is, who have no H relation between them, action opportunities are shared equally. In the same way, among subgroups of actors whose members do not have an H relation to actors from different subgroups, action opportunities will be allocated in proportion to the number of actors in each subgroup. These ideas can be expressed more precisely.

ASSUMPTION 2

If D, the digraph of the system, is disconnected, then action opportunities are distributed between each of its weak components in proportion to the number of points in each of the weak components.

Since isolated points are considered weak components, the above assumption is quite general.

The next assumption deals with the distribution of action opportunities among actors who stand in the H relation to each other. The basic notion involved is that an actor will tend to defer to actors for whom he has high expectations. When an action opportunity is given to the group, each actor will defer to those other actors for whom he has high expectations, and may accept the action opportunity if, and only if, those others do not accept it. The action opportunity is passed from actor to actor down the expectation structure of the group until it is accepted. If it passes through the entire structure without being accepted, then it is returned to the top level of the structure and the process of the passing of the action opportunity repeats itself. When an actor accepts the action opportunity and performs, the new action opportunity he creates (either explicitly or implicitly) when he finishes performing is given to the top level of the structure. More precisely,

ASSUMPTION 3

a. Within each weak component of D, action opportunities will be given to each actor in ascending order of level value either until one of the actors accepts the action opportunity or the order is exhausted. Between actors with the same level value, action opportunities are equally distributed.
b. If an action opportunity reaches the lowest level of D without being accepted, then it will be returned to the top level of D.

This assumption constitutes a generalization of Horvath's (1964) assumption. In considering it, it is obvious that at least two types of verbal interaction constitute violations of this assumption. The first type are interruptions, where an actor creates an action opportunity for himself where there is none, and the second type are specifically directed action opportunities such as, "What do you think, John?" Although both types of acts are quite common, when their frequency of occurrence is compared to the frequency with which action opportunities are created and taken in discussion groups, it seems reasonable that their occurrence be considered within a margin of error.

One further assumption is needed to complete the basic formulation. This assumption is taken directly from Horvath (1964).

ASSUMPTION 4

If an actor is offered an action opportunity, he will accept it with probability θ.

The probability of an actor accepting an action opportunity when it is offered to him can be treated as a constant for a homogenous population under similar conditions.

The four assumptions above are sufficient to determine completely the interaction and the structure processes. It may be instructive to point out that the formulation developed here is entirely compatible with the general formulation of Expectation States Theory (see chapter two of this volume), and it represents the case where all interaction parameters are equal for the actors to begin with except for differences in the rates of positive reward actions received by the actors. These differences result in the differentiated power and prestige order and its concomitants.

III. THE MODEL

The assumptions of the previous section completely define the stochastic properties of the interaction process. However, it is necessary to derive a model that can make specific predictions about a particular case before the formulation can be empirically evaluated. It seems best to derive the model for the group size of three, this being the smallest group size that preserves the properties of the general system.

There are five different status structures that can exist in a three-actor group. The digraphs of these structures are given in Figure 3-1.

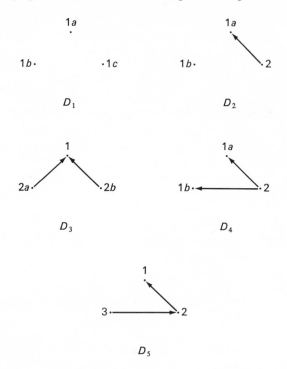

FIGURE 3-1
Possible states of the system

On the digraphs the points have been labeled with their level values. Where there is more than one point with the same level value the points have been arbitrarily assigned letter suffixes. Different structures are, of course, identified in terms of different configurations of positions, not in terms of actors who may occupy them. If points were identified as actors instead of positions, the digraphs of different structures with the same configuration of positions would be isomorphs.

Given these digraphs, it is quite straightforward to calculate the probabilities of each actor accepting an action opportunity and producing a performance output when the system is in each state by applying assumptions 2, 3, and 4. The following representation is adapted: $P_j^{(i)}$, which stands for the probability that A_j—the actor identified by level value j—performs on a given trial, given that the system is in the ith state, state D_i, on that trial.

In the equivalence state, D_1, it follows immediately from Assumption 2 that the performance probabilities are equal for each actor, that is,

$$P_{1a}^{(1)} = P_{1b}^{(1)} = P_{1c}^{(1)} = \tfrac{1}{3}$$

To determine the performance probabilities for the asymmetric state, D_2, it is helpful to use a tree diagram as shown in Figure 3-2. The symbol S stands for the action opportunity offered to the group—to the top level of the status structure.

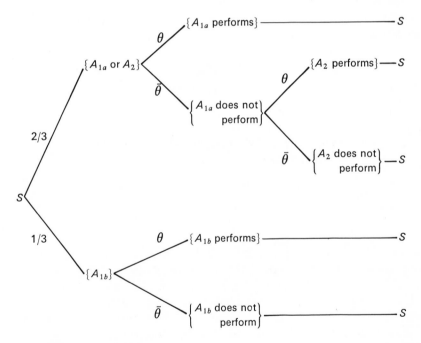

FIGURE 3-2
The tree diagram for state D_2

It is simplest to begin by deriving the probability of an action opportunity falling through the structure without being accepted by any of the actors, thus completing a "round":

$$P\{AO \text{ completes round}\} = \frac{2\bar{\theta}^2}{3} + \frac{\bar{\theta}}{3} = \frac{2\bar{\theta}^2 + \bar{\theta}}{3}$$

The probability of A_{1a} performing is the probability that the (A_{1a}, A_2) component is offered the action opportunity in the first round and A_{1a} accepts it, plus the probability that the action opportunity completes the first round and is again offered to the (A_{1a}, A_2) component, and A_1 accepts it, plus . . . ad infinitum.

$$P_{1a}^{(2)} = \frac{2\theta}{3} + \left[\frac{2\bar{\theta}^2 + \bar{\theta}}{3}\right]\frac{2\theta}{3} + \left[\frac{2\bar{\theta}^2 + \bar{\theta}}{3}\right]^2 \frac{2\theta}{3} + \cdots$$

$$P_{1a}^{(2)} = \frac{2}{3 + 2\bar{\theta}}$$

The probability of A_2 performing can be derived in the same way; in fact, the series for A_2 differs from the one for A_{1a} by a constant factor $\bar{\theta}$ in each term, which is the probability of A_{1a} not accepting the action opportunity in each round. That is,

$$P_2^{(2)} = \frac{2}{3}\bar{\theta}\theta + \left[\frac{2\bar{\theta}^2 + \bar{\theta}}{3}\right]\frac{2}{3}\bar{\theta}\theta + \left[\frac{2\bar{\theta}^2 + \bar{\theta}}{3}\right]^2 \frac{2}{3}\bar{\theta}\theta + \cdots$$

$$P_2^{(2)} = \frac{2\bar{\theta}}{3 + 2\bar{\theta}}$$

The performance probability for A_{1b} is the sum of the probabilities of A_{1b} being offered and accepting the action opportunity in each round. That is,

$$P_{1b}^{(2)} = \frac{\theta}{3} + \left[\frac{2\bar{\theta}^2 + \bar{\theta}}{3}\right]\frac{\theta}{3} + \left[\frac{2\bar{\theta}^2 + \bar{\theta}}{3}\right]^2 \frac{\theta}{3} + \cdots$$

$$P_{1b}^{(2)} = \frac{1}{3 + 2\bar{\theta}}$$

Comparing the performance probabilities for A_2 and A_{1b}, it is interesting to note that for θ less than 0.5, A_2 has a higher performance probability than A_{1a}. The actor who has accepted a lower position in the status order is "better off" than the actor who is as yet not part of the status structure. This result may perhaps be interpreted in terms of clique formation.

Proceeding in the same way for the top-determined state, D_3, whose tree diagram is given in Figure 3-3, the probability of an action opportunity completing a round can be seen to be

$$P\{AO \text{ completes round}\} = \bar{\theta}^3$$

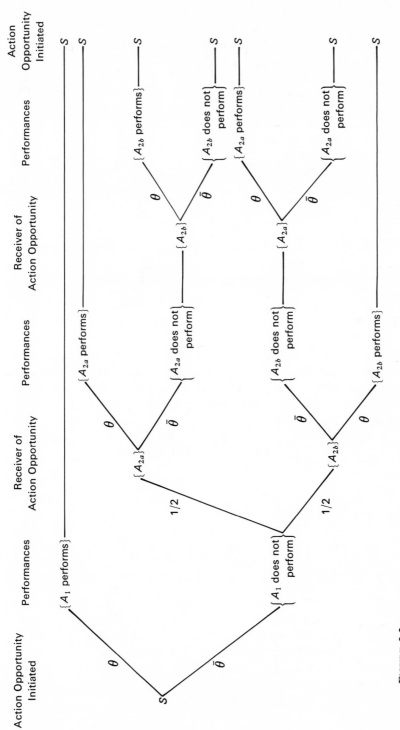

Figure 3-3
The tree diagram for state D_3.

Therefore, the probability of A_1 performing is the sum of the probabilities that he performs in the first round, the second round, etc.

$$P_1^{(3)} = \theta + \bar{\theta}^3\theta + \bar{\theta}^6\theta + \cdots$$

$$P_1^{(3)} = \frac{\theta}{1 - \bar{\theta}^3}$$

Since the above expression is one that appears frequently, let

$$\alpha = \frac{\theta}{1 - \bar{\theta}^3}$$

The probability of either of the A_2's performing must be equal because they have the same level value. Therefore, the probability of either one of the A_2's performing is one half the probability that A_1 does not perform.

$$P_{2a}^{(3)} = P_{2b}^{(3)} = \frac{\bar{\alpha}}{2}$$

The derivation of the performance probabilities follows the same steps for the remaining two states, the bottom determined state, D_4, and the stable state, D_5. The stable state, D_5, is identical with the Horvath model—the performance probabilities are exponentially distributed.

The performance probabilities can be arranged as a 5×3 matrix where each row gives the performance probabilities for each state of the system in order of level value. This matrix P is given in Figure 3-4.

Level Values*

D_1	⅓	⅓	⅓
D_2	$\dfrac{2}{3 + 2\bar{\theta}}$	$\dfrac{1}{3 + 2\bar{\theta}}$	$\dfrac{2\bar{\theta}}{3 + 2\bar{\theta}}$
D_3	α	$\tfrac{1}{2}\bar{\alpha}$	$\tfrac{1}{2}\bar{\alpha}$
D_4	$\tfrac{1}{2}(1 - \alpha\bar{\theta}^2)$	$\tfrac{1}{2}(1 - \alpha\bar{\theta}^2)$	$\alpha\bar{\theta}^2$
D_5	α	$\alpha\bar{\theta}$	$\alpha\bar{\theta}^2$

State of System

*The levels for each state are as follows: D_1: 1a, 1b, 1c; D_2: 1a, 1b, 2; D_3: 1, 2a, 2b; D_4: 1a, 1b, 2; D_5: 1, 2, 3.

FIGURE 3-4

The matrix of performance probabilities, P

In order to make the model empirically testable it is necessary to work with the probabilities of making a "run of performance outputs" rather than the probabilities of making unit performance outputs, since it is quite difficult to identify unit performance outputs empirically (Fisek, 1968). To obtain the probabilities of making runs of performance outputs, the expected length of runs of performance outputs for each actor in each state is calculated and used as a correction factor for each performance probability. The expected run lengths are simply $1/(1 - p)$, where p stands for a performance probability. These probabilities are then normalized—each being divided by the sum of the corrected probabilities. Thus the P matrix is transformed into a new P' matrix, each of whose entries gives the probabilities of runs of performance outputs.

In order to avoid needless complexity, from this point on the elements of the P' matrix are given as $p_j^{(i)}$ instead of $p_j'^{(i)}$ since the elements of the P matrix are never used in expressions.

The assumptions of the formulation define the structure process to be a Markov chain. The probability of the process being in state D_i on trial n is only dependent on what state the process is in on trial $(n - 1)$, and is completely independent of what state the process might have been in on any previous trials. The probability that a new expectation relation will form that will change the status structure and thus shift the state of the system is dependent only on the parameter (π) and the performance probabilities of the actors, which in turn depend on the current state of the system.

The probability that the process moves from state D_1 to state D_2 is twice the probability that one of the actors performs (which is equal to 1 by definition of a trial), and that one of the other actors forms a high expectation relation with regard to him (which is π by Assumption 1), and that the other actor does not form a high expectation relation with regard to him (which is $\bar{\pi}$). That is, the probability is $2\pi\bar{\pi}$. The factor of 2 comes in since this configuration can occur in two different ways. Likewise, the probability of the process moving into state D_3 is the probability that both nonperforming actors form high expectation relations with regard to the performing actor, that is π^2. The process cannot move in one step from state D_1 to either state D_4 or D_5; therefore, the one-step transition probabilities for these states are zero. The probability of remaining in state D_1 is equal to 1 minus the probabilities of moving into states D_2 and D_3. Therefore, the first row of the transition matrix is:

$$(\bar{\pi}^2, 2\pi\bar{\pi}, \pi^2, 0, 0)$$

The transition probabilities starting out in each of the other states are derived in analogous ways. The one-step transition matrix of the structure process, S, is given in Figure 3-5.

$$D\text{-State on Step } n + 1$$

	1	2	3	4	5
1	$\bar{\pi}^2$	$2\pi\bar{\pi}$	π^2	0	0
2	0	$\bar{\pi}(1 - \pi p_{1b}^{(2)})$	$p_{1a}^{(2)}\pi$	$p_{1b}^{(1)}\pi\bar{\pi}$	$(p_{1b}^{(2)} + p_2^{(2)})\pi$
3	0	0	$1 - (p_{2a}^{(3)} + p_{2b}^{(3)})\pi$	0	$(p_{2a}^{(3)} + p_{2b}^{(3)})\pi$
4	0	0	0	$1 - (p_{1a}^{(4)} + p_{1b}^{(4)})\pi$	$(p_{1a}^{(4)} + p_{1b}^{(4)})\pi$
5	0	0	0	0	1

(rows labeled: D-State on Step n, values 1, 2, 3, 4, 5)

FIGURE 3-5
The one-step transition matrix of the structure process, S

The matrix S, together with the matrix of performance probabilities P', and an initial probability vector W, completely determine the stochastic properties of the interaction process. The initial probability vector is defined to be $[1, 0, 0, 0, 0]$ by the initial condition that the process starts out in the equivalence state, with all actors status equals.

The one-step transition matrix makes obvious the one basic feature of the structure process: the process is, in fact, an absorbing chain with a single absorbing state. There is only one stable expectation structure for the three-person group, and provided that the value of π, the change of state parameter, is not too small, the process will eventually reach this stable state.

The estimation of the two parameters of the model, π and θ, is somewhat complicated, as is usually the case with Markovian models with unobservable states. It is not possible to derive maximum likelihood estimates for the parameters of the model. However, it is possible to construct less rigorous estimation systems, which yield estimates for the parameters.

The actors, or rather the positions they occupy, are identified by level value in the theoretical system. However, in the empirical system actors are identified by their "basic initiation rank." The actor who has the largest number of performance outputs for the entire session is assigned basic initiation rank 1, the actor with the next largest number of performance outputs is assigned rank 2, etc. In order to estimate parameters and to evaluate the model, the correspondence between the two systems of identification must be established. We assume that the level values of actors in the stable state correspond directly to their basic initiation ranks. That is, the actor with basic initiation rank 1 is assumed to be the actor with level value 1 in the stable state and similarly for ranks 2 and 3.

Estimating the parameter θ is easy if we assume that the process has stabilized, that it entered the absorbing state over the last n trials of the process.

$R_i^{(n)}$ represents the observed mean proportion of participation by actors of basic initiation rank i in the last n trials of the process. The following relations can be used to estimate θ:

$$R_i = \hat{P}_i^{(5)} = \frac{\hat{\theta}\hat{\theta}^{(i-1)}}{1 - \hat{\theta}^3} \qquad i = 1, 2, 3$$

This is a nonlinear, but overdetermined, system of simultaneous equation in one unknown, $\hat{\theta}$. The system can be solved by numerical methods.

The estimation of π is somewhat more complicated. Analytic expressions for the overall probability of participation can be obtained for each basic initiation rank and equated to the observed values of the total proportions of participation. Basic initiation ranks have been assumed to be equivalent to levels for the stable state: now it is necessary to determine the probabilistic relations between basic initiation rank and level value for each of the states. These probabilities are designated as $Z_{ij}^{(k)}$, that is, the probability that the actor with basic initiation rank j is in level i in state k. These probabilities can be arranged as five 3×3 matrices $Z^{(1)}$ through $Z^{(5)}$, each matrix giving the probabilities for one of the states of the system.

For the first state the probabilities have a very simple form. There is only one level in state 1, therefore the probability of each basic initiation rank being associated with it is 1. The probability of a rank being associated with a particular level 1 (that is, la, lb, or lc) is 1/3. For state 2, these probabilities are somewhat more complicated. Both A_{1a} and A_{1b} can achieve first basic initiation rank, A_{1b} and A_2 can both achieve third basic initiation rank, and all these actors can achieve second basic initiation rank. Let S_{ij} be the probability that the system moves from state i to state j. Consider:

$$Z_{1a, 1}^{(2)} = \frac{S_{23} + (S_{24}/2) + P_2^{(2)}\pi}{S_{23} + S_{24} + S_{25}}$$

The numerator is the sum of the probability that the system moves to state 3, half the probability that the system moves to state 4, and the probability that the system moves to state 5 by way of A_{1b} forming an expectation relation with regard to A_2. These are the different paths through which A_{1a} can achieve first basic initiation rank. The denominator is the sum of the probabilities of the system changing at all, which normalizes the probability that A_{1a} achieves first rank. All other expressions are derived in similar ways and are given in Figure 3-6.

The fundamental matrix, N, of the process (Kemeny and Snell, 1960), defined as

$$N = (I - Q)^{-1}$$

where I is the identity matrix and Q is the matrix of the transient states of the

Initiation Rank

$$Z^{(1)} \quad \text{Level} \quad \begin{array}{c} 1a \\ 1b \\ 1c \end{array} \begin{array}{ccc} 1 & 2 & 3 \\ \left[\begin{array}{ccc} \frac{1}{3} & \frac{1}{3} & \frac{1}{3} \\ \frac{1}{3} & \frac{1}{3} & \frac{1}{3} \\ \frac{1}{3} & \frac{1}{3} & \frac{1}{3} \end{array} \right] \end{array}$$

Initiation Rank

$$Z^{(2)} \quad \text{Level} \quad \begin{array}{c} 1a \\ 1b \\ 2 \end{array} \begin{array}{ccc} 1 & 2 & 3 \\ \left[\begin{array}{ccc} 1-x & x & 0 \\ x & 1-x-y & y \\ 0 & y & 1-y \end{array} \right] \end{array}$$

where $\quad x = \dfrac{\frac{1}{2}s_{24} + p_{1b}^{(2)}\pi}{s_{23} + s_{24} + s_{25}}$

$\quad y = \dfrac{p_{2}^{(2)}\pi + \frac{1}{2}s_{23}}{s_{23} + s_{24} + s_{25}}$

Initiation Rank

$$Z^{(3)} \quad \text{Level} \quad \begin{array}{c} 1 \\ 2a \\ 2b \end{array} \begin{array}{ccc} 1 & 2 & 3 \\ \left[\begin{array}{ccc} 1 & 0 & 0 \\ 0 & \frac{1}{2} & \frac{1}{2} \\ 0 & \frac{1}{2} & \frac{1}{2} \end{array} \right] \end{array}$$

Initiation Rank

$$Z^{(4)} \quad \text{Level} \quad \begin{array}{c} 1a \\ 1b \\ 2 \end{array} \begin{array}{ccc} 1 & 2 & 3 \\ \left[\begin{array}{ccc} \frac{1}{2} & \frac{1}{2} & 0 \\ \frac{1}{2} & \frac{1}{2} & 0 \\ 0 & 0 & 1 \end{array} \right] \end{array}$$

Initiation Rank

$$Z^{(5)} \quad \text{Level} \quad \begin{array}{c} 1 \\ 2 \\ 3 \end{array} \begin{array}{ccc} 1 & 2 & 3 \\ \left[\begin{array}{ccc} 1 & 0 & 0 \\ 0 & 1 & 0 \\ 0 & 0 & 1 \end{array} \right] \end{array}$$

FIGURE 3-6
The relations between levels and basic initiation rank in each state

process (the matrix obtained from S by suppressing the fifth row and the fifth column), gives the expected number of times the process is in each state given that it began in a particular state. Since the present process can start only in state 1, the vector that is the first row of this matrix, v, contains the relevant information. The vector v' can be obtained from the vector v by adding one more element that gives the expected number of times the process is in the stable or absorbing state. This is equal to the number of trials of the process T, minus the expected number of times the process is in one of the transient states (which is the sum of the first four elements of the vector v). This vector is given below:

$$v' = \left\{ \frac{1}{(1 - S_{11})}, \frac{S_{12}}{(1 - S_{11})(1 - S_{22})}, \frac{S_{12}S_{23} - S_{13}(1 - S_{22})}{(1 - S_{11})(1 - S_{22})(1 - S_{33})}, \right.$$
$$\left. \frac{S_{12}S_{24}}{(1 - S_{11})(1 - S_{22})(1 - S_{44})}, \quad T - \sum_{i=1}^{4} v'_i \right\}$$

Given these quantities and K_i—the observed mean number of participations for rank i—the following system of equations can be set up:

$$\sum_{n=1}^{5} v'_n \sum_{j=1}^{3} Z_{ji}^{(n)} p_j^{(n)} = K_i \qquad i = 1, 2, 3$$

As the value of θ has already been obtained, the above is an overdetermined system of nonlinear simultaneous equations in one unknown, π. The system can be solved by numerical methods.

IV.   THE STUDY

A series of experimental discussion groups were conducted to gather data for evaluating the model. The group discussions were held in a soundproof laboratory room, one wall of which contained a one-way mirror. The three subjects were seated around a triangular table and provided with notebooks and pencils. The room also contained a large-faced clock.

The subjects were male freshmen at Stanford University who were paid for their participation in the study. Each subject was contacted by telephone (after initial recruitment in class) approximately two days before the study and scheduled for a session. Care was taken to schedule subjects from different living groups for each session.

Subjects were told that they would be participating in a "group problem-solving study" and that their conversation would be tape-recorded and that they would be observed from behind the one-way mirror. The task was then presented to them; it consisted of constructing a discussion problem for a group such as their own that would satisfy certain conditions. The task had to be such that it did not involve any specific abilities or skills that could serve as an immediate dimension of differentiation among group members. It had to minimize the probability of a split on a major value dimension, such as conservative–liberal, among the subjects. Furthermore, the task had to have a minimum of intrinsic interest to obtain the commitment of the subjects to its solution. It became clear during pretests that, as hoped, finding such a discussion problem is itself a task that satisfies these conditions.

The subjects were given forty-five minutes to work on the task. The experimenter left the laboratory room after presenting the task and answering questions, and he returned forty-five minutes later. A postsession questionnaire designed to gather relevant sociometric data was administered to the subjects at the completion of the study. The purposes of the study were explained to the subjects at length before they left the laboratory.

Eighteen pretest groups were conducted for purposes of selecting task- and training-observers. For the study proper a total of seventy-six experimental groups were conducted. Of these groups, seventeen were discarded from the sample for failing to meet the initial conditions of the study. These groups either were not task oriented, or contained visible minority group members or previous acquaintances. Fifty-nine groups were included in the final sample.

All sessions were tape-recorded. The coding of the interaction was done directly by two observers. To obtain satisfactory reliability, only the initiator of each act was recorded. It was found that attempts to code targets of acts and to categorize the content of acts resulted in lowering the reliability. (Waxler and Mishler, 1966).

The same two observers coded the data for all groups. They listened to the conversation through stereophonic earphones from behind the one-way mirror and recorded the data by speaking the seat number of the initiating actor into a dictating machine. The data record was broken up into three-minute intervals by a special signal.

Any speech not interrupted by an action opportunity, arbitrarily defined as a pause $1\frac{1}{2}$ seconds long (as judged by the observers), was coded as a single act. Nonverbal meaningful acts such as head shaking were coded as acts if they were performed in response to an action opportunity. Interruptions were coded if the actor managed to output a meaningful unit.

The general level of interobserver reliability for the entire study was quite satisfactory. Three rank inversions out of a possible 174 occurred for the basic initiation ranking of the two observers. In all three cases the participations for the actors whose ranks were inverted were nearly equal. A reliability coefficient, constructed after Bales (1950), as the proportion of the sum of the differences between the scores of the observers for each rank to the average number of acts scored for the group, has a mean value for all groups of 0.936.

The formula for this coefficient is given as:

$$R_1 = 1 - \frac{1}{2} \sum_{i=1}^{3} \frac{|X_i - Y_i|}{X_i + Y_i}$$

where X_i and Y_i are the scores of each of the observers for actor i. The very high value of this coefficient is somewhat misleading since scoring errors tend to cancel out over large time segments. A finer reliability measure that is equivalent to calculating the coefficient R separately for three-minute segments and averaging for each group provides a better idea of the actual reliability. The formula for this coeffieient is given as:

$$R_2 = 1 - \frac{\sum_{j=1}^{14} \sum_{i=1}^{3} |x_{ij} - y_{ij}|}{\frac{1}{2} \sum_{i=1}^{3} X_i + Y_i}$$

where x_{ij} and y_{ij} stand for each observer's score for actor i in time slice j. The mean value of this coefficient is 0.876, which seems to reflect a fair degree of reliability.

A further check on reliability, providing a statistical measure of the similarity of the two sets of data, is given by the χ^2 statistic. For each group, the chi-square was computed for the two sets of observations—each time slice being regarded as one cell of a frequency table. The mean chi-square value over all groups is 6.23 with 28 degrees of freedom. The associated probability level with this chi-square value is greater than 0.99, indicating a satisfactory degree of agreement between the two sets of data.[1]

V. THE RESULTS

A cursory examination of the data is sufficient to indicate that there are problems with the fit of the model to the data (Fisek, 1968). The model is a process model in the sense that it predicts time trends in the probabilities of participation for the actors. Since the process starts out in the status equality state, the probabilities of participation of the three actors should be equal to begin with and then change over time, with the probability of participation for the first basic initiation rank increasing and the probability for the third basic initiation rank decreasing.

---

[1] The data presented here and in the rest of the analyses are from the data record of one of the observers.

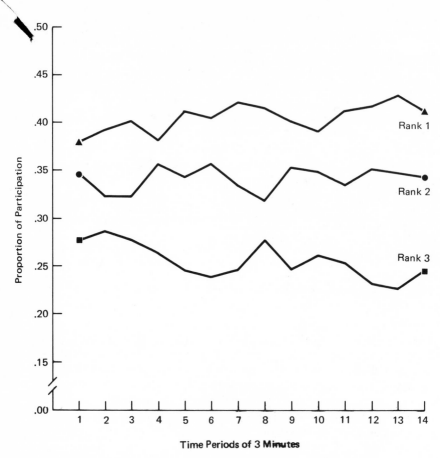

FIGURE 3-7
Proportion of participation over time for each basic initiation rank for time periods
of 3 minutes (first period approximately 1 minute): entire sample.

Figure 3-7 gives the proportions of participation over time for each basic
initiation rank.[2] It is quite obvious that the probabilities of participation are
differentiated for the different ranks to begin with. The proportions remain
reasonably constant over time. For the first basic initiation rank the proportion of participation in the first time segment is 0.38 and in the last is 0.41, a
change of three percentage points. For the third rank, the proportion of participation in the first time segment is 0.28 and in the last it is 0.25, again a
change of three percentage points. Although these changes are in the expected

[2]For these graphs the basic initiation rank has been determined from the last four time
periods (twelve minutes) of the interaction, excluding the final period, during which a
number of the groups had actually stopped interacting.

directions, the magnitudes of the changes are not large enough to seriously consider the goodness-of-fit of the model.

What seems to be happening in these groups is that processes other than the evaluation–expectation process are operating in the evolution of the status structure. It is not possible to determine what these processes are by means of formal analysis and one has to offer explanations based on the largely subjective impressions of the observers (See Fisek, 1968). These impressions were that for some of the groups the evaluation–expectation process did indeed seem to be operating, and the group seemed to evolve differentiated status positions over time. However, for other groups it seemed that the group had already established a status order at the very outset. As has been already remarked, the unit evaluation process is not the only process that can be instrumental in the formation of expectation states. Some of the other processes can occur very rapidly and could account for groups with an already established status order. One alternative is a process in which status characteristics are activated (or made salient) and performance expectations are formed on the basis of these status characteristics. In the open interaction situation the activation of status characteristics, particularly *specific* status characteristics and diffuse status characteristics, which, unlike age, sex, and race are *not* identified with visually discriminable cues, typically is achieved through extremely subtle and indirect forms of verbal as well as nonverbal behavior.[3] If in some of our groups such status characteristics were activated or made salient, then this would have determined at an early stage in the process the expectation structure of the group and its power and prestige order. For an analysis of the mechanisms involved in these processes, see Berger and Fisek, chapter six of this volume.

Another alternative is that individual differences in such variables as disposition to perform, persuadability, and presentation of the self have resulted in initial differences in performance outputs. The Expectation States Theory by Berger and Conner (see chapter four, this volume) describes how differences in performance outputs can result in differentiated performance expectations, which, once formed, will maintain the initial order. Such differences among the actors were in fact not controlled in the composition of the discussion groups.

There is no independent criterion for separating the types of groups that may be called initially differentiated and initially undifferentiated. Chi-square provides a measure of the degree to which a group deviates from the expected state of equality of participation. Calculating a chi-square between the observed distribution of participation during the first seven minutes of the

---

[3] From this standpoint, an individual communicating to others (ever so subtly) the fact that he attended a prestigious private school (rather than a normal public school) may be engaged in activating in his group a diffuse status characteristic that is not identified with visual cues.

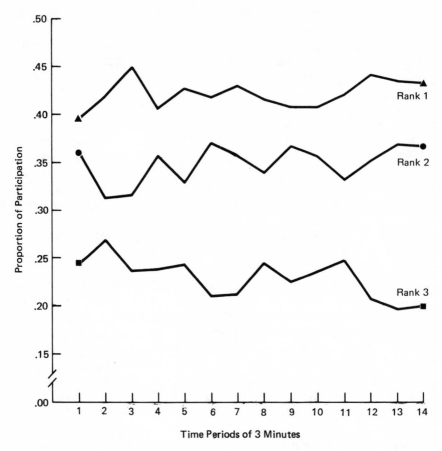

FIGURE 3-8
Proportions of participation over time for each basic initiation rank for time periods
of 3 minutes (first period approximately 1 minute): initially differentiated subset.

group session and the distribution that could be expected under the hypothesis
of equal probabilities of participation for each group yields a distribution of
chi-square values that has a reasonable break point corresponding to a 0.20
probability value (Fisek and Ofshe, 1970). In this way the groups can be
partitioned into two subsets—thirty groups that are initially differentiated
and twenty-nine groups that are initially undifferentiated.

Figure 3-8 gives the proportions of participation over time for the three
ranks of the subset of initially differentiated groups. After examining the
curves, it seems fair to say that the characteristic rates of participation for
each rank are determined from the very start and remain stable for the rest of
the session (cf. Lewis, 1970). The inference is that the status order of the group
had already evolved at the start of the interaction. Determining *what specific*

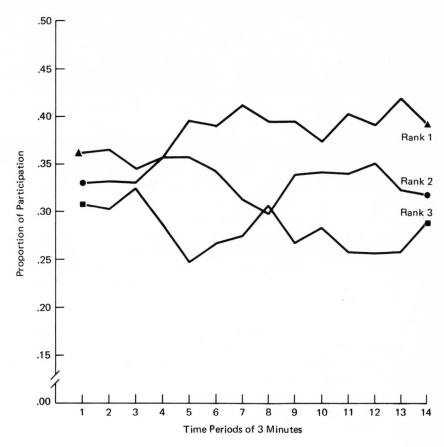

FIGURE 3-9

Proportions of participation over time for each basic initiation rank for time periods of 3 minutes (first period approximately 1 minute): initially undifferentiated subset.

process of expectation formation was involved would require further investigation.

Figure 3-9 gives the proportions of participation over time for the subset of initially undifferentiated groups. The curves for the different ranks do start out together and then diverge over time. It seems worthwhile to investigate the model's goodness-of-fit to this subset of groups.

To evaluate the goodness-of-fit of the model the data is first edited by removing all runs. That is, consecutively scored participations by the same actor are reduced to a single participation because the model's predictions are in terms of total participations rather than unit participations. Further editing is required since the model is formulated as a discrete-time process where each trial is defined as an act. That is, the model's predictions over time are in terms of number of acts elapsed since the start of the process rather than real or "clock" time. (See Reynolds and Fisek, 1971.) The proportions of participation over time need to be calculated on blocks of a given number of acts (that is, the first thirty acts, the second thirty acts), rather than on segments of clock time. Therefore, the amount of data that can be analyzed is determined by the minimum number of acts produced by any group in the sample. The smallest number of acts produced by any group in the sample after runs have been taken out is 140. Therefore the model is evaluated for the first 140 acts output by each group. This means that considerable amounts of data from some groups are ignored. However, this is not a serious problem, since the model is concerned with the evolution of the power and prestige order, which takes place early in the course of interaction.

The general strategy of evaluation of the goodness-of-fit of the model is that of Monte Carlo simulation on a digital computer. The parameters of the model are estimated from the data and are used to simulate the interaction process as described by the model on a computer. The real and simulated results can be compared to see how close the model comes to describing the data. This technique avoids the difficulties that would be faced in trying to derive predictions from the model by analytical methods.

The parameters were estimated by solving the two sets of simultaneous equations derived in the last section on a digital computer, using a grid-search method and least-squares minimization criteria. Both systems of simultaneous equations were well behaved in the sense that each had a single well-defined minimum within the permissible range of parameter values, that is, the interval (0, 1). The values obtained were

$$\theta = 0.354$$
$$\pi = 0.027$$

These parameter values were used to conduct 40 simulations of the experiment, each of 29 groups run for 140 trials or acts.

The proportions of participation over time for each rank for both the observed and simulated results are given in Figure 3-10. The dotted lines represent the simulated results—the mean values of the forty simulations, and the solid lines represent the observed values.

To smooth out the curves the values have been graphed as running averages of thirty acts slipping by ten acts. That is, the first point on each curve gives the proportion for acts one through thirty, the second point for acts eleven through forty, and so on.

There appears to be fairly good agreement between the observed results and the simulated results—the general shapes of the two systems of curves are quite similar. The proportions for each rank begin approximately equal, and then diverge over time. The proportions for the first rank increase, those

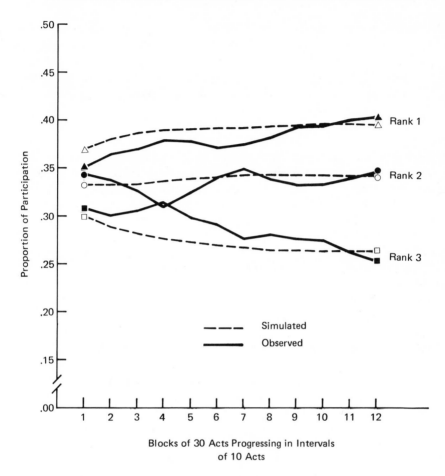

FIGURE 3-10

Proportion of participation over time for observed and simulated data. Proportions are computed over blocks of 30 acts progressing in intervals of 10 acts (acts 1–30, 11–40, 21–50, etc.)

for the second rank remain fairly constant, and those for the third rank decrease over time. The maximum discrepancy at any point between the observed and simulated curves for rank 1 is 0.020 and the average discrepancy is 0.012. The corresponding values for the curves for rank 2 are 0.026 and 0.008. Similarly, the values for the curves for rank 3 are 0.037 and 0.016. Of course, these last values do not provide any new information, since each system of three curves has only two degrees of freedom. The proportions for the three ranks add up to 1 at every point. The overall average discrepancy is 0.012. Whether this degree of agreement between the data and the predictions of the model can be considered satisfactory is largely a subjective question.

A more formal measure of goodness-of-fit, the chi-square measure, can be applied to the two sets of curves. This cannot be done with the curves as represented in Figure 3-10; the points are for overlapping blocks, so they are not independent. However, the chi-square can be calculated for the equivalent curves of seven blocks of twenty trials each. The chi-squares were calculated, in order to avoid inflating the number of cases, on the mean for all simulations of the number of acts of each rank in each block and the corresponding observed values. The chi-square value obtained for the curves for rank 1 is 0.079. This chi-square has six degrees of freedom and the associated probability with this chi-square value is greater than 0.99. The value obtained for the rank 2 curves is 0.128. Again, with six degrees of freedom the associated probability level is greater than 0.99. Similarly, the result for rank 3 is—note it is not independent of the results for ranks 1 and 2—a chi-square value of 0.291, with an associated probability greater than 0.99. These results seem to indicate a fair degree of agreement between the observed and predicted results.

Another statistic that is sensitive to trend—that reflects the evaluation of a status structure over time—is the proportion of commuting two-tuples. The commuting two-tuple (1, 2) is an occurrence of actor 1 performing on trial n followed by actor 2 performing on trial $(n + 1)$ or actor 2 performing on trial n and actor 1 performing on trial $(n + 1)$. Thus, commuting two-tuples reflect interchanges between the actors in the system. In a three-person group there are three commuting two-tuples, the (1, 2) two-tuple, the (1, 3) two-tuple and (2, 3) two-tuple. Figure 3–11 gives the proportions of commuting tuples over time as running averages. As in the case of the simple proportions, the dotted lines represent the results of the simulations and the solid lines the observed results.

It is fairly clear that the tuple statistics are indeed sensitive to trend; the trends to be observed in the data and the simulated results are quite similar. Considering the curves for the (1, 2) two-tuple, the maximum discrepancy at any point is 0.071 and the average discrepancy is 0.030. For the curves for the (1, 3) two-tuple the maximum discrepancy is 0.051 and the average discrepancy is 0.016. The curves for the (2, 3) two-tuple are, as in the case of the simple proportions, not independent of the other curves; however, considering their goodness-of-fit as well tends to complete the picture. For these curves the maximum discrepancy is 0.042 and the average discrepancy is 0.022. The overall average discrepancy is 0.023. The chi-square statistic can be used in this case as well, as a measure of goodness-of-fit. The chi-square is again calculated for equivalent curves of seven (twenty act blocks) on the simulated and observed mean numbers of acts in each block. The chi-square value obtained for the curves for the (1, 2) two-tuple is 0.604; with six degrees of freedom the associated probability is greater than 0.99. For the (1, 3) two-tuple curves the chi-square value is 0.493 and the associated probability is

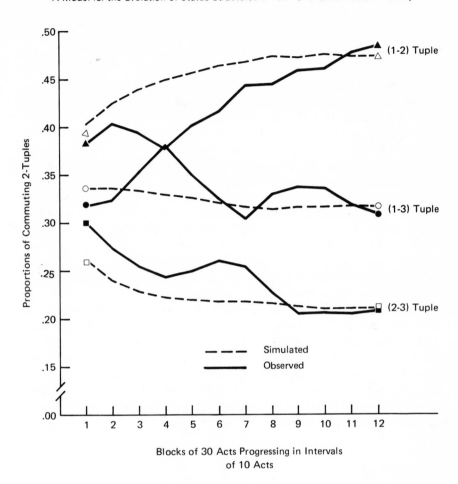

FIGURE 3-11
Proportion of commuting 2-tuples over time for observed and simulated data. Proportions are computed over blocks of 30 acts progressing in intervals of 10 acts (acts 1–30, 11–40, 21–50, etc.)

again greater than 0.99. The curves for the (2, 3) two-tuple yield a chi-square of 0.488 with an associated probability greater than 0.99. The results do seem to indicate a fairly good fit between the model and the data.

The model does quite poorly in predicting the variances of these statistics, the proportions of participations, and the properties of commuting two-tuples, across groups. The variances predicted by the model are consistently greater than the observed values (Fisek, 1968). It is not clear what interpretation can be placed on this fact.

VI. SUMMARY AND CONCLUSIONS

Our studies of task-oriented discussion groups began with the basic finding that inequalities develop over time in the rates at which members participate in the group discussion. Building on the early efforts to model the distribution of participation rates in such groups, and using the theoretical framework of Expectation States Theory, we constructed a model for the evolution of status orders capable of providing a precise stochastic description of the interaction process.

The basic substantive process incorporated into the model was the evaluation–expectation process that describes the emergence of status orders as a function of the expectations for task performance that group members came to hold for each other as a result of evaluating each other's task performances.

The results of a study conducted to evaluate the empirical validity of the model indicate that the model cannot describe the evolution of differences in participation ratios over time for *all* groups studied. Processes other than the evaluation–expectation process may be involved in forming expectation states in a substantial set of the groups in the study. However, the model does quite well in describing the time changes in the participation rates for a significant subset of the groups in the study—those which appear to satisfy the initial condition of status equality at the start of the group session. It seems reasonable to infer that the evaluation–expectation process was operating in a substantial proportion of the groups in this study.

REFERENCES

BALES, R.F. 1950. *Interaction process analysis*. Cambridge, Mass.: Addison Wesley.

————. 1953. The equilibrium problem in small groups. In *Working papers in the theory of action*, eds. T. Parsons, R. F. Bales, and E. A. Shils, pp. 111–65. Glencoe, Ill.: The Free Press.

BALES, R. F., F. L. STRODBECK, T. M. MILLS, and M. E. ROSEBOROUGH. 1951. Channels of communication in small groups. *American sociological review* 16 (August): 461–68.

BALES, R. F., and P. E. SLATER. 1955. Role differentiation. In *Family, socialization and interaction processes*, eds. T. Parsons, R. F. Bales, et al., Glencoe, Ill.: The Free Press.

BERGER, J., B. P. COHEN, and M. ZELDITCH, JR. 1966. Status characteristics and expectation states. In *Sociological theories in progress*, eds. J. Berger, M. Zelditch, Jr., and B. Anderson. Boston: Houghton Mifflin Company.

BERGER, J., and T. CONNER. 1969. Performance expectations and behavior in small groups. *Acta sociologica* 12: 186–98.

BERGER, J., T. CONNER, and W. MCKEOWN. 1969. Evaluations and the formation and maintenance of performance expectations. *Human relations* 22 (December): 481–502.

BERGER, J., J. L. SNELL. 1961. A stochastic theory for self-other expectations. *Technical report no. 1*. Stanford University. The Laboratory for Social Research.

CARTWRIGHT, D., and F. HARARY. 1956. Structural balance: a generalization of Heider's theory. *Psychological review* 63 (September): 277–93.

COLEMAN, J. S. 1960. The mathematical study of small groups. In *Mathematical thinking in the measurement of behavior*, ed. H. Solomon. Glencoe, Ill.: The Free Press.

FISEK, M. H. 1968. The evolution of status structures and interaction in task oriented discussion groups. Ph. D. dissertation, Stanford University.

FISEK, M. H., and R. OFSHE. 1970. The process of status evolution. *Sociometry* 33 (September): 327–46.

HARARY, F., R. NORMAN, and D. CARTWRIGHT. 1965. *Structural models*. New York: John Wiley & Sons.

HEIDER, F. 1946. Attitudes and cognitive organization. *Journal of psychology* 21 (January): 107–12.

HORVATH, W. J. 1964. A mathematical model of participation in small groups. *Behavioral science* 10 (April): 164–66.

KADANE, J. B., and G. LEWIS. 1969. The distribution of participation in group discussions: an empirical and theoretical reappraisal. *American sociological review* 34 (October): 710–22.

KADANE, J. B., G. LEWIS, and J. RAMAGE. 1969. Horvath's theory of participation in group discussions. *Sociometry* 33 (September): 348–61.

KEMENY, J. G., and J. L. SNELL. 1960. *Finite Markov chains*. Princeton, N.J.: Van Nostrand Reinhold Company.

LEIK, R. 1965. Type of group and the probability of initiating acts. *Sociometry* 28 (March): 57–65.

———. 1967. The distribution of acts in small groups. *Sociometry* 30 (September): 741–51.

LEWIS, G. 1970a. Bales' Monte Carlo model of small group discussions. *Sociometry* 33 (March): 20–36.

———. 1970b. The assumption of stationary parameters in theories of group discussion. *Behavioral science* 15: 269–73.

REYNOLDS, P. D., and M. H. FISEK. 1971. Alternatives for measuring temporal change in the development of status hierarchies in small discussion groups. Seventeenth Annual West Coast Conference for Small Group Research. Honolulu, Hawaii.

STEPHAN, F., and E. G. MISHLER. 1952. The distribution of participation in small groups: an exponential approximation. *American sociological review* 17 (October): 598–608.

WAXLER, N., and E. G. MISHLER. 1966. Scoring and reliability problems in interaction process analysis: a methodological note. *Sociometry* 29 (March): 28–40.

Performance Expectations and Behavior in Small Groups: A Revised Formulation*

JOSEPH BERGER

THOMAS L. CONNER

I. INTRODUCTION

A major portion of the literature on interaction in informal task-oriented small groups is concerned with four fundamental and related problems. First, there is the problem of systematically describing interaction. A solution to this problem requires both a typology of kinds of behavior and a set of assertions as to how types of behavior are related to each other and form predictable patterns. Second, there is the problem of the emergence of role and status systems based on interaction. Third, there is the problem of the effect of established role and status systems upon interaction. Finally, there is the question of the stability of role and status systems: How are role and status systems maintained and how are they changed?

*Research for this paper was supported in large part by grants from the National Science Foundation (NSF G-13314, G-23990, GS-1170) and by a grant from the National Institute of Mental Health (MH-16580–01). We would like to acknowledge the help given us at various stages of this investigation by Bernard P. Cohen, Hamit Fisek, Bonnie Hole, J. Laurie Snell, Murray Webster, and Morris Zelditch, Jr.

In this paper we deal with all of these problems as they are conceptualized in the context of Expectation States Theory. We develop a categorization of behavioral acts as they occur in problem-solving groups. We specify how kinds of acts follow each other and how such sequences of acts are grouped into units to structure a discussion. A set of assertions is then developed that specifies how performance expectation states emerge from patterns of interaction; how expectation states determine rates of initiation and receipt of types of behavior; and how the patterning of behavior due to expectation states serves to maintain those states.

II. THE THEORY

A. KINDS OF BEHAVIOR AND THE STRUCTURE OF INTERACTION

Our analysis applies to a group of at least two persons who must accomplish a task together. We assume that it is both necessary and legitimate to take into account the behavior of others in solving the task—that the members are collectively oriented. We also assume that task completion takes precedence over such things as maintaining friendly relations, reducing tension and antagonism, and producing personal satisfaction. That is, we assume that the group is "task focused."

Kinds of Behavior

We are going to restrict our analysis to four kinds of task related behavior. We will not include "social-emotional" or "process" behavior (Bales, 1953). We exclude from analysis any type of behavior that is related exclusively to social and emotional relationships in the group. So, for example, behavior aimed at increasing morale or commitment to the task or smoothing tension or establishing friendship does not fall within the scope of our theory.

We begin as Bales and others have by dividing all of the behavior that is reasonably classified as social into units called *acts*. An act may be a simple verbal sentence and could also be a gesture, a look, or some other form of nonverbal communication. But in the strict sense, an act is the smallest unit of social behavior that can be classified within our system. Any behavior that is not an instance of one of our concepts is, of course, ignored. The kinds of acts we are primarily concerned with are *action opportunities, performance outputs, positive reactions*, and *negative reactions*.

An *action opportunity* is an act that communicates a request for activity—a socially distributed chance to perform. It is usually a question but may also be a glance, a stare, or a hand gesture. Verbal action opportunities would include such comments as "Why?"; "How old is he?"; "Does anyone know?"; or "What about you?" A *performance output* is an act that is an attempt to solve or partially solve a task-related problem and that can be evaluated as a unit. It may be the suggestion of a course of action, a decision, or a solution; the statement of an idea, fact, observation, generalization, or assertion; or a statement in a chain of reasoning, a hypothesis, or logical assertion. But it must be of sufficient length and content so that persons can say of it "I agree" or "that's wrong," or some other evaluative statement. A *reaction* is any act that communicates the unit evaluation of a performance output, such as agreeing with a suggestion, concurring with a fact, or disputing an idea. It is frequently a verbal act but may often be a frown, a grimace, or a nod. The following are all reactions: "Uh-huh," "Yeah," "Well, I don't know . . . ," "Sure," "But . . . ," and "No . . . ." We will distinguish *positive reactions* from *negative reactions* based on the kind of evaluation being communicated.[1]

Theoretical Constructs

The above terms are all observable behaviors. Not all of the terms of our theory are observable, however. Some of our concepts refer to unobservable states and processes that are assumed to be related to the kinds of observable behavior we are concerned with. The first of these is the concept *performance expectation state*, which is a generalized belief that an actor holds about the capacity of himself or others to contribute to task completion.[2] In the simplest case, performance expectations are in a one-to-one relationship to actual abilities, but this is not a requirement and may not even be a common situation. In fact, performance expectations can be created through a variety

[1] We assume that in task focused groups, the sign of a unit evaluation tends to correspond to the sign of the reaction expressed. If a person believes an idea is unsound he will ordinarily say so. This assumption may not be true of process-oriented groups and may be one of the characteristics that distinguishes them. However, even in task focused groups, the correspondence may not be perfect. Persons ranked high in the expectation structure are more likely to have their positively evaluated performance outputs reacted to positively, and low ranking persons are more likely to have their negatively evaluated performance outputs reacted to negatively.

[2] Although we describe expectation states, structures and rankings in such phenomenological terms as "generalized beliefs," this is primarily a heuristic device that we use here and shall use elsewhere. However, expectation states, structures and rankings are unobservable states in our theory, and no assumptions are being made as to how these states do in fact relate to the structure of an individual's cognitions and particularly to his conscious and verbalizable cognitions. Although by experimental manipulation or by assumption, we attempt to assign an individual to a specific expectation state at the *outset* of the interaction process, inferences about how such states emerge or change *during the course of the interaction process* are made on the basis of behavior that is either postulated to lead to such states or behavior that is postulated to be consequences of such states.

of processes that do not depend on the existence of differential task ability of the actors. Some of these processes are described in this paper; others are described in chapters five and six. We will be concerned with whether the expectations are held for self or other(s) and will usually deal only with relative expectations, that is, with rankings rather than with some concept of absolute expectations.

A *unit evaluation* is a specific, momentary evaluation of whatever composes the unit. By momentary we mean the evaluation is relatively temporary rather than enduring, thus leaving out sentiments such as liking, loving, hating, etc. The unit evaluated is ordinarily a performance output and for the purposes of this paper we will restrict ourselves to these kinds of unit evaluations. Examples would include thinking that a fact is accurate, an idea is unsound, or a suggestion is acceptable. We will distinguish only positive and negative evaluations.

Defined Terms

The above terms are all primitive terms whose meaning is given by general understanding and example. Other terms that we use can be formally defined using the primitive terms. We will now briefly state them for later use.

Acceptance of an action opportunity occurs when an action opportunity is directed at some person (x) and he responds with some other categorizable behavior, such as a performance output. Otherwise the action opportunity is *declined*. If x initiates a performance output, then an *influence attempt* is a negative reaction to x's performance output accompanied with one or more counter performance outputs. *Acceptance of an influence attempt* is any change of the evaluation of a performance output following an influence attempt.

Informal Characterization of the Interaction

Let us now imagine that a group of persons, all strangers, come together to collectively complete some task—say a discussion problem. As they concern themselves with their task, they are continually initiating performance outputs and giving action opportunities. They are also engaged in evaluating each other's performance outputs and communicating these evaluations with positive and negative reactions. During the early parts of the discussion we believe that who will engage in what kinds of behavior depends largely on idiosyncratic characteristics of the members. However, as the members continue to interact, a ranking of the members by performance expectations will often develop. Should this happen, it will markedly affect the future behavior of the members. Specifically, it will affect who is given action opportunities, who will on his own initiate performance outputs, whose performance outputs are positively or negatively evaluated, and who will be influenced by whom. We further argue that the patterning of these behaviors will in general maintain the performance expectation ranking.

Sequences of Kinds of Behavior

The occurrence of one kind of behavior will affect what other kind of behavior comes next. Kinds of behavior follow each other in specifiable orders. The crucial idea to understanding such patterning of the interaction as it proceeds is the *full fundamental sequence of behaviors.* As a sequence it forms a discrete unit from which the entire discussion is built by repetition of the sequence, hence the term "fundamental."

The sequence begins with the initiation of an action opportunity by some member, followed by initiation of a single performance output by another member. The initiator of the performance output then initiates an action opportunity of his own and the others respond with one or more positive reactions. For example, the following bit of conversation follows this pattern exactly:

A: How much should we spend? (action opportunity)
B: Five thousand is enough, (performance output)
   isn't it? (action opportunity)
C: Sure. (positive reaction)
D: Fine. (positive reaction)

We believe that all task-relevant interaction either follows this pattern exactly or is some simple variation of it. There are three major classes of variation: omissions from the sequence (hence the term "full sequence"), additions resulting from the occurrence of a negative reaction, and nesting or overlapping of sequences.

Let us first analyze omissions from the full fundamental sequence. Consider the initial action opportunity. Its function is ordinarily to allow social control of who talks and of what he talks about. But not only is it awkward always to precede a performance output by a question, it is frequently unnecessary. If for some reason it becomes necessary and legitimate for some members to participate more than others in the discussion, then people will tend to control their own performance rates without the group having to direct action opportunities to some but not to other members. So, in actual discussions, the initial action opportunity is often missing, although the person who initiates a performance on his own probably does so only to the extent that he feels that no one would have objected to asking him to perform.

The action opportunity following a performance output is also often missing. Its function is usually to request evaluations of the performance and to control both who does the evaluating and what aspects of the performance are to be evaluated. It can also be used to communicate the end of a string of performance outputs in the case of overlapping sequences (see below). So, as with the initial action opportunity, the action opportunity after a performance is often omitted because it is not always necessary that its functions be performed.[3]

Finally, some performance outputs are never reacted to. From the standpoint of "public consumption" it is ordinarily the case that positive evaluations are understood and assumed by the members. So if a person initiates a performance output, he will assume that the others accept it and will positively evaluate it unless they say otherwise.

We can describe the full fundamental sequence and its deletion variations in terms of a simple diagram such as that shown in Figure 4-1.

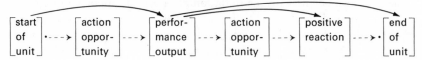

FIGURE 4-1

We regard any path that follows the arrows through the diagram as a unit and as equivalent from an interaction point of view to the path that is the full fundamental sequence (indicated by all broken lines). Figure 4-1 also shows how we believe the omissions are related to each other. Notice that if the second action opportunity is initiated, then there is no path that allows omissions of the positive reaction. Otherwise, the omissions can occur independently of each other.

The initiation of a negative reaction following a performance output is the beginning of a social influence process. At the end of the process either the performer must decide that the negative reactor (or reactors) is correct or the negative reactor must be convinced to change his mind. The central feature of this process is the "counter performance output"—a performance output initiated as a substitute or partial substitute for the original. Consider the following conversation between A and B:

> B: I think he should be put in a foster home. (performance output)
> A: Well, I'm not sure. (negative reaction) Foster homes are only temporary. (performance output)
> B: That may be, (positive reaction) but it doesn't really matter. (performance output)
> A: Sure it does. (negative reaction) Finding somebody to adopt him will give him a sense of security. (performance output)
> B: Yes, I guess that's right. (positive reaction)

---

[3] The infrequency of this act should not be overemphasized, however. There are subtle ways, which are often difficult to objectively record, of initiating an action opportunity, such as raising the pitch of the voice or pausing.

Person *B* finally accepts *A*'s negative reaction to his original proposal by agreeing with subsequent performance outputs.

The basic structure of the influence process sequence can be seen clearly from the above example. After the initial performance output and negative reaction, one or more additional performance outputs are initiated and reacted to until consensus is achieved (or can be assumed) on the evaluation of the original performance output. The unit sequence that begins with "Foster homes are only temporary" terminates with positive consensus when *B* says, "That may be." The unit sequence that begins with, "It doesn't really matter," terminates with *B*'s final comment. The original unit sequence that began with *B*'s first comment also terminates on *B*'s final comment with negative consensus. Finally, the unit sequence that begins with *A*'s last comment terminates on *B*'s last comment with positive consensus. The final fate of the first performance output is decided indirectly by the fates of the second, third, and fourth performance outputs. Thus, the example contains four unit sequences, all of which have terminated by *B*'s last remark.

Each of these unit sequences can be identically described *so long as we give up the idea that the parts of a unit sequence have to be contiguous*. Acts of any kind from another sequence can occur at any point in the original sequence, but, of course, are not included as a part of it. So if we confine ourselves to the first unit sequence of the example, we have only two observable acts:

1.   *B* initiates a performance output.
2.   *A* initiates a negative reaction.

It is also implied, however, that *B* has been influenced, although this is an event that is not directly observable. One way to represent this series of events is shown in Figure 4-2. The unobservable event "acceptance of influence" is enclosed in braces.

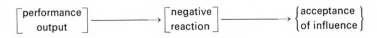

FIGURE 4-2

The full representation of the unit sequence is now as shown in Figure 4–3.

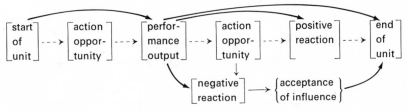

FIGURE 4-3

The behavior that occurs between [negative reaction] and {acceptance of influence} can also be described by Figure 4-3 and is considered separately.

In analyzing the influence process we have already encountered the third possible kind of modification of the full fundamental sequence—overlapping of unit sequences. We argued that a modification was not necessary because such sequences could be considered separately and analyzed just as if they were independent sequences. The same order of events would characterize any sequence, whether it overlapped with another or not.

The idea of overlapping sequences leads directly to the idea of units larger than a simple, nonoverlapping sequence. As a group attempts to complete their task they partition their activities into the completion of a series of smaller "tasks" or subtasks. For example, if the group has met together to consider their budget for some coming period of time they might partition their meeting into review of the previous budget, consideration of future needs, and construction of a new budget. These in turn would be broken down into smaller and smaller questions. At the end of this process, if it continued for a long time, the discussion would consist of a series of small, indivisible subunits. We do not believe that groups consciously carry this process to its ultimate conclusion. Recognition of subunits probably ends early in the process. Yet from the point of view of the observer-analyst, very small subunits can be distinguished and analyzed. We will recognize as the smallest subunit a *simple subtask unit*, defined as a single unit sequence of behaviors that does not overlap with any other unit sequence. Ordinarily we would not expect simple subtask units to be recognized by group members. A *complex subtask unit* is defined as a set of two or more overlapping unit sequences such that the set includes:

1. The first unit sequence.
2. All other unit sequences begun before termination of the first unit sequence.

If we let B_1 indicate the beginning of unit sequence 1 and E_1 the termination of unit sequence 1, then the following are both examples of complex subtask units:

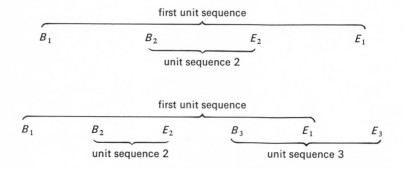

Complex units are again not ordinarily recognized unless they are very large. A group discussion consists of a time-ordered series of simple and complex subtask units.

Groups, however, normally do recognize large task units. That is, they recognize partitions of the discussion into major, self-contained parts. The defining property of these parts is difficult to specify aside from the fact that the group members are aware of them (and have probably explicitly established them) and the group "product" at the end of each part can be evaluated as a "success" or "failure." Based on these ideas we will call a *full task unit* a set of subtask units, which has associated with it differentially valued outcome states.

Unit Sequences in the Two-Man Group

The preceding analysis applies to groups of any size and does not take into account who initiates a particular act or to whom it is directed. In order to use the formulation as we intend, the diagram in Figure 4-3 must be expanded to include both initiator and receiver. However, because our attempts to accomplish this for groups of size 3 or larger presented theoretical complications that have yet to be solved, the remainder of our analysis is confined to two-man groups. But we believe that this type of analysis can be extended to larger groups.

As a convenience we adopted a simple notational system for designating each act and its initiator and receiver. The two members are A and B. A single act is recorded in the form "initiator (type of act) receiver," with abbreviations for each type of act. For example, by $A(PO)B$, we mean person A initiated a Performance Output to person B. The abbreviation AO means "action opportunity," and $+R$ means "positive reaction," $-R$ means "negative reaction," and IB means "influenced by." When we write $B(IB)A$, it means B is influenced by A, or that B has been persuaded to change his mind by A.

At the start of a unit, one of the members may initiate either a performance output or an action opportunity (see Figure 4-3). The target of either act is automatically given once the initiator is specified, a special property of the two-man group, so that a unit may be begun in one of four mutually exclusive ways: $A(PO)B$, $B(AO)A$, $A(AO)B$, or $B(PO)A$. These correspond to the first four branches of Figure 4-4.

In the case where the unit begins with an action opportunity, Figure 4-3 specifies that it be followed by a performance output. This is represented by the arrows from $B(AO)A$ to $A(PO)B$ and from $A(AO)B$ to $B(PO)A$ in Figure 4-4. We do not imagine, however, that an action opportunity will always be accepted. The receiver may decline the opportunity to perform. But the opportunity must be responded to and we believe this will take the form of a second action opportunity directed at the original initiator. The arrows

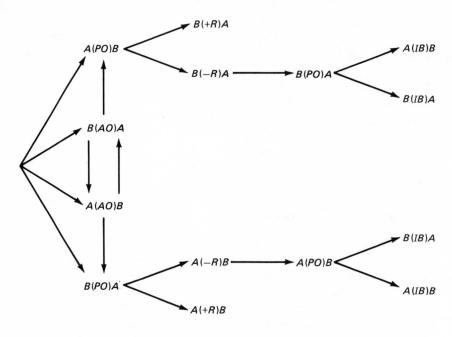

FIGURE 4-4

from $A(AO)B$ to $B(AO)A$ and back again represent this in Figure 4-4.

Following a performance output, Figure 4-3 specifies three alternatives: a positive reaction, a negative reaction, and no reaction (interpreted in the text as implying positive evaluation). To simplify the analysis, we will assume here that the alternative of no reaction is not available—that explicit reaction (positive or negative) is forced. This restriction will have no effect upon any of our conclusions. Figure 4-4 contains arrows from both $A(PO)B$ and $B(PO)A$ to the two kinds of reactions to represent these ideas.

The final part of Figure 4-3 to be expanded is the behavior that follows a negative reaction. We argued above that the crucial idea to understanding this part of the sequence is that of a second performance output (or third, or fourth, or more) that is an alternative to the first. We will confine ourselves here to the case of a single counter performance output that is always initiated by the negative evaluator. This restriction simplifies the analysis that follows but still allows us to deal with the most important predictions. Extension of the analysis to include more possibilities is not difficult but it is also not particularly instructive. Following the mandatory single counter performance output, one or the other of the members will finally be influenced. In Figure 4-4, arrows from the counter performance outputs [following $B(-R)A$ and $A(-R)B$] are drawn to both $A(IB)B$ and $B(IB)A$ to represent this final part of the sequence.

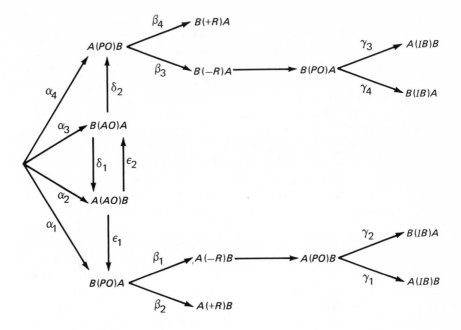

FIGURE 4-5

Figure 4-4 represents the ordering of possible behaviors, under the conditions stated, that defines a simple subtask unit for a two-man group. A discussion in a two-man group would be a collection of such units, and to make predictions about the discussion we need only make predictions about the units. The kinds of predictions we have in mind involve essentially assertions about the likelihoods of various paths through the unit. For example, is it more likely that A will initiate a performance output that B positively evaluates (the path from $A(PO)B$ to $B(+R)A$ in the diagram) or that B will initiate a performance output that A positively evaluates (from $B(PO)A$ to $A(+R)B$ in the diagram)?

We will derive probabilities of paths from simple probabilities assigned to each of the branches of the diagram in Figure 4-4. We associate with each branch a constant (that is, neither time-dependent nor dependent upon any but the most immediate behavior in its unit) probability that the behavior indicated by that branch will occur. These probabilities are assigned as indicated in Figure 4-5.

The Probability of an Accepted Performance Output

A key idea in our analysis is that at some stage in the group's activities members come to hold stable performance expectations for each other. We assume, for the task and group conditions we are considering, that such performance expectations are based on differences in rates at which members have had performance outputs accepted. We specify this argument in detail below. As a preliminary step, we now want to derive from Figure 4-5 an expression for the probability of an accepted performance output.

The probability that A has a performance output accepted can be found by summing the probabilities of each sequence of behaviors that results in an accepted performance output for A. The probability of any sequence is the product of the probabilities on each branch of the sequence. For example, the sequence in which A initiates a performance output and B initiates a positive reaction (the path from $A(PO)B$ to $B(+R)A$ in Figure 4-5) has probability $\alpha_4\beta_4$ of occurring. The probability that A initiates a performance output, B reacts negatively, but B is influenced by A is $\alpha_4\beta_3\gamma_4$.

If A receives an action opportunity before initiating a performance output, the computation is more complex because as the diagram is constructed, A and B can exchange several action opportunities before A performs. Let us consider the case in which B reacts positively to A's performance. Suppose B initiates the first action opportunity to A. If A performs after the first opportunity, the probability is $\alpha_3\delta_2\beta_4$. After one exchange of opportunities the probability is $\alpha_3\delta_1\epsilon_2\delta_2\beta_4$. After two exchanges it is $\alpha_3\delta_1^2\epsilon_2^2\delta_2\beta_4$. It is clear that the expression for the probability that B initiates the first action opportunity and A subsequently performs is

$$\sum_{n=0}^{\infty} \alpha_3(\delta_1\epsilon_2)^n\delta_2\beta_4$$

Since $\delta_1\epsilon_2 < 1$, the expression becomes[4]

$$\frac{\alpha_3\delta_2\beta_4}{1 - \delta_1\epsilon_2}$$

Suppose, on the other hand, that A initiates the first action opportunity to B, but B does not perform. If A performs after his first opportunity, the probability is $\alpha_2\epsilon_2\delta_2\beta_4$. After one exchange of opportunities the probability is $\alpha_2\epsilon_2\delta_1\epsilon_2\delta_2\beta_4$. After two exchanges it is $\alpha_2\epsilon_2^2\delta_1^2\epsilon_2\delta_2\beta_4$. In a manner similar to that above, the expression for the probability that A initiates the first action opportunity and subsequently performs is

$$\frac{\alpha_2\epsilon_2\delta_2\beta_4}{1 - \delta_1\epsilon_2}$$

The probability that A performs after an action opportunity and gets a

---

[4]For $S = \sum_{i=0}^{\infty} x^i$ and $|x| < 1$ it is known that $S = 1/(1 - x)$.

positive reaction is the sum of the probabilities over the two possible initial conditions, or

$$\frac{(\alpha_3 + \alpha_2\epsilon_2)\delta_2\beta_4}{1 - \delta_1\epsilon_2}$$

In a similar fashion, the probability that A receives the first action opportunity from B and A performs and B reacts negatively, but B is influenced is

$$\frac{\alpha_3\delta_2\beta_3\gamma_4}{1 - \delta_1\epsilon_2}$$

And the corresponding probability for B receiving the first action opportunity is

$$\frac{\alpha_2\epsilon_2\delta_2\beta_3\gamma_4}{1 - \delta_1\epsilon_2}$$

Thus, the probability that A performs after an action opportunity, B reacts negatively, but B is influenced is the sum of the probabilities above, or

$$\frac{(\alpha_3 + \alpha_2\epsilon_2)\delta_2\beta_3\gamma_4}{1 - \delta_1\epsilon_2}$$

A can also get a performance output accepted by reacting negatively to B's performance and successfully influencing him. This could happen when B receives an action opportunity and when he does not. The two expressions for these probabilities are $\alpha_1\beta_1\gamma_2$ and

$$\frac{(\alpha_2 + \alpha_3\delta_1)\epsilon_1\beta_1\gamma_2}{1 - \delta_1\epsilon_2}$$

The complete expression for the probability that A has a performance output accepted (which we will label P_A) can now be written and is shown below with the corresponding expression for B. The order of the parts of the expression has been rearranged to facilitate comparison.

$$P_A = \alpha_4\beta_4 + \frac{(\alpha_3 + \alpha_2\epsilon_2)\delta_2\beta_4}{1 - \delta_1\epsilon_2} + \alpha_4\beta_3\gamma_4 + \frac{(\alpha_3 + \alpha_2\epsilon_2)\delta_2\beta_3\gamma_4}{1 - \delta_1\epsilon_2}$$
$$+ \alpha_1\beta_1\gamma_2 + \frac{(\alpha_2 + \alpha_3\delta_1)\epsilon_1\beta_1\gamma_2}{1 - \delta_1\epsilon_2}$$

$$P_B = \alpha_1\beta_2 + \frac{(\alpha_2 + \alpha_3\delta_1)\epsilon_1\beta_2}{1 - \delta_1\epsilon_2} + \alpha_4\beta_3\gamma_3 + \frac{(\alpha_3 + \alpha_2\epsilon_2)\delta_2\beta_3\gamma_3}{1 - \delta_1\epsilon_2}$$
$$+ \alpha_1\beta_1\gamma_1 + \frac{(\alpha_2 + \alpha_3\delta_1)\epsilon_1\beta_1\gamma_1}{1 - \delta_1\epsilon_2}$$

To simplify our further discussions we will designate the parts or components of the expressions for P_A and P_B as follows:

$$C_{1A} = \alpha_4 \beta_4 \qquad\qquad C_{1B} = \alpha_1 \beta_2$$

$$C_{2A} = \frac{(\alpha_3 + \alpha_2 \epsilon_2) \delta_2 \beta_4}{1 - \delta_1 \epsilon_2} \qquad\qquad C_{2B} = \frac{(\alpha_2 + \alpha_3 \delta_1) \epsilon_1 \beta_2}{1 - \delta_1 \epsilon_2}$$

$$C_{3A} = \alpha_4 \beta_3 \gamma_4 + \frac{(\alpha_3 + \alpha_2 \epsilon_2) \delta_2 \beta_3 \gamma_4}{1 - \delta_1 \epsilon_2} \qquad C_{3B} = \alpha_4 \beta_3 \gamma_3 + \frac{(\alpha_3 + \alpha_2 \epsilon_2) \delta_2 \beta_3 \gamma_3}{1 - \delta_1 \epsilon_2}$$

$$C_{4A} = \alpha_1 \beta_1 \gamma_2 + \frac{(\alpha_2 + \alpha_3 \delta_1) \epsilon_1 \beta_1 \gamma_2}{1 - \delta_1 \epsilon_2} \qquad C_{4B} = \alpha_1 \beta_1 \gamma_1 + \frac{(\alpha_2 + \alpha_3 \delta_1) \epsilon_1 \beta_1 \gamma_1}{1 - \delta_1 \epsilon_2}$$

Thus

$$P_A = C_{1A} + C_{2A} + C_{3A} + C_{4A}$$

and

$$P_B = C_{1B} + C_{2B} + C_{3B} + C_{4B}$$

The Emergence of Performance Expectation States

The circumstances under which performance expectation states emerge include scope conditions beyond those we have already stated. As additional scope conditions we assume, first, that there is some single ability or a perfectly correlated set of abilities, seen by both A and B as relevant to *every part* of their collective task. We call such a task a *unitary task*. Ruled out are circumstances, for example, in which some parts of the task require one ability while other parts require a different, uncorrelated, ability, or in which several abilities are required by the task but the abilities are unrelated. Second, we require that A and B begin their work with no prior or immediate knowledge of their respective abilities. Thus, there must be no apparent characteristics of either that activate differences in social status, such as sex, race, and occupation, and they must be strangers with no prior history of interaction. We will refer to this condition as the assumption of *initial status equality*. This does not imply, however, that A and B are in fact equal in ability, nor does it imply that there are no characteristics they possess that differentiate them. Rather, we require only that A and B begin in ignorance with no established relationships.

In outline, our argument for how expectation states are established under these task conditions is as follows. Beginning as presumed status equals, collectively oriented and task-focused, and working on a unitary task, A and B will each have performance outputs accepted at a particular rate in the course of their interaction. If, say, A is getting performance outputs accepted at a higher rate, then as the discussion progresses there is an increasing likelihood that A and B will develop performance expectation states. We believe a full task unit is normally sufficient time for this process to occur so that by the end of the unit A and B will have established differentiated expectation states based on the differentiated rates of accepted performance outputs.

Let us now present the argument more formally. The number of performance outputs accepted for A and for B are obviously governed by the *probability* that A has a performance accepted, P_A, and that B has a performance accepted, P_B, respectively. Recall that

$$P_A = C_{1A} + C_{2A} + C_{3A} + C_{4A}$$
$$P_B = C_{1B} + C_{2B} + C_{3B} + C_{4B}$$

Assume now, that there are no characteristics whatsoever that differentiate A and B—that, for example, they are equally persuadable, equally talkative, equally intelligent, and so on. In these idealized circumstances, A and B should not differ in any tendency to initiate or receive any kind of behavior. (See Figure 4-5.)

$$\alpha_4 = \alpha_1$$
$$\beta_4 = \beta_2$$
$$\alpha_3 = \alpha_2$$
$$\delta_2 = \epsilon_1$$
$$\gamma_4 = \gamma_3$$
$$\gamma_1 = \gamma_2$$

A direct consequence of the equality of these probabilities is the equality of P_A and P_B. That is, since $\alpha_4 = \alpha_1$ and $\beta_4 = \beta_2$, then $\alpha_4\beta_4 = \alpha_1\beta_2$, or $C_{1A} = C_{1B}$. Similarly, $C_{2A} = C_{2B}$, $C_{3A} = C_{3B}$, and $C_{4A} = C_{4B}$. Since all four components of P_A and P_B are respectively equal, P_A and P_B are equal, and A and B should, on the average, have the same number of performance outputs accepted.

If, however, A and B are alike except for, say, A's higher tendency to initiate performance outputs, then P_A and P_B are no longer equal. All the equalities stated above would hold except that α_4 would be larger than α_1. This would result in $C_{1A} > C_{1B}$ while $C_{2A} = C_{2B}$, $C_{3A} = C_{3B}$, and $C_{4A} = C_{4B}$. Thus, with some of the components ordered in a consistent fashion while the remaining components are equal, P_A and P_B are ordered. In this example $P_A > P_B$, so over a period of time it is expected that A will have more performance outputs accepted than B.

In ordinary groups, meeting under the conditions of collective orientation, task focus, and initial status equality, we believe that it is very common for some of the C's to be ranked even though none of the group members have as yet formed performance expectations. This produces inequalities in rates of accepted performance outputs that will lead members eventually to form performance expectations consistent with these inequalities.

We will distinguish three sets of circumstances that may hold with respect to the C's in the initial phase of a group's discussion:

Partial component inequality (condition 1)

$$C_{iA} > C_{iB} \text{ for some } i \text{ and}$$
$$C_{iA} = C_{iB} \text{ for the remaining } i$$

Complete component inequality (condition 2)

$$C_{iA} > C_{iB} \text{ for all } i$$

Complete component equality (condition 3)

$$C_{iA} = C_{iB} \text{ for all } i$$

This does not exhaust the possibilities, since mixed cases are not included. Mixed cases, however, create problems in analysis that have yet to be solved.

Because of its importance in further theoretical analysis, we want to indicate a special case of complete component inequality. This is the case of consistent inequality of all the constituent probabilities of the components. That is, when

$$\alpha_4 > \alpha_1$$
$$\beta_4 > \beta_2$$
$$\alpha_3 > \alpha_2$$
$$\delta_2 > \epsilon_1$$
$$\gamma_4 > \gamma_3$$
$$\gamma_2 > \gamma_1$$

we will say the condition of *complete constituent inequality* holds.

If we are given a full task unit, call it U_1, and A and B are collectively oriented, task-focused, but initially status equals, then, if either condition 1 or condition 2 holds, this results in A having more performance outputs accepted than B and will result in A and B forming consistent performance expectations at some time t within U_1. We will designate this by $E_A > E_B$ meaning that both A and B are in states in which the expectations held for A are greater than those held for B. These ideas are stated formally in the emergence assumption below.

ASSUMPTION 1: EMERGENCE OF EXPECTATION STATES

If at the beginning of a full task unit U_1, complete or partial component inequality holds, then at some time t in U_1, $E_A > E_B$.

There is a wide variety of circumstances that might result in complete or partial component inequality. It is beyond the scope of this paper to fully specify them, but we can give an informal description of some of them. Consider, for example, "talkative" people—persons who have a high propensity for initiating interaction. If we placed a talkative person and a quiet person together who were, according to some measurement, equally competent but unaware of this, we would expect from the emergence assumption that the talkative member, under the given task conditions, would eventually come to be perceived as the member with more task capacity. It is widely believed that some people are easier to influence than others; such a difference would again be sufficient to produce inequalities in accepted performance outputs and ultimately differentiated performance expectations. Other possible factors would include differences in self-esteem, differences in general intelligence, differences in interactive skills, and differences in knowledge of relevant information.

Behavioral Consequences of Ranked Performance Expectation States

Bales has argued that any group discussion involves a compromise between two principles—completing the task efficiently and well, and dealing with social and emotional requirements of the group and its members. In task-focused groups, emphasis is upon efficient completion of the task. If this goal were strongly emphasized and ruthlessly pursued, the group would rely almost exclusively upon those members who are perceived as more competent to contribute ideas and make decisions. If the emphasis were reversed and pursued equally ruthlessly, the group would spread participation and decision making among the members in a more nearly equal fashion. Presumably it would be less important for a contribution to be a "good" one, or for a decision to be a "correct" one, and more important that every member have his chance to contribute and influence whatever is decided. Groups between these two extremes, especially those which are moderately task-focused, would legitimize and require some inequality in order to complete the task well but would control it so as not to completely disregard its social and emotional requirements.

If the above is correct, then rankings of expectation states between A and B ought to produce inequalities in rates of kinds of behavior between A and B.

ASSUMPTION 2: BASIC EXPECTATION ASSUMPTION

For A expected to perform at a higher level than B, $E_A > E_B$, then

2.1 A is more likely to initiate a performance output than B.

2.2 A is more likely than B to receive a positive unit evaluation of, and a positive reaction to, his performance output.

2.3 A is more likely than B to receive an action opportunity.

2.4 A is more likely than B to accept an action opportunity.

2.5 A is less likely than B to be influenced.

In terms of the probabilities specified in Figure 4-5, it follows from the above, respectively, that

(2.1) $\alpha_4 > \alpha_1$
(2.2) $\beta_4 > \beta_2$
(2.3) $\alpha_3 > \alpha_2$
(2.4) $\delta_2 > \epsilon_1$
(2.5) $\gamma_4 > \gamma_3$ and $\gamma_1 < \gamma_2$

These inequalities will be recognized as the condition of complete constituent inequality. Thus we can restate Assumption 2 as

ASSUMPTION 2*:

If $E_A > E_B$ then complete constitutent inequality will hold.

The basic expectation assumption is one of the central assertions of Expectation States Theory. It specifies the fundamental relationship between ranked expectation states and rates of behavior. As a consequence of this, all of the task-relevant activity in a discussion group is structured in a pervasive pattern of inequality that corresponds to the expectation states. In particular, it follows from Assumption 2* that A will now have more performance outputs accepted.

We argued previously that if $\alpha_4 > \alpha_1$ and $\beta_4 > \beta_2$, then $C_{1A} > C_{1B}$. Note that $\delta_2 = 1 - \delta_1$ and $\epsilon_1 = 1 - \epsilon_2$ so that if $\delta_2 > \epsilon_1$ and $\alpha_3 > \alpha_2$, then

$$\alpha_3(1 - \delta_1) > \alpha_2(1 - \epsilon_2)$$

or equivalently,

$$(\alpha_3 + \alpha_2\epsilon_2) > (\alpha_2 + \alpha_3\delta_1)$$

Thus if $\delta_2 > \epsilon_1$ and $\alpha_3 > \alpha_2$ and $\beta_4 > \beta_2$ then

$$\frac{(\alpha_3 + \alpha_2\epsilon_2)\delta_2\beta_1}{1 - \delta_1\epsilon_2} > \frac{(\alpha_2 + \alpha_3\delta_1)\epsilon_1\beta_2}{1 - \delta_1\epsilon_2}$$

or $C_{2A} > C_{2B}$. If all the C's are examined, it will be clear that $C_{iA} > C_{iB}$ for all i. So we have

THEOREM 1

If $E_A > E_B$, then $P_A > P_B$.

In words, Theorem 1 asserts that if A and B have formed expectation states such that A is expected to perform at a higher level than B, then A is more likely to have performance outputs accepted.

The Maintenance of Performance Expectations

Assumption 1 and Theorem 1 together lead to the maintenance of expectation inequalities. In outline the argument is that one consequence of ranked expectation states is a pattern of behaviors that is a sufficient condition for the creation of those same ranked expectation states. Ranked expectation states produce differences in rates of accepted performances that in turn support and maintain expectations. Let us begin the detailed argument by considering a group that has developed a ranked expectation state structure at some point t within a full task unit U_1. We assume, as before, that $E_A > E_B$ at time t. Bear in mind that we are still assuming collective orientation, task focus, initial status equality, and a unitary task.

The question to be considered is what happens to the expectation, formed at time t, for the rest of the unit U_1? For the kind of emergence process we have described, and assuming no change of scope conditions, it would be reasonable to take as axiomatic that the expectations are maintained unchanged. Only if they were expected to change would an explanatory problem be posed. Nonetheless, suppose change were possible. There are two possibilities. Either the members return to having no performance expectations and this continues to the end of the unit, or they disappear and are replaced by other performance expectations.

It is important to recall now that in the section on emergence we distinguished three initial circumstances that result in some, all, or none of the components of P_A and P_B (probabilities of an accepted performance output) to be ranked. In particular, if either partial component inequality (condition 1) or complete component inequality (condition 2) holds, then this is sufficient for ranked expectation states to emerge. For our present argument, we must assume that, whatever the circumstances were that ordered some of the probabilities to produce condition 1 or 2 at the beginning of the unit, they remain unchanged *throughout* the unit and their effects would have continued except for the formation of expectation states. So, for example, if B began the unit easier to influence than A, this must also hold throughout the discussion. Thus, if unequal expectations emerge at time t in u_1 but disappear later, then we have reverted to exactly the same circumstances that obtained at the start of the discussion and would expect the same results— the re-emergence of ranked expectation states.

For example, if partial component inequality holds initially, then, by definition $C_{iA} > C_{iB}$ for some i and $C_{iA} = C_{iB}$ for the remaining i. According to Assumption 1, ranked expectation states will emerge at some point t in u_1, with $E_A > E_B$. Theorem 1 then implies that *after* emergence of $E_A > E_B$, $C_{iA} > C_{iB}$ for all i (complete component inequality). This will continue so long as $E_A > E_B$. Hence, so long as $E_A > E_B$, one of the conditions sufficient for the emergence of $E_A > E_B$ will always be true. Moreover, should the expectations disappear, as long as other conditions are unchanged we still have a sufficient condition for the emergence of $E_A > E_B$ and the same expectations must reappear. Thus once ranked expectations emerge, Assumption 1 and Theorem 1 together assure that no other expectation states are possible. These ideas are stated formally in Theorem 2 on the *Maintenance of Expectations*:

THEOREM 2

If at the beginning of a full task unit U_1, complete or partial component inequality holds, and if at some time t in U_1, $E_A > E_B$, then for the remainder of U_1 after t, $E_A > E_B$.

It is important to emphasize that Theorem 2 does *not* imply that expectation states never change. Rather, only that *given no change in initial scope conditions*, expectation states will not change. Should a change of expectations occur, we would assume that some scope condition has been altered or some new condition has been introduced, and an explanation for that change would have to be constructed. For example, if, as we believe may have happened in some of Bales' groups (Heinike and Bales, 1953), task focus begins to weaken and the group becomes more process-oriented, the whole expectation structure may undergo change. Or, as a further example, if an external source began to evaluate either the behavior of group members or the decisions of the group, then the expectation states structure they had developed might change to correspond to the external evaluations.

The Spread and Maintenance of Inequality

The Emergence Assumption and the Basic Expectation Assumption imply a process that we call the *Spread of Inequality*. Let us consider an example of this process as a way of developing the argument. Assume a two-person group in which A and B are alike save for one characteristic—B is more influenciable than A. That is, when A performs, B will influence A less often than A will influence B when B performs. Or, $\gamma_2 > \gamma_3$.[5] Let us call this stage 1 of the process. The relationships between probabilities and components at this stage are summarized in the first two columns of Table 4-1.

Since the circumstance described represents partial component inequality,

[5]Notice that this is a *weaker* assertion than that made in the Basic Expectation Assumption, which states that B, for whom A and B hold lower expectations, is more likely to change his mind no matter who has performed. Or B will lose more influence struggles than A, no matter who is trying to exert influence. Our assumption here is only that when B is compared to A as a target for influence, B loses more often than A does.

TABLE 4-1

Stage 1		Stage 2	
Probabilities	Components	Probabilities	Components
$\alpha_4 = \alpha_1$	$C_{1A} = C_{1B}$	$\alpha_4 > \alpha_1$	$C_{1A} > C_{1B}$
$\beta_4 = \beta_2$	$C_{2A} = C_{2B}$	$\beta_4 > \beta_2$	$C_{2A} > C_{2B}$
$\alpha_3 = \alpha_2$	$C_{3A} > C_{4B}$	$\alpha_3 > \alpha_2$	$C_{3A} > C_{3B}$
$\delta_2 = \epsilon_1$	$C_{4A} > C_{3B}$	$\delta_2 > \epsilon_1$	$C_{4A} > C_{4B}$
		$\gamma_4 > \gamma_3$	
$\gamma_2 > \gamma_3$		$\gamma_1 > \gamma_2$	

according to the Emergence Assumption, at some time t in the discussion, expectations will form with $E_A > E_B$. Then according to the Basic Expectation Assumption, complete constituent inequality will result as specified in the third column of Table 4-1.

Stage 2 differs from stage 1 in the following ways. First, pairs of probabilities that were unranked in stage 1 are ranked in stage 2. For example, in stage 1, $\alpha_4 = \alpha_1$, but in stage 2, $\alpha_4 > \alpha_1$. Thus inequality has spread to formerly unranked pairs of probabilities. Second, pairs of components that were unranked in stage 1 are ranked in stage 2. For example, $C_{1A} = C_{1B}$ in stage 1, but $C_{1A} > C_{1B}$ in stage 2. Thus inequality has spread to formerly unranked pairs of components.[6]

All of these differences represent a more pervasive inequality. Inequality has spread to more kinds of behavior. More generally, we can then state two theorems that we call the *Spread of Inequality* theorems.

THEOREM 3.1

If at the beginning of a full task unit (U_1), partial component inequality holds, then by the end of U_1, complete constituent inequality holds.

THEOREM 3.2

If at the beginning of a full task unit (U_1) complete component inequality but not constituent inequality holds, then by the end of U_1 complete constituent inequality will hold.

It is possible at the beginning of a unit for complete constituent inequality

---

[6]It should be noted here that in stage 1, C_{3A} is compared to C_{4B} rather than C_{3B}, and C_{4A} is compared to C_{3B} rather than C_{4B}. Also, the weaker ranking $\gamma_2 > \gamma_3$ is replaced by the stronger ranking $\gamma_4 > \gamma_3$ and $\gamma_1 > \gamma_2$. That is, in stage 1, it is still possible for B to win influence struggles more than 50 percent of the time in those cases where B has initiated the original performance output. If he wins, for example, 55 percent of such struggles, then $\gamma_2 > \gamma_3$ says that A will win more than 55 percent when A has initiated the original performance output. In stage 2, however, B will lose the majority of *all* influence struggles.

to exist even though expectation states have not formed. According to the Emergence Assumption, ranked expectation states will develop, but there will be no spread of inequality. Inequality is complete to begin with. According to the Emergence and Maintenance Assumptions, under these conditions the inequality is maintained. We state this in the following theorem which we call the *Maintenance of Complete Constituent Inequality*:

THEOREM 3.3
If at the beginning of a full task unit (U_1) complete constituent inequality holds, then it will persist through the entire unit.

III. SUMMARY AND DISCUSSION

The central idea of this paper is that patterns of behavioral inequalities in task focused small groups can be explained by positing an underlying structure of ranked performance expectation states. Our approach to the construction of such an explanation began with the development of a typology of kinds of behavior and the specification of how types of behavior follow each other in unit sequences. With this as a base we have developed a set of assumptions and theorems that specify how

1. Ranked performance expectation states emerge as a consequence of patterns of behavioral inequality.
2. Ranked performance expectation states in turn determine patterns of behavioral inequalities by affecting initiation of performance outputs, receipt of action opportunities, receipt of positive reactions, and acceptance of influence—and hence produce and maintain inequalities in accepted performance outputs.
3. Ranked performance expectations states are maintained.
4. Behavioral inequalities spread to more types of behaviors once ranked performance expectation states are established.

As formulated, the theory allows us to more fully understand previous experiments and gives guidance for developing new experiments. In particular, three experiments have been designed and carried out to provide empirical information relevant to various parts of our formulation. First consider the experiment described in chapter two of this volume in which three subjects were asked on repeated trials to decide which of two answers was correct in a binary decision task. Each subject made a private, independent choice between the binary alternatives, was told what the two others selected, and then made a private final choice. Information about the choices of others was a deception, however, in that the experimenter led each subject to believe that the others unanimously disagreed with him. He had to decide on each trial whether he or the others were right. Given our characterization of the interaction process, each such trial then consists of:

1. An action opportunity that cannot be declined (the opportunity to make an initial choice).
2. A performance output (the initial choice).
3. An influence attempt: a negative reaction with a counter performance output (exchange of disagreement information).
4. Either acceptance of influence (subject changes his mind) or non-acceptance of influence.

In other words, each trial is a direct operationalization of Figure 4-5, with all parameters controlled except the probability of acceptance of influence. The emergence assumption of this paper predicts the formation of ranked performance expectation states after some unspecified number of trials, and the probability model of chapter two specifies the process of such formation. Once expectation states are formed, the Basic Expectation Assumption of this paper predicts corresponding inequalities in rates of acceptance of influence. The model in chapter two uses this assumption to detect formation of expectations. Hence the experiment represents a test of the emergence assumption given that the Basic Expectation Assumption is correct. The data clearly show that rates of acceptance of influence shift as time goes on, and, furthermore, an increasing number of subjects evidence this shift.

An earlier experiment reported by Berger and Conner (1969) used the same trial structure as the above experiment but involved only two subjects. There were two parts to the experiment. In part 1 subjects were given a test reputed to measure the ability required for part 2 of the experiment. Fictitious results were publicly returned to the subjects so as to assign subjects specific states at the outset of the process. Of interest here are two conditions—where one subject is told he is high and his partner low (designated [+ −]) and where the other subject is told he is low and his partner high (designated [− +]). Part 2 consisted of a series of trials identical in all respects to those in the Berger, Conner, and McKeown experiment above. Each subject repeatedly had to decide to accept influence or not. Hence in this experiment emergence was not problematic, but whether rates of acceptance of influence would differ because of ranked performance expectation states was problematic. Subjects in the [+ −] condition accepted influence considerably less than subjects in the [− +] condition (22 percent compared to 56 percent respectively). These differences were consistent and stable over all trials.

Finally, in chapter three of this volume, Fisek (see also Fisek, 1969) describes an open interaction experiment in which he systematically recorded the initiation of performance outputs in three-man discussion groups. His results were mixed in that only 29 of his 59 groups displayed the increasing and then stable inequality in initiation of performance outputs that one would expect with the development of expectation states. The remaining 30 groups displayed inequality from the beginning and maintained it without detectable change. The data from the 29 groups that displayed increasing inequality provides support for the emergence assumption presented in this paper. Expectation States Theory can also provide an explanation, moreover, for the other 30 groups. One interpretation is that there may have been initial complete constituent inequality in these 30 groups. Fisek in no way controlled for factors that would be expected to produce such inequality. If this is correct, then by the Maintenance of Complete Constituent Inequality theorem, differential rates of initiation of performance outputs would persist for the entire experiment. We have no direct evidence for this interpretation and further research would be required to establish it.

The bulk of our theory has been presented in the context of a model for interaction in the two-man group.[7] But as the discussion above indicates, we believe that the principles that lie behind the model are of more general applicability than two-man groups. Given the conditions we have specified, particularly initial status equality, inequality in number of accepted performance outputs will lead to ranked performance expectation states in larger groups, although the process will be more complicated. Ranked expectation states will order initiation of performance outputs, receipt of positive reactions, acceptance of action opportunities, receipt of action opportunities, and acceptance of influence beyond the scope of conditions we have stated. And we believe ranked expectation states tend to generally produce the conditions for their own stability, unless external conditions change. What remains to be done is progressively to remove the special restrictions imposed upon our formulation and to reformulate the statement of the theory so as to increase its generality. Such efforts are presently under way.

REFERENCES

BALES, R. F. 1953. The equilibrium problem in small groups. In *Working papers in the theory of action*, eds. T. Parsons, R. F. Bales, and E. A. Shils, pp. 111–61. Glencoe, Ill.: The Free Press.

BERGER, J., and T. L. CONNER. 1966. Performance expectations and behavior in small groups. *Technical report no. 18.* Laboratory for Social Research, Stanford University.

———. 1969. Performance expectations and behavior in small groups. *Acta sociologica* 12: 186–98.

[7]Lakatos (1968) distinguishes between a theory and a model. A model is the formal application of the principles of the theory to a highly restricted, possibly a very special set of circumstances as a procedure for developing and refining the theory.

BERGER, J., T. L. CONNER, and W. L. MCKEOWN. 1969. Evaluations and the formation and maintenance of performance expectations. *Human relations* 22 (December): 481–502.

FISEK, M. H. 1969. The evolution of status structures and interaction in task oriented discussion groups. Unpublished Ph. D. dissertation, Stanford University.

HEINICKE, C. M., and R. F. BALES. 1953. Developmental trends in the structure of small groups. *Sociometry* 16: 7–38.

LAKATOS, I. 1968. Criticism and the methodology of scientific research programmes. In *Proceedings of the Aristotelian Society* 68: 149–86.

SOURCES OF EVALUATION AND SOCIAL INTERACTION

INTRODUCTION TO PART THREE

The task of this section is to extend some basic concepts and assertions of
Expectations States Theory to the problem of how a special class of
"significant others" and "multiple significant others" (sources of
evaluations) determines the behavior of individuals in interpersonal
situations. Webster and Sobieszek base their work on a long-standing
perspective in social psychology which claims that the individual's
self-image arises as the result of knowing others' opinions, that he comes to
view himself in the "looking glass" of others' ideas regarding him.
Reformulating this idea in terms of Expectation States Theory, they
describe the formation of an individual's conception of his own task ability
(self-expectations), and his conception of others' ability as well
(expectations for other). The theory is extended to include
conceptualization of a particular type of person, a *source*, whose evaluative
opinions will be used by individuals in forming their expectation states for
self and other. Other propositions of Expectation States Theory then
enable description of specific, testable consequences of the expectation
states formed in this manner.

A set of experiments designed to test the original expectation states
"source theory" is described, and in general they support the formulation.
The initial source theory is generalized to apply to the much more complex
social situation in which an individual is faced simultaneously with two
sources of evaluations. A second set of experiments designed to test this
generalization provides support for most of the derivations from the
generalized theory.

Webster and Sobieszek's research leads them to the problem of: How
does the individual accept information from two highly influential
individuals who usually contradict each other? In many ways this is
analogous to the classical situation of reconciling two conflicting
"significant others." In order to refine their understanding of the
mechanism by which an individual processes information from conflicting
sources of evaluation, a third set of experiments is designed and carried
out. Analyses of the results of these experiments suggest a choice between
several formulations of the resolution mechanism, and the propositions of
the source theory are appropriately modified.

The first set of experiments presented in this chapter were previously
reported (Webster, 1969)—though without the complete theoretical
background presented here—and the second set of experiments were
similarly reported (Sobieszek, 1972). A further extension of the propositions
of the basic theory to describe effects of known status characteristics of the

source, along with relevant empirical data, are presented in Webster, 1970. Attempts to differentiate between various modes of source acceptance, other than that formulated in this chapter, are reported in Sobieszek and Webster, 1973. Finally, the complete research program, including theoretical work and experimental research not reported here, appears in *Sources of Self-Evaluation*, a research monograph by Webster and Sobieszek published by John Wiley & Sons, 1973.

We would also like to call the reader's attention to additional research that is related to or has evolved out of the work presented in this chapter. Two mathematical treatments of problems arising from the research described in this chapter have been published. The first mathematical treatment (Savage and Webster, 1971) presents a probabilistic reformulation of the basic source theory, isolates and eliminates some indeterminacies in the earlier formulation, and presents a simple model for the process of source acceptance described here. The second mathematical treatment (Webster et al., 1972) proposes and tests several alternative models in order to specify precisely the process of information utilization in cases where different sources of evaluation are providing either consistent or inconsistent information to the individual. General issues of information processing models for situations similar to this one are discussed in Berger and Fisek (1970), and preliminary data are presented to aid in evaluating two general types of models. A formal information processing theory, along with a mathematical model of the process, has also been recently developed by Kervin (1972); and experimental tests comparable to both those of Berger and Fisek, and Webster et al. are reported.

REFERENCES

BERGER, J., and M. H. FISEK. 1970. Consistent and inconsistent status characteristics and the determination of power and prestige orders. *Sociometry* 33 (September): 287–304.

KERVIN, J. B. 1972. An information processing model for the formation of performance expectations in small groups. Unpublished doctoral dissertation, The Johns Hopkins University.

SAVAGE, I., and M. WEBSTER. 1972. Source of evaluations reformulated and analyzed. *Proceedings of the sixth Berkeley symposium on mathematical statistics and probability.* Vol. IV: 317–27. Berkeley, Calif.: University of California Press.

SOBIESZEK, B., and M. WEBSTER. 1973. Conflicting sources of evaluation. To be published in *Sociometry*.

WEBSTER, M. 1969. Source of evaluations and expectations for performances. *Sociometry* 32 (June): 243–58.

WEBSTER, M., and B. SOBIESZEK. 1973. *Sources of self-evaluation.* Research monograph to be published by John Wiley & Sons.

WEBSTER, M., L. ROBERTS, and B. SOBIESZEK. 1972. Accepting significant others: six models. *American journal of sociology* 78: 576–98.

CHAPTER FIVE

Sources of Evaluations

and Expectation States*

MURRAY WEBSTER, JR.

BARBARA I. SOBIESZEK

In this chapter we are interested in adapting the perspective of Expectation States Theory to some issues in the literature on self-evaluation. Our interests seem to be central to this tradition and, at the same time, to be amenable to the theoretical and experimental approach of the expectation theory research. The general question is "How does the individual form his conceptions of his ability at various tasks?" In attempting to answer this question, more specific issues—the role of others in influencing the self-conception, the precise characteristics of the influential others, the nature of the influence process by which others' opinions become incorporated into the self, the

*We would like to acknowledge intellectual and practical assistance from, in particular, Joseph Berger, Doris Entwisle, M. Hamit Fisek, David Grafstein, John B. Kervin, and Morris Zelditch, Jr. The research program was partially supported by NSF grant GS-2169 and by Office of Education grant OEG-2-7-061610-0207 (administered through the Center for Study of Schools, The Johns Hopkins University). Of course we bear responsibility for any intellectual flaws in this chapter. The financial support does not imply any sponsoring or approval of the respective granting agencies.

consequences of disagreement among influential others, among other considerations—arise and must receive at least partial solutions.

We begin with a selective review of the self-evaluation literature, emphasizing those theoretical and empirical treatments that seem most directly relevant to these issues.

I. THE SELF-EVALUATION TRADITION

Sociological interest in the development of the self is usually traced to the writings of Charles Horton Cooley (1902), though many of the same sorts of ideas were expressed earlier by William James. The central idea of this tradition is that the individual's conception of himself—who he is, what kind of a person he is, how much ability he has at various tasks—is directly dependent upon the opinions and evaluations he perceives from others. He "sees himself" as an object in a way that is dependent upon the ways that he thinks others see him. When the individual looks at himself as he might look in a mirror, what he sees reflected back are the opinions of others. The individual accepts these opinions, and comes to think of himself in the same ways as others appear to.

> In a very large and interesting class of cases the social reference takes the form of a somewhat definite imagination of how one's self—that is any idea he appropriates—appears in a particular mind, and the kind of self-feeling one has is determined by the attitude toward this attributed to that other mind. A social self of this sort might be called the reflected or looking-glass self:
>
> > "Each to each a looking-glass
> > Reflects the other that doth pass."
>
> As we see our face, figure, and dress in the glass, and are interested in them because they are ours, and [are] pleased or otherwise with them according as they do or do not answer to what we should like them to be; so in imagination we perceive in another's mind some thought of our appearance, manners, aims, deeds, character, friends, and so on, and are variously affected by it. [Cooley, pp. 183–84]

Of central significance in this sort of view of the self is the crucial role played by *others* in forming the individual's self-referent ideas. The individual must interact with others so that he can form his self-conceptions, and consequently, it is important for us to understand precisely the roles played by these others.[1]

---

[1]A very different point of view might be called the "developmental self," which many personality theorists and psychoanalysts espouse. According to this view, the self (or per-

In addition to focusing attention on the others, there is implicit in the looking-glass self description the idea that the looking glass may be distorted; it may not be a perfect reflection of others' opinions. Several sources of distortion may be postulated. First, the individual may incorrectly interpret the words or the nonverbal communication of others; he may not understand perfectly the evaluations they try to transmit. Second, there are norms governing polite means of expression that can act to produce intentional distortion of evaluations. Third, something about the individual's past experience, such as previous evaluations from others, may interact with immediate evaluations to modify their effect.

Intentional and unintentional distortion of others' communications are important in most real-life instances of forming a self-evaluation, but they are not necessarily the initial concerns in building a theory of how the self is formed. Having noted these two possibilities of imperfect communication, we shall say no more about them. The third possibility, that past history modifies the effect of future experiences, is theoretically very important. Cooley did not develop this idea, but it appears clearly in the work of Mead, in the discussion of a cognitive structure.

George Herbert Mead (1934) adopted the looking-glass perspective and developed Cooley's ideas further. Two of Mead's contributions are important to the theory to be developed here. The first is the idea of the "generalized other"; the second is the idea of the development of a cognitive structure.

In explicating the relationship believed to exist between the opinions of others and the individual's self-concept, Mead asserted:

> But only by taking the attitude of the generalized other toward himself, in one or another of these ways, can he think at all, for only thus can thinking—or the internalized conversation of gestures which constitutes thinking—occur. [Mead, 1934: 156]

---

sonality) is importantly influenced by biological development. The maturing individual develops his personality and his self-referent ideas during the maturation of the mind, which grows in a way analogous to the growth of the body. The self that is formed is usually considered to be the product of the growth of inborn tendencies of the individual, perhaps somewhat altered by his experiences with others.

By contrast, according to the "social self," or looking-glass orientation, *there is nothing there before the individual engages in interaction with others.* Any "personality" traits and any self that is visible are solely the products of the individual's interaction with and perception of others in regard to himself. Whatever inborn tendencies there may be, they are insignificant by comparison to the importance of the others with whom the individual interacts. At most, adherents of the looking-glass point of view would say that the individual is probably born with some sort of undifferentiated psychic energy, and a propensity to engage the world in interaction. Specific traits that are evident in an individual, and any individual differences in habits, behavior patterns, etc., are attributed, not to the individual's biological composition, but to his experiences with others.

Our intent here is not to compare or evaluate these two approaches, but simply to acknowledge that we have adopted one of them: that of the "social self."

The generalized other is usually considered to be a sort of mental image that the individual forms from his interactions with various specific others. By observing the responses of a large number of other individuals to himself, a person learns to expect responses from them that fall within a certain "typical" range; he comes, in other words, to understand how "most people" regard him. According to Mead, this generalized other is the most important determinant of the individual's self-image. Intuitively this is plausible. If we assume that the variety of individuals with whom most people have contact will differ slightly in their opinions of him—or, more precisely, that they will differ slightly in the opinions he *thinks* they hold of him—then in order for an individual to form a specific and definite self-image, he must find some way to combine their opinions. The combined opinions of the total community with whom he has interaction constitute the generalized other. Exactly how it is that the various discrete opinions are combined to form the generalized other—whether it is a simple additive process, a weighted average, or some other process—is a further question with which Mead did not deal explicitly (see Webster et al., 1972, for some models of the process). In the theory to be presented here we will present a partial answer to the question of how individual others' opinions are combined. At this point, we simply note the importance of the concept of a generalized other to a theory of development of self-concept.

The generalized other appears to imply another idea; namely, that not every other with whom the individual interacts is equally important in determining the self-image. If it is the case that the opinions of "most others" hold more importance for the individual than the opinions of any single other, then the idea of differential significance of various sources of opinions has been suggested. It is also plausible on an intuitive basis that some individuals will be more effective than others, not only in contributing to the generalized others' opinion, but also as individuals. Specifying the characteristics that determine the differential effectiveness of those others is in fact a central issue in constructing a theory of the looking-glass self. Differential importance is implied in Mead's discussion of the generalized other, but neither at this point nor elsewhere is it developed further. The issue is considered in the writing of Sullivan (see below), though as will be seen, it is not completely specified there, either.

A second major contribution of Mead was his explicit reference to a semipermanent sort of cognitive structure that gets built up as the result of the evaluations of others.

> I do not now want to discuss metaphysical problems, but I do want to insist that the self has a sort of structure that arises in social conduct that is entirely distinguishable from this so-called subjective experience of these particular sets of objects to which the organism alone has access—the common character of privacy of access does not fuse them together.

The self to which we have been referring arises when the conversation of gestures is taken over into the conduct of the individual form. When this conversation of gestures can be taken over into the individual's conduct so that the attitude of the other forms can affect the organism, and the organism can reply with its corresponding gesture and thus arouse the attitude of the other in its own process, then a self arises. [Mead, 1934: 166–67]

If we take the writing literally, Cooley's looking-glass self has no permanence; the looking-glass reflections are constantly changing, and with them, presumably, the individual's self-image is constantly changing. Such a result is certainly counter-intuitive. The idea that an individual has some sort of semi-permanent idea of who he is and of his various ability levels is clearly something we would like to incorporate into a theory of formation of self (yet it is curiously absent in some other recent theories; for example, Kinch, 1963; Zetterberg, 1957). More importantly, the idea of a constantly changing self-image is inconsistent with empirical evidence. For example, some of the Expectation States Theory research described in earlier chapters has shown quite clearly that as the result of having received a series of evaluations, individuals come to hold a specifiable set of ideas concerning their own task abilities. Moreover, it has been shown in these studies that the set of self-referent ideas produces a relatively determinate set of subsequent behaviors. Individuals who have received a large proportion of positive evaluations come to hold high self-expectations; those who have received a large proportion of negative evaluations come to hold low self-expectations; *and* the subsequent behaviors of these two groups of individuals differ markedly.

Mead, in the passage just quoted, indicates awareness of the importance of conceptualizing some sort of structure that gets "built up" as the result of receiving the opinions of others. It is not clear in this passage whether he conceptualizes the self as a set of cognitions or as a behavioristic set of learned responses; either conceptualization would be consistent with his famous example of learning how to catch a ball, for instance. In theoretical terms, this means that the precise nature of the self is still inadequately specified. But the idea that there is some semi-permanent effect upon the individual as the result of the opinions of others is there, and it is crucial to an adequate theory of the development of the self.

The final contribution to a theory of the self to be noted here is the idea of the "significant other," usually attributed to Harry Stack Sullivan (1947). A significant other is one whose opinions "matter" to the individual, someone whose approval he desires and whose censure he wishes to avoid.

The importance of conceptualizing the differential significance of the others with whom the individual interacts has already been noted. Anyone has available a wide variety of opinions concerning himself, and intuitively it is reasonable to suppose that he will not use all of them equally. It is more pleasing to have one's manners praised by someone known to have good taste than by an obvious boor, more satisfying to win a prize in a national contest than in a local one, more enjoyable to have one's classwork praised by the teacher than by the classroom dunce. Quite simply, for most people, it seems reasonable to believe that some others' opinions are crucially important to development of the self-image, and others' opinions matter not at all.

In clinical applications such as those of interest to Sullivan, it is usually a fairly simple matter to determine who are the significant others in the individual's life: most often they are the parents; sometimes, other relatives, close friends, or teachers. Consequently, in Sullivan's writings there is no need to specify in a more general way the *characteristics* that make a particular other significant. However, for developing a theory it will be crucial to specify in more abstract terms the characteristics of parents—more properly, the characteristics of people in general—that allow them to become significant others. Such specification will permit constructing an explanation for the significance of parents' opinions, and also for the significance (or lack of significance) of any other person's opinions.

To summarize the ideas discussed so far, we began by adopting the Cooley orientation to a theory of the self-image, which argues that it is from the opinions and evaluations of others that the individual develops a particular set of ideas concerning himself. Exactly how the opinions of others are translated into the individual's self-image is a problem that we shall have to consider later. Building upon the looking-glass self idea, Mead introduces the idea of the generalized other—some combination of the opinions of the others with whom the individual interacts. However, the result of disagreement between others and the combining mechanism for consistent opinions are left unspecified. In addition, Mead introduces the idea of a semi-permanent "self structure," which tends to persist and which produces effects upon future behavior. Mead also introduces the idea of differential importance of others, explicitly addressed by Sullivan in his discussion of significant others. However, the very important task of specifying clearly, precisely, and generally the characteristics of significant others at this point remains uncompleted.

The theoretical ideas in the self-evaluation literature have formed the basis for a large amount of empirical research that has been, for the most part, confirmatory. With some changes of emphasis, this research also suggests answers to some of the open questions just noted. We will be concerned with only a part of the looking-glass self literature, though it is by far the largest area of interest so far as empirical research has been concerned. We will not be concerned with all areas of self-concept, but only with self-*evaluation*, the individual's ideas concerning his own abilities. The reason that most empirical research in the looking-glass self tradition has dealt with self-evaluation instead of more global ideas of self-concept is probably measurement. It is relatively easy to measure an individual's ideas of his own abilities because such ideas can be scaled; they can be high or low, and the standards for deciding whether they are high or low can be specified. By contrast, there are no universally-accepted standards for what constitutes being a "good person," or a "successful partner." However there is no reason to suppose that the ideas in the looking-glass self are inapplicable in principle to areas where measurement is difficult, or that such elements of self-concept are unimportant. They simply have not received so much attention as the more strictly evaluative areas.

One of the earliest, as well as one of the most direct, tests of the looking-glass self ideas was performed by Miyamoto and Dornbusch (1956). Using rating scales on a number of personal attributes, they found strong support for the following assertions: (1) self-evaluation will be highly correlated with actual rating by others in the immediate group; (2) self-evaluation will be highly correlated with subjects' perceived rating by "most people"; (3) the correlation of self-rating and perceived rating by "most people" will be greater than the correlation of self-rating and actual rating by others of the immediate group. The first finding is consistent with the basic Cooley idea, and the second and third findings are consistent with Mead's ideas of the generalized other. We may also note that these findings are consistent with the idea that some distortion can exist in perception of others' actual opinions, and with the differential significance of others. However, specification of the characteristics of a significant other was not pursued in this study.

Backman et al. (1963), Haas and Maehr (1965), and Jones et al. (1968) have studied conditions surrounding change in an existing level of specific self-evaluations. Their work has shown both that it is reasonable to speak of a relatively enduring self-structure, and that the self may be affected by new information in the form of evaluations from certain others. The nature of these others, clearly intended to be what Sullivan called significant others, has varied in these studies: "experts," "professionals," and "authorities" have evaluated subjects in order to affect their self-evaluations. Implicitly, these are expected to be significant others, and intuitively it is plausible that they would be. However, no clear or consistent specification of the characteristics that make their evaluations significant is given.

A study by Reeder et al. (1960) may suggest some of the characteristics necessary to a significant other. Using a design similar to Miyamoto and Dornbusch, they found that for some of their subjects (Air Force enlisted men) self-rank and objective rank by others of the immediate group were quite discrepant. They hypothesized that the discrepancy might be due to what they called "extensity of interaction," and tested this hypothesis by constructing an index of the number of significant reference groups available to the men. Variables in the index included amount of education, marital status, urban or rural background, age, and military rank. Subjects with high "extensity" on this index showed the greatest discrepancy between self-rating and rating by members of their military work groups.

However we may note that it is not necessarily the *number* of alternative reference groups, but perhaps rather the particular characteristics of the others in these groups that is crucial. It seems reasonable to suppose that the opinions of others who are, by these variables, better educated, of urban background, older, and of higher military rank (omitting marriage) would be more likely to be significant to subjects than would people low on these variables. This alternative interpretation suggests a number of possible characteristics of significant others—for example, age, intelligence, formal status—an idea that we introduce in the theory of the following section as "competence to evaluate."

Four central issues seem to emerge from this brief review of the self-evaluation literature. First, what are the characteristics of a significant other, an other whose evaluative opinions are accepted by the individual and used as the basis for forming his own opinions regarding himself? Second, how is it that the evaluations of the significant other are "translated" into some overall conception of one's own abilities? Third, what happens in the case in which there is more than one potential significant other present, and they either agree or disagree in their evaluations of the individual? Fourth, what are the nature and the behavioral consequences of the self-evaluation that is produced? The self-evaluation literature is rich in ideas and suggestions, and certainly it possesses intuitive appeal. Yet as many others have noted, the generality and the broadness of the ideas usually do not provide specific research directives. Important questions are left open or are dealt with in a way that does not permit direct empirical testing. In the next section we undertake the task of explicating the characteristics of the significant other, and of incorporating answers to the four questions above in a formal theory for which determinate tests may be designed.

II. SOURCES OF EVALUATIONS AND EXPECTATIONS FOR PERFORMANCE: AN INITIAL FORMULATION

As we have noted, the looking-glass self tradition provides a number of ideas regarding the way in which an individual comes to hold a certain set of ideas regarding himself, but for the most part these ideas are not developed sufficiently to provide either a formal theoretical expression or a set of specific research directives. By contrast, Expectation States Theory does provide both a formal theoretical framework and the possibility of deriving determinate empirical predictions. However, previous versions of this theory have not included the ideas of the importance of others' opinions or of the differential opinions of others in forming the individual's expectation states. In this section we propose a version of Expectation States Theory designed to incorporate in a formal way some of the ideas of the looking-glass self, and thus to extend the theory to include a conceptualization of the source of expectations.

Previous versions of Expectation States Theory have been concerned primarily (although not exclusively) with specification of either a "unit-evaluation process" for the formation of expectations (Berger and Conner, 1969; Berger, Conner, McKeown, 1969; and chapter two of this text), or the *consequences for observable future interaction* of a given expectation state (Berger and Conner, 1969; also see Berger and Conner, chapter four). Here we propose to add the concept of a *source* of expectations, similar to the idea of a significant other in the looking-glass self tradition. What this means is a further specification of *determinants* of expectations. It is the attempt to specify characteristics of an other that make his opinions important enough that they will be used by the actor in forming his expectations for himself and for others.

The approach adopted involves several goals. First, of course, such an extension of Expectation States Theory should improve the determinacy of the theory. Adding one or more concepts to a theory, along with one or more substantive assertions—such as an explicit specification of exactly what kind of individual can produce the expectations held by members of a group and the process by which the expectations are produced—can increase the number and the precision of predictions that can be made from the theory. Second, the extension is intended to provide theoretical links between Expectation States Theory and the ideas in the self-evaluation literature. Third, we hope to perform the extension in a way that will enable us to make use of previous theory building and empirical research, and at the same time to provide enough flexibility for future extension. On this last point, we wish to preserve the formal structure of Expectation States Theory from previous chapters, so as to be able to build upon previous experimental confirmation of parts of the theory not centrally at issue here—for example, confirmation of the assertion that differentiated patterns of expectation states will produce specifiable differences in observable behavior, such as rejection of influence. In addition, though the first version of the theory extension will deal with the simplest possible case in order to test the basic specification of the characteristics of the significant other, if this task proves successful, we wish to have a formal theoretical structure and experimental design that may be adapted for more complex situations in the future.

We have already noted several areas in which it is desirable that the ideas of the looking-glass self be explicated. The term "self-evaluation" has a variety of meanings in common usage, and a somewhat smaller set of meanings in current professional discourse. To some it connotes a strictly defined idea of ability at one task; to others, abilities at most tasks; to others, a measure of overall satisfaction; to still others, a measure of discrepancy between ideal self and actual self. For many purposes of communication, such diversity of meaning causes no problems, but for building an explicit theory, it is undesirable for any of the terms to have this indefinite or "surplus" meaning. An idea of an "expectation state" does have a determinate and precise meaning as it is used in the propositions of expectation theory, but this meaning does not correspond exactly to many of the common usages of self-evaluation. Thus it is desirable to specify the relations between the term "self-evaluation" and the term "expectation state."

The first distinction is that expectation states refer only to *task performance*; expectations are held for how well an individual is likely to do at some measurable activity. Thus such "dimensions" of self-evaluation as "morality" and "luck" are not reflected in expectation states.

Second, the primary, though not the exclusive, focus of expectation states is upon a single task at one time, such as an individual's expectations for his own ability at solving mathematical problems.[2] Self-evaluation is sometimes used to refer to a more global trait, such as generally high intellectual ability, or even "overall quality as a person." For the former meaning, generally high intellectual ability, some versions of Expectation States Theory (for example, Berger et al., 1966) have used the term "General Expectation State," or GES; the latter concept has no equivalent in our theory. In our usage, we restrict the usage of "expectation state" to conceptions about a specific task ability and situation. The second important distinction, then, is task-specificity of expectation states.

Finally, self-evaluation is frequently considered to be a trans-situational characteristic of an individual, an idea of his ability that he carries about from one place to another. By contrast, expectation states speak of conceptions of ability *relative* to two or more individuals, such as holding high-low expectations for self and a given other, or for self and a given pair of others. We might note that the idea of a self-evaluation that does not incorporate relativity between specific others seems unlikely to be of much use in predicting behavior in any empirical circumstances; but it is the case that, as the term is usually used, this *relative* self-evaluation aspect is left unspecified. With these restrictions in mind, assertions to be made about expectation states are consistent with most assertions that would be made about self-evaluation.

To review briefly, Expectation States Theory, as presented in earlier chapters of this book, was originally developed to account for phenomena associated with the emergence and maintenance of power and prestige structures in informally organized, task-focused groups, such as Bales-type discussion groups, juries, study groups, or ad hoc committees. Observable differences between members of such groups (such as public evaluations, acceptance or

---

[2]We may conjecture that the individual's overall self-evaluation is composed of some weighted average of his expectations for various tasks, perhaps weighted by the importance he attaches to being able to perform highly at each task.

rejection of influence, number of chances to perform) are assumed to reflect an underlying structure of *expectation states*, which develop through the various interaction processes described in part two of this text. The persistence of established differences is explained by the self-maintaining nature of expectation states: once they exist, they affect the very conditions (such as the nature of the unit evaluations) that led to their establishment.

What is particularly important from our point of view is the role of individual unit evaluations of performances in the formation of expectation states, for this appears to be the principal way that ability conceptions arise. In other words, how individuals evaluate performances in early phases of group interaction determines the expectation states that develop and, through the expectations states, determines most important features of the interaction patterns for the group. Because the formation of expectation states is for our purposes analogous to the process of forming an overall self-evaluation, the theory must specify just how it is that the individual makes his unit decisions about the individual performances. If we know how the individual has evaluated the performances of any actor (including himself), then we may use the version of the theory presented in chapters two and four to derive predictions for the formation of expectation states and for subsequent behaviors.

For an individual who is interested in evaluating a given performance output, there are basically two means he can use. First, he may evaluate the performance himself; he may decide, on the basis of past knowledge, experience, or some objective criterion (such as an answer key to a test, or a book on athletic performance records) whether the performance is a good one. This is the method assumed in previous versions of the theory. Second, the individual might rely upon the opinion of someone else in the group; he may observe the evaluation made by some other individual and decide to agree with it. There are probably several considerations that influence the decision to rely upon the opinion of another. One case in which the individual will probably prefer to use the opinion of another is the case of his own performances. If a performance is his own, he may feel a particular need to have it validated by others. If he hadn't considered the performance a good one *before* he voiced it, he never would have done so—though whether it sounded good to him *while* he was saying it is another matter. Also, he may realize that it is difficult to be objective about the quality of one's own work, and for that reason he may prefer to accept the evaluations made by others. A second major factor that seems likely to impel the individual to rely upon the opinions of others is task difficulty. The more difficult the task, or the more unclear the evaluative standards, the more difficult it will appear to the individual to evaluate a performance output; and consequently, the more willing he probably will be to use the opinion of someone else. Certainly in the limiting case of complete subjective uncertainty about the accuracy of the performance, along with a lack of objective evaluative standards, the opinion of someone else could be crucial.

At this point we are ready to state the foregoing considerations more formally, in a version of expectation theory designed to take account of the influence of others' evaluations.

We begin with the two scope restrictions common to all versions of Expectation States Theory: *task-orientation* of group members, and *collective orientation*. The former condition means that the individuals are strictly concerned with solving the group's problem, as opposed to a concern with having a smooth, friendly, social interaction. Collective orientation means that not only is it legitimate, it is also necessary for the group members to consider each other's opinions in solving the problem.

DEFINITION 1

An interaction situation is *task situation S* if and only if:
a. there are at least two actors, *p* and *o*, making performance outputs;
b. there is one actor, an evaluator, *e*, with the right to make evaluations of the performance outputs of *p* and *o*.
c. *p* and *o* have no prior expectations for their own or each other's performance at the task;
d. all actors are task-oriented;
e. all actors are collectively oriented.

We will also have occasion to refer to p'—*p* as he perceives himself—but only in an analytic sense is p' an additional actor in situation *S*.

Since the theory is concerned with the differential effectiveness of evaluators, it is convenient to designate a special type of evaluator, a *source*. The concept of a source constitutes a major addition to previous versions of Expectation States Theory. A source will be defined as an evaluator whose evaluative opinions "matter" to *p*, one whose performance evaluations are likely to be accepted by *p* and used as the basis for forming his expectations for himself and other actors. He is, in other words, a "significant" evaluating other. Because of the central importance of the source to this version of the theory, the question arises as to precisely what characteristics will enable an evaluator to become a source. One answer to this question becomes apparent from a consideration of the task-orientation of the group.

If we assume that in a problem solving group of the type under discussion, actors are actively "trying" to form conceptions of their own and of each other's abilities, then it seems likely that they will be more willing to pay attention to the evaluations made by an actor whom they already know has high ability at the task than to one whose ability is already known to be low. In other words, if an actor *p* is trying to decide whether to agree with the performance evaluations *e* makes of *o*, it seems more likely that *p* will decide that *e*'s opinions are valuable when *e* is known by *p* to have high task ability than when *e* is known to have low ability. As the first statement, we define a *source* as an actor whom *p* considers to have more ability at the task then he himself possesses.

DEFINITION 2

E is a *source* for *p* in *S* if and only if *p* believes that *e* is more capable of evaluating performances than *p* is.

Assumption 1 then specifies the effect of a source upon *p*'s evaluations.

ASSUMPTION 1

In *S*, if *e* is a source for *p*, then *p* will agree with *e*'s unit evaluations of any actor's performances.

Note that by Assumption 1, *p* may be interested in evaluating any actor's performances, either those of another actor or those of himself. Also note that by this statement of Assumption 1, if *p* does not know the ability of *e*, then the theory cannot be used to predict the expectation states *p* will come to hold. In other words, the theory being developed here will be useful to predict the formation of expectations only in cases where there is an evaluator *e* who is a potential source (or "significant other"), and where *p* has an idea of *e*'s ability to perform the task.[3]

It may not be immediately apparent that Assumption 1 and Definition 2 are intended to deny one intuitively plausible empirical outcome; namely, that *any* actor who is permitted to play the socially-defined role of evaluator will become an effective source. We argue that it is not necessarily sufficient that an individual be in a formal position where he has the right to make evaluations in order for him to affect the ability conceptions (expectation states) of the performing actors. He must, in addition, be believed to have greater ability at the task than the actors, or they may well ignore his evaluations.

Definition 2 and Assumption 1 may be represented as balance diagrams, following the conventions developed by Cartwright and Harary (Harary et al., 1965). Unit evaluations of performances are represented by directed lines, with + or − signs to indicate positive or negative evaluations, respectively. Expectation states will be represented by directed double lines with + and − signs indicating, respectively, high and low expectations. Unit relations, which by definition are always positive, will be represented by a bracket.

In Figure 5-1, *p* has accepted *e* as a source, as shown by the unit relation "acceptance," and *e* has made a positive evaluation of a performance output. Assumption 1 then asserts that because of the acceptance relation between *p*

---

[3] The theory as constructed can be used to make predictions even if *p* does not know for sure the ability of *e*, if *p* can make some inference as to *e*'s ability. This would be the case, for example, if *p* knew *e*'s rank on a status characteristic, but not his task ability. Thus it might be possible to extend this theory to assume explicitly that *p* will use knowledge of a status characteristic to form an ability conception for *e* in the manner described by Berger et al. (1966). We do not undertake this extension here, but it is our intent to formulate the theory in such a way that it will be possible at a later time.

FIGURE 5-1

Positive evaluation of a performance output by an evaluator whom *p* has accepted as a source

and *e*, *p* will make the same evaluation of the performance that *e* has made. This means that, in terms of the diagram, *p* will complete his cognitive structure in a balanced fashion—in this case, with three positive relations. By the standard rules of balance theories, if the *p–e* relation exists, then the *p–p.o.* relation depends upon the *e–p.o.* relation. Specifically, the unit relation *p–e* is always positive; therefore, if *e–p.o.* is negative, then *p–p.o.* must be negative also in order to avoid imbalancing the structure. This feature of the diagram may be said to constitute a partial explanation of Assumption 1 of the theory and of the definition of the source. Completion of the structure is shown in Figure 5-2. As may be seen in Figures 5-1 and 5-2, if *p* has *not* accepted *e* as a

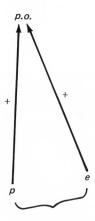

FIGURE 5-2

Positive evaluation of the performance by *p*

source, then the *p–e* unit relation will not have formed, and the structure would be "vacuously balanced" no matter what sign were put on the *p–p.o.* evaluation. This illustrates the previous statement that if *p* has *not* accepted *e* as a source, then the theory cannot be used to predict *p*'s evaluation of the performance.

Assumption 2 is concerned with the relation of unit evaluations and the formation of expectations for an individual's future performance.

ASSUMPTION 2

In *S*, if *p* evaluates a series of performances of any actor, then he will come to hold an expectation state for that actor which is consistent with those evaluations.

It is not the intention of Assumption 2 to specify details of the unit-evaluation process in the formation of expectation states; this has been done elsewhere (Berger, Conner, McKeown, chapter two; and Fisek, chapter three of this text). All that Assumption 2 asserts is that with time, a series of unit evaluations of an actor's performances will generalize into an expectation state held for that actor, and that the type of expectation state (high or low) will be consistent with these positive or negative evaluations.

Let us assume that the performance outputs represented in Figures 5-1 and 5-2 were made by *o*. This is represented by adding *o* to the diagram, and unit relations between *o* and performance outputs, as in Figure 5-3. Further, because *p* has positively evaluated these performance outputs, Assumption 2 asserts that he will come to hold consistent expectations (in this case, high expectations) for the actor who made these outputs. (For evaluating *p*'s own performance, we would put *p'*—*p* as viewed by self—in place of *o* in Figures

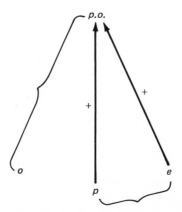

FIGURE 5-3
P's perception of a unit relation between *o* and the performance

5-3 and 5-4.) In other words, Assumption 2 again asserts that p will complete a set of relevant cognitive structures in a balanced fashion, as shown in Figure 5-4.

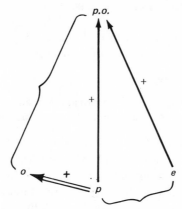

FIGURE 5-4

Formation of high expectations for the actor o after a number of positively evaluated performances

The complete Assumption 3 specifies the effect of p's expectations for *other* actors (where the other actors can include e, an evaluator) upon his observable interaction with them. Assumption 4 specifies the effect of the expectations p holds for both *himself and others* upon his observable interaction with those others. Many of the ideas expressed in Assumptions 3 and 4 have been adapted from previous versions of Expectation States Theory presented in this book.

It is the special task of Assumption 3d to specify the circumstances under which p will accept the evaluator e as a source. From the perspective of Expectation States Theory, the major requirement for e to be accepted as a source is that p must hold high performance expectations for him. More precisely, Assumption 3d asserts that the higher are the expectations p holds for e, the more likely is p to believe that e is "more capable of evaluating performances than p," thus fulfilling the conditions of Definition 2 for acceptance as a source.

ASSUMPTION 3

In S, if p holds higher expectations for any actor (o_1) than for another actor (o_2):

a. p will be more likely to give o_1 action opportunities than o_2
b. p will be more likely to evaluate positively o_1's future performance outputs than o_2's
c. in case of disagreement between o_1 and o_2, p will be more likely to agree with o_1
d. p will be more likely to accept o_1 than o_2 as a source

ASSUMPTION 4

In *S*, the higher the expectations an actor *p* holds for self relative to the expectations he holds for *o*:

a.   the more likely he is to accept a given action opportunity and make a performance output

b.   in case of disagreement with *o*, the more likely he is to reject influence

This completes the theory. The attempt has been made to make most parts of the theory consistent with other versions of expectation theory. This version differs from previous versions in three ways: first, it adds and defines the concept of a source, an actor whose evaluations will be accepted by others in the system; second, it specifies the effects of a source upon formation of expectation states; and third, it makes acceptance of an actor as a source probabilistically dependent upon the expectations held for him by others.

Since the main interest here is in the concept of the source, derivations that were tested were those involving acceptance by *p* of an evaluator as a source and the effects of his evaluations upon *p*'s subsequent observable behavior. In order to state the derivations succinctly, it will be helpful to introduce some abbreviated notation. An evaluator for whom *p* holds high expectations will be referred to as a high evaluator, or *H*; an evaluator for whom *p* holds low expectations will be referred to as a low evaluator, or *L*. If *p*'s performances have been positively evaluated and *o*'s have been negatively evaluated, then *relative to o*, *p* will be said to be in the $(+ \ -)$ experimental condition; if *p*'s performances have been negatively evaluated and those of *o* have been positively evaluated, this is the $(- \ +)$ condition. We do not say that *p* holds a $(+ \ -)$ or $(- \ +)$ expectation state at this point, for whether this is true depends upon whether *p* accepts the evaluations of *e*. If *p* *does* accept the $(+ \ -)$ or $(- \ +)$ evaluations from *e*—as the theory predicts he will depending upon his expectations for *e*—then relative to *o*, *p* will form $(+ \ -)$ or $(- \ +)$ expectations, respectively. Thus, formation of a given $(+ \ -)$ or $(- \ +)$ expectation state is a function of two things in this theory: the high or low expectations held by *p* *for* the evaluator, and the positive or negative evaluations of performance made *by* the evaluator.

Combining the notation for evaluators with that for evaluations yields the following four experimental conditions: (1) if *p* has received positive evaluations and *o* has received negative evaluations from a high evaluator, this is the $H(+ \ -)$ condition for *p*; (2) if *p* has received negative, and *o* positive evaluations, then *p* is in the $H(- \ +)$ condition; (3) if the evaluations are the same as in condition 1 but *p* holds low expectations for the evaluator, this is the $L(+ \ -)$ condition; (4) if the evaluations are the same as in condition 2 and *p* holds low expectations for the evaluator, this is the $L(- \ +)$ condition.

Combining Assumptions 1, 2, and 3d yields the prediction that when *p* holds high expectations for *e*, performance evaluations from *e* are quite likely to affect *p*'s expectation state. In fact, if the expectations held by *p* for *e* were extremely high, and if the number of evaluations made by e were infinite, then p's expectation state would be completely determined, according to these assumptions. In any empirical situation, an infinite number of evaluations is impossible, but tests of the theory should provide a fairly large number of evaluations, so as to make Assumption 3d (acceptance of the evaluator as a source) problematic, and not Assumption 2 (generalization of performance evaluations into an expectation state). Adding Assumption 4b relates acceptance of influence to expectation state, and enables derivation of the following empirical consequence:

DERIVATION 1

In case of disagreement with o, the probability of p's rejecting influence is greater in the $H(+ -)$ case than in the $H(- +)$ case.

Since p has no idea of his own ability in S, it is assumed that there is some non-zero probability that even an evaluator for whom p holds low expectations will become a source to him. Thus the same set of assumptions yields:

DERIVATION 2

In case of disagreement with o, the probability of p's rejecting influence is greater in the $L(+ -)$ case than in the $L(- +)$ case.

Because Assumption 3d asserts that an e for whom p holds low expectations is less likely to become a source, holding constant the nature of the performance evaluations and varying the expectations p holds for e, we would expect the H to be more "effective" than the L.

DERIVATION 3

In case of disagreement with o, the probability of p's rejecting influence is greater in the $H(+ -)$ case than in the $L(+ -)$ case;

DERIVATION 4

In case of disagreement with o, the probability of p's rejecting influence is *less* in the $H(- +)$ case than in the $L(- +)$ case.

Combining the four derivations yields the predicted ordering of the four conditions:[4]

---

[4]Interestingly, the predicted ordering of probabilities in Derivation 1 may be derived from the orderings predicted by Derivations 2, 3, and 4. Derivations 2, 3, and 4 also may be combined to yield the substantively less interesting derivations $H(+ -) > L(- +)$ and $L(+ -) > H(- +)$, which are more obviously contained in Derivation 5. Thus Derivations 1 and 5 are both "second order" derivations, which need not be stated explicitly for empirical tests of the theory. They have been stated explicitly because of their substantive interest in terms of the theoretical issues of the significant other and the effects of expectation states. The facts that Derivation 1 is logically eliminable and that Derivation 5 implies

DERIVATION 5

In case of disagreement with o, the probabilities of p's rejecting influence will be in the following order: $H(+ -) > L(+ -) > L(- +) > H(- +)$.

III. AN EXPERIMENTAL TEST OF THE INITIAL FORMULATION

Eighty subjects were run in an experiment designed to test the above derivations from the theory; twenty subjects were assigned randomly to each of the four conditions. All subjects were males between the ages of eighteen and twenty-four, and were students recruited from a junior college for "a study in group interaction."

Each group consisted of two subjects, previously unacquainted with each other. The physical layout of the laboratory, and all details of the experiment were designed to be as close as possible to those of previous Expectation States Theory experiments, including those reported in chapters two and six. As subjects arrived at the laboratory, they were greeted by a secretary or by one of the two experimenters, and were led to the interaction room. Each subject was seated at a table with number 1 or 2 on it, and the subjects were separated from each other by a curtain so that they could see the experimenters and a slide projection screen, but not each other.

The host experimenter introduced herself as "Dr. Gordon," and read a standardized experimental procedure to the subjects. The experiment was described as being a study in individual and group problem solving that consisted of two parts. In the first part, each subject in the interaction room was to make choices about a series of twenty slides. As each judgment was made it would be communicated to a (fictitious) third student who would evaluate it and tell each subject whether he thought the answer was correct. It was emphasized that "Person Number 3 does *not* have an answer key to these slides. However before he makes his choice for each slide, he will see your choices, and he will evaluate them according to his ability to judge."

The evaluator was described as being another student like themselves at the same college as the subjects. They were told that he had been scheduled to arrive half an hour before them so that his ability at the task could be measured.

---

two other derivations are not immediately obvious, either intuitively, or in terms of the substantive issues of this work. The simplification and clarity permitted by translating substantive concepts such as those used here into mathematical concepts are well illustrated by this example. We are indebted to Professor I. Richard Savage, Department of Statistics, Florida State University, for bringing these relations to our attention. For some other results of Professor Savage's analysis, as well as a simple probability model of the theory, see Savage and Webster, 1971.

Subjects were then shown a sample of the task on which they would be working. In order to minimize the effect of previous performance expectations, the task was described to the subjects as being, and in fact was, quite unlike anything they had ever done before. It consisted of a series of slides, each of which contained two patterns composed of black and white rectangles arranged in a random checkerboard design. Subjects were told to decide which of the patterns, the top one or the bottom one, contained the greater area of white. Each pattern was actually approximately 50 percent white, and extensive pretesting had established the empirical probability of choosing either alternative as very close to 0.50 (Ofshe, 1968). Thus the situation contained neither an objective nor a subjective basis for evaluating choices; only a social basis, Number 3's opinions, which could be ignored.

All choices were indicated by subjects on a panel each had before him. The communication machine has been described in detail elsewhere (Webster, 1967; chapter two of this text); here it is sufficient to state that it is a system of buttons to indicate binary choices, and lights which indicate the choices of others in the group. All communication through the machine is under full control of the experimenter.

After the task was explained, the second experimenter described a set of "standards" for the task. A score of 11 to 15 correct out of 20 was described as a "usual, or average score"; 16 to 20 correct was "unusual, and clearly indicates a superior individual performance"; and 0 to 10 correct was also "unusual, but indicates a poor individual performance." Thus an "average" score was described as being clearly better than chance guessing would produce; a "poor" score was clearly worse than chance success.

After making certain that the subjects understood the task and the standards, the second experimenter left the room, ostensibly to determine whether the evaluator had finished having his ability measured. A few minutes later, this tape recording of the second experimenter's voice was played through the intercom in the interaction room:

> Pardon me, Dr. Gordon. (Pause.) Person Number 3 has finished the first set of slides. Out of the 20 slides, he got a total of [8 or 17] correct, and [12 or 3] incorrect. (Pause.) This is an unusual score, and would fall into the [*lower* or *upper*] category for an individual performance.

This constituted the *L-H* manipulation. Then the host experimenter presented subjects with the first set of slides. After viewing a slide for five seconds, each subject indicated his choice by pressing the appropriate button on his panel. This act was the operationalization of giving each subject an action opportunity that he had to accept, and of his making a performance output. After another five-second delay, during which time Person Number 3 was presumably studying the slide along with both subjects' answers, a light appeared on each subject's panel beside the words "Number 3's choice." This was the operationalization of the evaluator's making a unit evaluation of each subject's performance output. Person Number 3 agreed with one of the subjects 17 times out of 20; he agreed with the other subject 9 times out of 20.

After the series of slides the second tape recording was played over the intercom:

> Experimenter: Person Number 3, how many of the slides did you think Person Number 1 gave the correct answer to?
> Number 3: Number 1? I think he got 17 out of 20.
> Experimenter: And Number 2?
> Number 3: Uh, 9 out of 20.

This constituted the $(+ -)$ and $(- +)$ expectation manipulation. At this point, *if a subject has accepted Number 3 as a source*, the theory predicts that he is very likely to hold an expectation state for himself and for the other subject that is congruent with Number 3's evaluations.

It is worth noting that the recording used for the expectation manipulation was the same whether Number 3 was described as having low ability or high ability. This means that such factors as his tone of voice, "confidence," etc., were constant across all conditions of the experiment.

Data for test of the theoretical derivations were gathered in Phase II of the experiment. This time, the host experimenter explained, both subjects were to work together "as a team" on another set of slides. Each would make an "initial choice" and would see the other's initial choice, they would both have five more seconds to restudy the slide, and then each of them would make a private "final decision."

Since initial choice feedback was under control of the experimenter, subjects were told that they disagreed with each other on 20 out of the 23 trials. The proportion of times that subjects in each condition resolved the disagreements in favor of self, $P(s)$, was then computed as the measure of *rejecting* influence.

Following the disagreement trials, each subject was interviewed separately by one of the experimenters. After questions designed to ascertain whether the subject did meet the initial scope conditions of the theory, the entire study was explained to him. All false information given during the study was corrected, the necessity for the deception was explained, and any questions he had were answered. After this, he was asked not to discuss the study in detail with any friends who might participate in the future, he was thanked, and was paid for his time.[5]

---

[5] Of the 80 subjects in the experiment, it was clear from the interviews that 4 of them did not meet the scope conditions of the theory. Two expressed a definite belief that the initial choice disagreements in Phase II were not real, and hence that they were not concerned with resolving them; one had previously participated in deception research and hence did not believe many of the manipulations; and one reported that he was more concerned with *agreeing* with his partner than with getting the right answer. Data from these four, constituting 5 percent of the sample, were excluded from analyses.

If we may assume that, in this controlled laboratory situation, no feature of the situation except those specified in the theory has important, systematic effects upon acceptance of influence, then the five derivations from the theory become predictions for empirical testing. The data in Table 5-1 are in accord with all five predictions.

TABLE 5-1.   Overall $P(s)$ for Subjects by Condition

Condition	N	$P(s)$
1. $H(+ -)$	19	0.80
2. $L(+ -)$	19	0.65
3. $L(- +)$	20	0.58
4. $H(- +)$	18	0.46

Table 5-2 presents the results of statistical tests of the derivations. Derivations 1–4 are tested using the Mann-Whitney U statistic, and Derivation 5 is tested using the Jonckheere test (1954); this is a distribution-free test for any number of samples, and evaluates the probability of obtaining a particular ordering of discrete conditions. Rows 1, 3, and 5 show that the confidence level of the difference of the first, third, and fifth predictions is beyond 0.05; row 2 shows that the confidence level of the difference of the second prediction is 0.062; and row 4 shows that the confidence level of the difference of the fourth prediction is 0.085.

TABLE 5-2.   Statistical Tests of Derivations

Derivation	Predicted Relation of Conditions	N's	U	P
1	$1 > 4$	19, 18	38.0	<0.05
2	$2 > 3$	19, 20	135.5	0.062
3	$1 > 2$	19, 19	61.0	<0.05
4	$3 > 4$	20, 20	141.5	0.085
5	$1 > 2 > 3 > 4$	19, 19, 20, 18	($Z = 4.35$)	<0.05

It seems fair to conclude that the results of the overall $P(s)$ figures in Table 5-1 and Table 5-2 are consistent with the predictions of the theory. The difference between the $(+ -)$ and the $(- +)$ cells of the H condition (row 1) is large, and is in the direction expected. The difference between the two cells of the L condition (row 2) is smaller, and is also in the expected direction. The relative effectiveness of the H and the L may be compared by examining the data in rows 2 and 4 of Table 5-1; in both rows, the difference is as predicted by the derivation from the theory. The complete predicted ordering of Derivation 5 is also supported (row 5 of Table 5-2).

For purposes of specifying the empirical scope of application of the theory, data from this experiment may be compared to the data from a previous experiment, reported previously (see Berger and Conner, 1969). The situation was very similar in both experiments except that previously it was the *experimenter* who evaluated subjects' performances in Phase I. We assume that the experimenter had a high probability of becoming a source and of having his evaluations accepted by subjects, but the reasons for acceptance would be different. In the earlier experiment it was not the perceived ability of the experimenter to perform the task, but rather the fact that he had access to evaluative information that was denied to subjects: *an answer key*. Access to an answer key would certainly fulfill the conditions of Definition 2 of this theory, for presumably subjects would believe that the key made the experimenter more capable to evaluate performances than they were themselves. However, it would make Assumption 3d of this version of the theory unnecessary—the expectations held for the experimenter's performance would be irrelevant in the earlier experiment. Because access to objective evaluative information fulfills the conditions of Definition 2 of this version of the theory, it is possible to use the theory to predict some results of the earlier experiment as well as for this one. The prediction would be the same as for the H conditions of the source experiment: $\exp(+\ -) > \exp(-\ +)$.

Table 5-3 compares the $P(s)$ data from the H conditions of the first source experiment to the comparable conditions of the previous experiment. As may be seen, the relations between the conditions of the previous experiment are as predicted from the theory.

TABLE 5-3.   P(s) of Subjects According to Evaluator of Performances

Evaluations	Evaluator	
	H	Exp.
(+ −)	0.80	0.78
(− +)	0.46	0.42

Moreover, the $P(s)$ data from comparable evaluation conditions of the two experiments are quite similar: $(+\ -)$ evaluations from the experimenter produce a $P(s)$ of 0.78, while $(+\ -)$ evaluations from the H produced a $P(s)$ of 0.80; $(-\ +)$ evaluations from the experimenter produced a $P(s)$ of 0.42, while $(-\ +)$ evaluation from the H produced a $P(s)$ of 0.46.[6]

[6] Several historical differences between the two experiments may make direct comparisons such as these tenuous; thus, these relations should be viewed as suggestive rather than definitive. Some of the theoretically nonrelevant differences are the following: (1) *subject population:* the previous study used male freshmen and sophomore students at Stanford

The significance for the theory of the comparison is that, for this experimental situation at least, it may be said that the effect of evaluations from sources with two different bases is virtually identical. Whether an evaluator's basis for accuracy is his own high ability or his access to objective evaluative standards, the behavioral effect of his evaluations—which is a function both of his likelihood of being accepted as a source and of the expectations induced as a result of his evaluations—will be the same.

On the basis of the experimental test of the theory, at this point it seemed reasonable to conclude that we had had some success, both at explicating ideas in the looking-glass self tradition, and at extending the propositions of Expectation States Theory. The data from these experiments provide support for the assertion that one characteristic of an actor that is crucial in determining the degree of effect of his evaluative opinions (that determines, in other words, whether he will become a "significant other" in this type of situation) is the ability level he is perceived to possess. If we know the level of expectations held for an evaluator and if we know the nature of the evaluations he makes of other actor's performances, then the source version of Expectation States Theory enables us to make predictions of the expectations that actors in this type of group situation will come to hold, and of important features of their observable future interaction as well.

IV. MULTIPLE SOURCES AND THE FORMATION OF PERFORMANCE EXPECTATIONS: AN EXTENDED FORMULATION

Our strategy up to this point had been to test a small number of ideas regarding the characteristics of a significant other in a highly simplified situation. Because of the experimental confirmation of these theoretical ideas, it was possible to extend the scope of this theory to more complex situations. In the following section we describe this extension of the initial formulation of our source theory to include situations involving more than one evaluator. Such an extension should enable us to make predictions for empirical situations in which individuals have their performances evaluated by more than one potential source, and where the evaluators possess either the same, or differing,

---

University; the source study used California junior college males; (2) *task:* the slides used for the previous study contained fictitious "foreign language words," and the task was to match them with English meanings; the task for the source study has already been described; (3) *critical trials:* the previous study used 25 trials, of which 22 were disagreements; the source study had three agreements in a series of 23 trials. In view of these differences in concrete features of the situation, the similarity of effect of expectation states, as measured by rejection of influence, is impressive.

levels of ability. The classical problem of conflicting significant others—evaluators who disagree in their opinions—will be considered, and a preliminary solution to this problem is formulated in this extension. (A revised solution is presented in the final section of this chapter.) In order to utilize the theoretical structure, as well as the results of empirical tests of our initial version of this source theory, our strategy was to introduce the smallest number of changes that would extend the scope of the original theory. Thus, this extension represents a generalization of the original theory. As such, it must cover the derivations of the original theory as well as provide additional derivations dealing with the more complex social situation of two evaluators.

In order to deal with situations involving two evaluators, two sorts of changes must be made in the theory. First, of course, the definition of situation S (Definition 1) must be expanded to apply to the case of two evaluators. Second, Assumption 1, which deals with acceptance of evaluations, must be expanded considerably, and the expansion performed in a way that permits maintaining the derivations of the initial version of the theory.

The change in Definition 1 is straightforward, and applies only to part b:

DEFINITION 1b

There are at least two actors, e_1 and e_2, with the right to make evaluations of the performance outputs of p and o.

The change in Assumption 1 is more complex. By splitting the assumption into three parts, it is possible to cover the logical range of situations. The first part will apply to the simplest situation; it is identical to the entire first assumption of the earlier version:

ASSUMPTION 1a

In S, if *only one* e is a source for p, then p will make the same unit evaluations of any actor's performances as does that e.

But in S there is more than one e, and therefore more than one potential source for p. The generalization therefore adds two parts to Assumption 1. Part b specifies the effects of two evaluators who agree in their evaluations when both have become sources for p:

ASSUMPTION 1b

In S, if *both* e_1 and e_2 are sources for p and both e_1 and e_2 make *the same* unit evaluations of any actor's performance, then p will make the same unit evaluations of performances as e_1 and e_2.

The case in which both evaluators have become sources for p but make different unit evaluations of any actor's performance is the most complex. Part c deals with that case:

ASSUMPTION 1c

In *S*, if *both* e_1 and e_2 are sources for *p* and e_1 and e_2 make *different* unit evaluations of a performance output of any actor, then *p* will not make a unit evaluation of that performance output.

The other definitions and assumptions of the theory are unchanged in this version.

Assumption 1c represents the simplest of three alternatives in dealing with the case of two conflicting significant others. It says that since *p* has accepted both evaluators as more capable than he is himself, he has no idea how to resolve the disagreement between them, and simply does not resolve it. Essentially, he withholds judgment.

This is not the only possible statement of Assumption 1c, and it may not be the most satisfactory one. However, it is the simplest statement, and for that reason we will use it here. In section VI we return to this question, consider alternatives, and attempt to develop and test a more precise statement of this part of the theory.

We may again represent Definition 2 and Assumptions 1a and 1b by the following balance diagrams. Directed lines represent unit evaluations of performances, brackets represent acceptance of an evaluator as a source, and double lines represent expectations held for an actor. Unit evaluations may be positive or negative ($+$ or $-$), and unit relations are positive if they form.

In Figure 5-5a, *p* has accepted one of the evaluators as a source (e_1), and that evaluator has made a positive evaluation of a performance output. By Assumption 1a, *p* will then also positively evaluate that performance output,

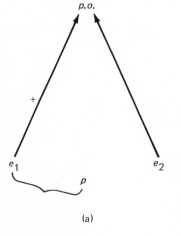

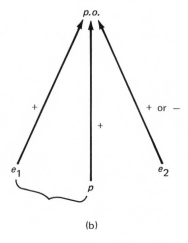

(a)   (b)

FIGURE 5-5
One evaluator accepted as a source

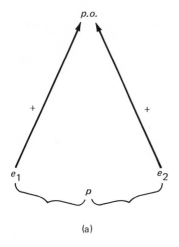

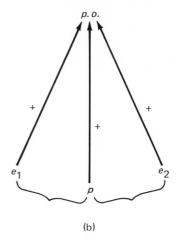

FIGURE 5-6

Two agreeing sources

as illustrated in Figure 5-5b. Note that the left cycle (p—$p.o.$—e_1) is balanced and stable, regardless of the evaluation made by e_2. The right cycle is incomplete and hence vacuously balanced, since the unit relation has not formed between p and e_2. This means that the entire cognitive structure is balanced and assumed to be stable, regardless of the evaluations made by any e who has not been accepted as a source.

Figure 5-6a illustrates the case where both evaluators become sources and both agree in their evaluations of a performance output. By Assumption 1b, p will evaluate the performance output the same as the two evaluators, and as shown in Figure 5-6b, the two cycles formed are balanced and hence assumed to be stable.

The case in which p has accepted both evaluators as sources and they make different performance evaluations is illustrated in Figure 5-7. Assumption 1c says that under these conditions, p will not assign a unit evaluation to the performance output. In Figure 5-7b, no matter how p evaluated the performance output, one cycle of the structure would be imbalanced and therefore unstable. Note also the *before* p is called upon to evaluate the performance output in Figure 5-7a the structure is also imbalanced—we would suppose from this fact, as well as on intuitive grounds, that a situation of disagreeing sources will produce psychological tension.

To draw derivations for empirical testing, a notation similar to that already introduced will be employed. For example, $H(+ \; -)L(+ \; -)$ indicates that a high ability evaluator gave p positive evaluations and o negative evaluations, and a low ability evaluator also gave p positive evaluations and o negative evaluations.

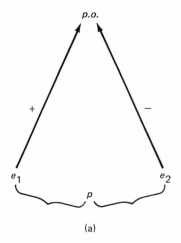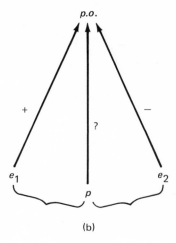

(a)   (b)

FIGURE 5-7
Two disagreeing sources

The cases selected for empirical testing are those which yield the maximum information about the extended version of the theory, and which are also the most interesting substantively. These four cases are $H(+ -)L(+ -)$, $H(+ -)L(- +)$, $H(- +)L(+ -)$, $H(- +)L(- +)$.[7]

Derivations 1 and 2 from the generalized theory are performed the same as for the first version.[8] Subjects in the $H(+ -)L(+ -)$ conditions are quite likely to form $(+ -)$ expectation states, and subjects in the $H(- +)L(- +)$ condition are quite likely to form $(- +)$ expectation states:

DERIVATION 1

Subjects in the $H(+ -)L(+ -)$ condition are more likely to reject influence than those in the $H(- +)L(- +)$ condition.

[7]Note that Assumption 4 of the theory applies to a large number of self-other expectation states. The cases of particular concern are $(+ -)$, $(0\ 0)$, and $(- +)$. Assume that if p is initially in an undefined state $[(0\ 0)]$ his expectations for self are equal to his expectations for other. Applying Assumption 4 to these cases, we may state that an individual in a $(+ -)$ state is more likely to reject influence than an individual in a $(0\ 0)$ state, and that an individual in a $(- +)$ state is less likely to reject influence. These inequalities are assumed to hold whether or not p differentiates expectations during the interaction; for example, in the manner described by Berger and Conner in chapter six. If p differentiates to a $(- +)$ state, *overall* he will reject influence more than if he *began* in a $(- +)$ state. Similarly, if he differentates to a $(+ -)$ state, *overall* he will reject influence less than if he *began* in a $(+ -)$ state. This application of Assumption 4 is used in all derivations below.

[8]For more complete exposition of the reasoning involved in these derivations from the generalized theory, the reader is referred to Sobieszek (1972), or to Webster and Sobieszek (1973).

In both the $H(+ -)L(- +)$ condition and the $H(- +)L(+ -)$ condition subjects are more likely to accept the high evaluator as a source, and to form expectations consistent with him, than with the low evaluator:

DERIVATION 2

Subjects in condition $H(+ -)L(- +)$ are more likely to reject influence than those in condition $H(- +)L(+ -)$.

Consider next the relation between the conditions $H(+ -)L(+ -)$ and $H(+ -)L(- +)$ and between conditions $H(- +)L(- +)$ and $H(- +)L(+ -)$. In $H(+ -)L(+ -)$ most subjects are expected to form $(+ -)$ expectation states, none to form $(- +)$ expectation states (this is precluded by Assumption 2) and a few to hold $(0\ 0)$ states. The latter category refers to those subjects for whom neither evaluator becomes a source, and who therefore are assumed to start out with undefined expectations for self and other (see footnote 7). In $H(+ -)L(- +)$ there is a somewhat different distribution. Most subjects, accepting the high evaluator as a source, will form high expectations for self and low for other, and some smaller number (those accepting only the low evaluator as a source) will form low expectations for self and high for other. Some will have undefined expectations because neither evaluator will become a source. Finally, an additional number for whom both evaluators become sources will (by Assumption 1b and Assumption 2) hold undefined expectations for self and other, because their sources have disagreed.

This line of reasoning indicates two types of subjects: those for whom expectations are defined and those for whom expectations are undefined. In the $H(+ -)L(+ -)$ condition more subjects will hold defined $(+ -)$ expectation states than in the $H(+ -)L(- +)$ condition. Similarly more subjects in $H(- +)L(- +)$ will hold defined $(- +)$ expectation states than in $H(- +)L(+ -)$. Thus the theory yields:

DERIVATION 3

Subjects in condition $H(+ -)L(+ -)$ are more likely to reject influence than subjects in condition $H(+ -)L(- +)$.

DERIVATION 4

Subjects in condition $H(- +)L(+ -)$ are more likely to reject influence than subjects in condition $H(- +)L(- +)$.

Combining D1, D2, D3, and D4 yields the complete ordering of conditions:

DERIVATION 5

$H(+ -)L(+ -) > H(+ -)L(- +) > H(- +)L(+ -) > H(- +)L(- +)$.

These five derivations will be referred to as the "primary derivations" for testing of the generalization.

Complete ordering and exact numerical predictions of the conditions of both source experiments would be possible if empirical values were known for the probabilities of accepting the high and low evaluators as sources. We are not yet in a position to determine these values. It is still possible, however, to construct partial orderings of conditions from the assumptions of the theory if we further assume that the probabilities of accepting the high and low evaluators as sources are the same across each condition of the two studies. With this intuitively plausible assumption the present formulation implies, other things being equal, that (1) two agreeing evaluators will have a greater effect than a single evaluator, and (2) evaluations from an evaluator described as possessing high ability will have a greater effect than the same evaluations from an evaluator described as having low ability. In other words, given situation S of the first source theory, with e_1, p and o present:

1. Adding an agreeing evaluator, e_2, increases the probability of forming expectations consistent with e_1's evaluations; adding a disagreeing e_2 decreases the probability of forming expectations consistent with e_1's evaluations.

2. The probabilities of forming expectations consistent with evaluations of either e_1 or e_2 are directly dependent upon the perceived relative abilities of e_1 and e_2.

The assumptions and derivations of the theory, together with the ideas stated above, enable us to predict that $H(+\ -)L(+\ -)$ should be more effective in producing $(+\ -)$ expectations than $H(+\ -)$, the comparable single high evaluator condition, which should in turn be more effective than $H(+\ -)L(-\ +)$. Similarly, $H(+\ -)L(+\ -)$ should be more effective in producing $(+\ -)$ expectations than $L(+\ -)$, the single low evaluator condition, which should in turn be more effective than $H(-\ +)L(+\ -)$. In producing $(-\ +)$ expectations, $H(-\ +)L(-\ +)$ should be more effective than $H(-\ +)$, which should be more effective than $H(-\ +)L(+\ -)$. And, to complete the partial orderings, $H(-\ +)L(-\ +)$ should be more effective than $L(-\ +)$, and $L(-\ +)$ should be more effective than $H(+\ -)L(-\ +)$. Considering these inequalities and applying Assumption 4, we have the following "secondary derivations," ordered in terms of probability of rejecting influence:

$$H(+\ -)L(+\ -) > H(+\ -) > H(+\ -)L(-\ +),$$
$$H(-\ +)L(+\ -) > H(-\ +) > H(-\ +)L(-\ +),$$
$$H(+\ -)L(+\ -) > L(+\ -) > H(-\ +)L(+\ -),$$
$$H(+\ -)L(-\ +) > L(-\ +) > H(-\ +)L(-\ +).$$

An observation concerning these derivations is in order. The extended theory predicts the ordering of the four cases selected for the present research, and as a generalization, it has also been constructed to predict the ordering of the first four cases in the initial source theory. But of the eight pair-wise inequalities contained in the secondary derivations, not all are independent. For example, if $H(+ -)L(+ -) > H(+ -)$, then since the first theory predicts the order: $H(+ -) > L(+ -)$, it follows that $H(+ -)L(+ -) > L(+ -)$. We therefore have selected for observation a subset of six pair-wise inequalities that are (a) independent and (b) entail a comparison between the *closest* pairs. This provides us with the most stringent test of the generalized theory that is presently possible. This selected subset of secondary derivations, ordered in terms of probability of accepting influence is:

$$H(+ -)L(+ -) > H(+ -)$$
$$H(+ -) \qquad > H(+ -)L(- +)$$
$$H(- +)L(+ -) > H(- +)$$
$$H(- +) \qquad > H(- +)L(- +)$$
$$L(+ -) \qquad > H(- +)L(+ -)$$
$$H(+ -)L(- +) > L(- +)$$

V. AN EXPERIMENTAL TEST OF THE EXTENDED FORMULATION

Eighty-four subjects were assigned randomly to each of the four experimental conditions, with twenty-one subjects per condition. All subjects were volunteers, recruited from large lecture classes at a junior college. Subjects were females between the ages of 18 and 22. The use of a female subject pool introduces a note of caution into comparisons between this experiment and the first experiment, as the first used a male subject pool. Although no evidence for sex differences exists to date in this research, it is possible that an unanticipated effect was introduced.

All details of the two source experiments were the same as those of the first experiment, except for the additional evaluator.

In Phase I, subjects were told that their choices would be evaluated by Persons Number 3 and Number 4, two junior college students like themselves in another laboratory room. Number 3 was always described as having unusually high ability to do the task, and Number 4 as having unusually low ability. As before, tape recorded voices were used to simulate the evaluators. Subjects were then presented 20 slides, and received evaluations after each slide from both evaluators.

Following the series of slides, the evaluations made by Number 3 and

Number 4 were reported to the subjects via a tape recording.[9] All details of Phase II were the same as the first experiment.

The $P(s)$ data on rejection of influence constitute the test of the five "primary derivations" of the theory.[10] Table 5-4 presents the data on overall $P(s)$ for each condition.

TABLE 5-4.   Overall $P(s)$ for Subjects by Condition, Two Evaluator Experiment

Condition	N	$P(s)$
1. $H(+\ -)L(+\ -)$	21	0.80
2. $H(+\ -)L(-\ +)$	20	0.76
3. $H(-\ +)L(+\ -)$	20	0.58
4. $H(-\ +)L(-\ +)$	20	0.42

[9]The scripts used are as follows: For the conditions where the evaluators agreed:

Experimenter: Person Number 3, how many of the 20 slides did *you think* Person Number 1 gave the correct answer to?
Number 3:   I think Number 1 got 17 out of 20.
Experimenter: And how many did you think Person Number 2 got the correct answer to?
Number 3:   I think Number 2 got 9 out of 20.
Experimenter: Person Number 4, how many of the 20 slides did you think Number 1 gave the correct answer to?
Number 4:   I think Number 1 got 16 out of 20.
Experimenter: And how many did you think Person Number 2 gave the correct answer to?
Number 4:   I think Number 2 got 8 out of 20.

For the conditions in which the evaluators disagreed:

Experimenter: Person Number 3, how many of the 20 slides did you think Person Number 1 gave the correct answer to?
Number 3:   I think Number 1 got 17 out of 20.
Experimenter: And how many did you think Person Number 2 got the correct answer to?
Number 3:   I think Number 2 got 9 out of 20.
Experimenter: Person Number 4, how many of the 20 slides did you think Number 1 gave the correct answer to?
Number 4:   I think Number 1 got 8 out of 20.
Experimenter: And how many did you think Person Number 2 gave the correct answer to?
Number 4:   I think Number 2 got 16 out of 20.

[10]Three of the eighty-four subjects run in the experiment clearly did not meet the scope conditions of the theory. One subject reported misunderstanding of the instructions and pushed buttons indicating her choices at random, a failure of task-orientation. One subject did not believe that the slides were different, and selected choices at random, another failure of task-orientation. A third subject did not believe that the evaluators existed, and disregarded them. This subject was not in situation S. Data from these three subjects, about 4 percent of the sample, were excluded from analysis.

The data from Table 5-4 are in accord with each of the five primary derivations. Table 5-5 presents statistical evaluation of the differences obtained, using the Mann-Whitney U and Jonckheere tests.

The first, second, and fifth rows of the table indicate that the confidence levels of the differences obtained for Derivations 1, 2, and 5 are at the 0.001 level or beyond. The confidence level of the difference for Derivation 3 is 0.288, and for Derivation 4, 0.02.

TABLE 5-5. Statistical Tests of Derivations, Two-Evaluator Experiment

Derivation	Predicted Relation of Conditions	N's	U	Z	p
1	$1 > 4$	21, 20	25.0	4.84	<0.05
2	$2 > 3$	20, 20	87.0	3.07	<0.05
3	$1 > 2$	21, 20	188.5	0.56	0.288
4	$4 > 3$	20, 20	125.0	2.04	<0.05
5	$1 > 2 > 3 > 4$			5.37	<0.05

The secondary derivations of the theory may be evaluated using the $P(s)$ figures from the original conditions and from the present experiment. Comparing Table 5-1 to Table 5-4 permits these comparisons.

The first predicted inequality, between $H(+ -)L(+ -)$ and $H(+ -)$, was not observed; the $P(s)$ figures are 0.80 for both these conditions. The remaining five inequalities are as predicted.

The principal tests of the generalization, the "primary" derivations concerning the ordering of pairs of conditions for the present experiment, are supported by the data. All differences are in the predicted directions, and the confidence levels of the magnitudes of the differences are significant beyond the 0.05 level for four of the primary derivations. Although the difference between the $H(+ -)L(+ -)$ and $H(+ -)L(- +)$ conditions is not so large as could be desired, there is reason to believe that the influence measure used may not be sensitive enough to reflect larger differences. Previous research using this influence measure suggests there may be a ceiling on the number of self resolutions subjects will make, because of decision-making properties of the situation. For subjects to have a $P(s)$ greater than 0.80, they would have to change their choices fewer than four times. Aside from this possibility, there is no apparent substantive explanation as to why the prediction does not hold.

Comparisons with the previous experiment must be interpreted with caution because of the difference in subject pools. However, we note that only one of the six predicted inequalities of the "secondary derivations" is not supported, and this again may be a function of properties of this experimental situation.

Considering the directions and magnitudes of the differences obtained in the tests of the primary derivations and the orderings obtained in both primary and secondary derivations, we observe that only one predicted inequality failed to be supported by the data. It seems reasonable to conclude that overall these data on rejection of influence provide support for the generalized theoretical formulation.

VI. CONFLICTING SIGNIFICANT OTHERS AND MECHANISMS OF RESOLUTION: REFINING THE EXTENDED FORMULATION

In the previous section we extended the source theory to cover the case of more than one evaluator. The extended theory was tested with one high-ability and one low-ability evaluator, who either agreed or disagreed in their evaluations of performances. Here we return to the case where two evaluators have been accepted as sources, but they disagree on their evaluations. In such a situation, the individual has accepted two others as significant others—and according to the theory, he should use their evaluations of performances, but their disagreement makes this impossible. This situation is the most extreme case of "conflicting significant others." Both intuitively, and in terms of the balance diagrams in Figure 5-7, this would be expected to be a tension-producing situation for the individual.

Assumption 1c was formulated to deal with this situation: it states that in case of disagreeing sources, the individual will make no unit evaluation of his own for the given performance output. Recall that we claimed that this was the simplest formulation, but not the only one that might apply. We now consider two alternative statements of Assumption 1c, and will then briefly describe some results of experiments conducted to distinguish between them.[11]

Alternative 1 has already been stated:

ASSUMPTION 1c

In S, if *both* e_1 and e_2 are sources for p and e_1 and e_2 make *different* unit evaluations of a performance output of any actor, then p will not make a unit evaluation of that performance output.

A second reasonable possibility is that p will try to simplify the conflicting situation by picking one of the evaluators and "sticking with" him;

---

[11]The theoretical rationale and the process of evaluating each alternative statement of Assumption 1c are quite complex. What we present here are abbreviated versions of the theoretical basis for the alternative formulations and the two empirical tests that we regard as most directly relevant to deciding among them. For more complete development of the ideas and presentation of other empirical results, the reader is referred to the Webster and Sobieszek research monograph, *Sources of Self-Evaluation*.

deciding, in effect, to ignore one of the sources and to form his evaluations based upon the other one. There is no obvious way to tell which of the evaluators p would select for this, and, at this stage, we are not prepared to specify any conditions that would dispose him towards selection of one or the other. What is central here is the notion that the individual in a situation of two conflicting sources will choose to adhere to only one of them:

ASSUMPTION 1c*

In S, if *both* e_1 and e_2 are sources for p and e_1 and e_2 make *different* unit evaluations of a performance output of any actor, then p will consistently make the same unit evaluations as those of only one of these sources, e_1 or e_2.

The third possibility to be considered here is that p will try to agree with both sources, if not on every unit evaluation (which of course is impossible), then on different particular evaluations. He will agree with e_1 some of the time and with e_2 some of the time. In this formulation, p may distribute agreements between the evaluators in a random pattern, such as an exact alternating pattern, or he may distribute them as a function of the expectations he holds for each: the higher the expectations held for an e, the more likely is p to agree with that e's evaluations on a given trial. Again, at this stage we are not ready to formulate *exactly* how p would distribute such agreements. What is central to this third alternative is that p continues to accept both sources, and his final set of cognitions (his expectation state) is determined by both of them:

ASSUMPTION 1c'

In S, if *both* e_1 and e_2 are sources for p and e_1 and e_2 make *different* unit evaluations of performance output of any actor, then p will distribute agreeing unit evaluations between e_1 and e_2.

In order to choose between the three alternative formulations of Assumption 1c, we may ask what sorts of expectation patterns would be found in our experimental situation, given each of the alternatives. Consider an experiment in which there are two evaluators, e_1 and e_2, both described as possessing *extremely high* task ability, and both of whom are therefore *very likely* to be accepted as sources. In Phase I, e_1 and e_2 disagree on nearly all their evaluations of the actors' performances; what e_1 thinks is correct is what e_2 thinks is incorrect, and vice-versa. If the first alternative formulation were to be supported, subjects in this situation would not have evaluated any performances, and hence would hold undifferentiated (0 0) expectations at the end of the series of evaluations.

For support of 1c*, either of two things would have to happen. (1) All subjects would have to choose the same evaluator. In this case, all of them would hold defined expectations, either all $(+ -)$, or all $(- +)$; virtually no subjects would hold undefined (0 0) expectations. (2) Some subjects would choose one evaluator, and some would choose the other. In this case, some would hold $(+ -)$ expectations, and the others would hold $(- +)$ expectations; again, virtually none would hold undefined (0 0) expectations. What is essential for support of this alternative is either evidence that all subjects formed the same $(+ -)$ or $(- +)$ expectations, or evidence that two distinct sub-populations have formed as the result of the evaluations.

If the alternative 1c' were to be supported, all subjects would form expectations, but the expectations would be intermediate to the $(+ -)$ and $(- +)$ states, since they were produced by the evaluations of both e_1 and e_2. Support for this alternative would require a homogeneous population of subjects, all of whom held expectations intermediate between $(- +)$ and $(+ -)$.

In order to decide between the three alternatives, two additional experiments were conducted. These may be called the "two-source experiment," or 2-S; and the "no source experiment," or 0-S. Subjects for these experiments were drawn from the same subject pool as those for previous experiments; all are females, and the same description as for the second experiment applies.

In the 2-S experiment, in Phase I both e_1 and e_2 were described as having achieved scores of 18 correct out of 20, but e_1 and e_2 disagreed on as many of their evaluations as possible. At the end of Phase I, e_1 reported her judgment that subject Number 1 got 17 correct and 3 wrong, and Number 2 got 9 correct and 11 wrong. E_2 reported her judgment that subject Number 1 got 8 correct and 12 wrong, and that Number 2 got 16 correct and 4 wrong. In other words, e_1 "tried" to produce $(+ -)$ expectations for subject Number 1 and $(- +)$ expectations for Number 2; e_2 "tried" to produce $(- +)$ expectations for subject Number 1 and $(+ -)$ expectations for Number 2. And both e_1 and e_2 had the same, extremely high, degree of competence to make judgments of performance.

In the 0-S experiment, the evaluators were described as in the 2-S experiment, but subjects were told that they would *not* see their evaluations in Phase I. Thus, subjects in the 0-S experiment had no evaluative basis for forming expectations in Phase I, and we assume that they began the disagreement (data collection) trials with undifferentiated self and other expectations, (0 0).

First, let us look at the overall mean $P(s)$ figures from both conditions, the measure we have been using for expectation states in all this research. These are reported in Table 5-6.[12] For the 2-S experiment, the $P(s)$ was 0.67; for the

[12]Data from three subjects, 10 percent of the sample, were excluded from analysis of the 2-S experiment. One expressed a definite conclusion that Number 3 and Number 4 did not exist, one did not believe the Phase II disagreements, and one completely misunderstood the situation. There were no exclusions from the 0-S experiment.

TABLE 5-6. Overall $P(s)$ for Subjects, by Condition 0-*S* and 2-*S*
Experiments

Condition	N	$P(s)$	p
0-*S*	30	0.64	
2-*S*	27	0.67	0.30

Figure given is confidence level, two-tail test.

0-*S* experiment, it was 0.64. As shown in row 3 of Table 5-6, the $P(s)$ data
from the two experiments are not sufficiently different to enable rejection of
the null hypothesis at the conventional 0.05 level.

For the 0-*S* experiment, the rejection of influence data show about what we
would expect. That is, subjects who hold differentiated (+ −) expectations in
these conditions have previously shown a $P(s)$ around 0.78–0.80, and for
subjects with (− +) expectations the figure is 0.42–0.46. The 0.64 figure for
the 0-*S* experiment is intermediate to this, which we would expect either if the
majority of subjects in this condition held undifferentiated (0 0) expectations,
or if through the Phase II disagreement process some subjects differentiated
into each [(+ −) and (− +)] state.

On the basis of $P(s)$ figures alone, we cannot distinguish satisfactorily
between the three alternative formulations of Assumption 1c. The first alternative predicts no difference between the 0-*S* and the 2-*S* experiments, and the
figures are very close. What may not be immediately apparent is that the other
two alternatives also could be consistent with close correspondence of the
$P(s)$ figures. In the extreme case, alternative 2 predicts that all subjects in the
2-*S* experiment will form the same differentiated expectation state, either
(+ −) or (− +). This clearly did *not* occur, for the $P(s)$ figure would have to
approximate either 0.78 or 0.44 for this. But it could also be that about half
the subjects in the 2-*S* experiment accepted each evaluator; thus, in fact half
formed (+ −) expectations, and half formed (− +) expectations. This
circumstance *could* produce an overall mean $P(s)$ within the range observed.
Alternative 3 predicts a uniform population of intermediate expectations in
2-*S*, and because the 0.67 value is intermediate to the previously-observed
(+ −) and (− +) values, the third alternative cannot be rejected.

It is in terms of the sorts of *distributions* of subjects expected in the 2-*S*
experiment that the three alternatives produce distinguishable outcomes. If
the first alternative is to be supported, subjects in the 2-*S* condition should be
distributed broadly about the mean proportion of rejecting influence. Exactly
how broad the distribution should be cannot be specified on theoretical
grounds, but because the first alternative predicts that no unit evaluations will
be made and therefore that subjects initially would start with (0 0) expecta-

tions, we should expect that the distribution for the 2-S experiment would approximate that from the 0-S experiment.

The second alternative could be supported in either of two ways: a single population of subjects, all holding either $(+ \ -)$ or $(- \ +)$ expectation states; or two populations, some $(+ \ -)$ and some $(- \ +)$. We already know from the $P(s)$ data that the first condition did not obtain, so support for the second alternative would require finding evidence for the existence of two populations in the 2-S experiment. Any cell containing two such distinct populations should have an extremely broad distribution; more precisely, the variance in the 2-S condition should be *as great as* or *greater than* the variance in the 0-S condition.

If the third alternative is to be supported, we expect to find a single, homogeneous population in the 2-S experiment, all holding intermediate expectations. This would mean a narrow distribution; *less* variance in the 2-S condition than in the 0-S condition.

Table 5-7 presents the overall variance about the mean *number* [not about the $P(s)$] of self resolutions per subject for the two experiments, and also pre-

TABLE 5-7.   Overall Variances and Variance Ratio Testing Differences between 0-S and 2-S Experiments

$\sigma^2$0-S	$\sigma^2$2-S	Degrees of Freedom	F
13.56	6.41	29,26	2.12

$0.05 < p < 0.10$, two-tail test.

sents the results of Snedecor's variance ratio test for differences between conditions. As can be seen, the variance in the 0-S experiment was over twice as great as that in the 2-S experiment, a difference which is significant beyond the 0.10 level. This result is consistent *only* with the third formulation of Assumption 1c.

The most important piece of data from the experiments that permits distinguishing predictions of the three formulations is the shape of the distributions, the variances. The greater variance in the 0-S condition than in the 2-S condition is inconsistent with the original formulation of Assumption 1c, and with the second formulation as well. In particular, the second formulation would lead us to expect a bimodal distribution of subjects in 2-S: a bimodal distribution would entail large variance, and, though we have not presented the actual shape of the distribution, the 2-S condition shows no evidence of bimodality. Thus, we find evidence for rejecting both the first and the second alternative formulations.

The third formulation leads us to expect greater variance in the 0-S experiment than in the 2-S, and this was observed. Since we have no empirical evidence that is in conflict with this alternative, and we have clear evidence consistent with it, we use this alternative to refine our theory. Thus the *present* version of our source theory incorporates the following reformulation of Assumption 1:

a.   In S, if *only one e* is a source for p, then p will make the same unit evaluations of any actor's performances as does that e;

b.   In S, if both e_1 and e_2 are sources for p and both e_1 and e_2 make *the same* unit evaluations of any actor's performance, then p will make the same unit evaluations of performances as e_1 and e_2;

c.   In S, if *both* e_1 and e_2 are sources for p and e_1 and e_2 make *different* unit evaluations of performance output of any actor, then p will distribute agreeing unit evaluations between e_1 and e_2.

The full set of definitions and assumptions that constitute the present version of our source theory is summarized in the appendix to this chapter.

VII. A GENERAL REVIEW AND FURTHER ISSUES

We began with the problem of how individuals form their conceptions of their own abilities. The social psychological literature indicates that the self-evaluation is the result of the influence of others' opinions upon the individual: he develops his self-evaluation as a function of what others think of him. In forming the self-evaluation, some others, called "significant others," are particularly important; these are such people as parents, teachers, and close friends. Exactly how the opinions of these significant others influence the individual's self-conception, however, is incompletely specified in this literature.

From our review of the self-evaluation literature, several problems became apparent. Foremost was the need to formulate in an abstract manner the important characteristics that make an other a significant other; that is, to state why some people's opinions and not others' are used in forming one's self-evaluations. Second, it is necessary to describe the process by which the opinions of others get built up into an enduring set of beliefs concerning the self. Third, the question of agreement and disagreement between evaluating others becomes important, as well as questions of what happens when two significant others disagree. Fourth, it was necessary to formulate the ideas in the self-evaluation literature and the answers we proposed to some of the unsolved problems emerging from this literature, in a form that would permit us to conduct determinate empirical tests of our theoretical ideas.

The strategy chosen was to extend the theoretical ideas in Expectation States Theory to include the concept of a *source*, an individual whose evaluative opinions would be accepted and used by others as the basis for forming their performance expectations for themselves and other people. The unit evaluation process was identified, for our purposes, as crucial in determining the individual's overall expectation level. A *source* for an actor *p* was defined as an individual who *p* believes is more capable than himself to evaluate performances in a given situation. It was assumed that the likelihood that some other (including an "evaluator") becomes a source to *p* is directly related to the performance expectations *p* holds for that other. Further, it was assumed that the evaluations of a source would determine the performance evaluations made by *p* and thus the performance expectations *p* comes to hold for self and other in the given situation. It was possible to modify the basic expectation experimental situation to test the ideas regarding the source in a very simple social situation.

Since these ideas were confirmed for the simple situation in which one important source existed, we extended the theory to the more complex social situation of two evaluators. This extension was also supported by empirical tests. However, there remained theoretical questions concerning the mechanism by which an individual processes the evaluations of two contradicting sources. Therefore, to increase the precision of the theory, we formulated three alternative statements as to what would happen when two sources (or significant others) disagreed, and as the result of a third series of experiments, were able to reject two of these alternatives.

Throughout, we have been concerned with proceeding from well-supported answers toward new questions. We began with some parts of Expectation States Theory that had received confirmation in studies designed to test them—namely, the propositions that the pattern of expectations held by individuals in group situations would determine their future likelihood of rejecting influence attempts—and added our ideas regarding the operation of a source in the formation of expectation patterns. Our initial ideas were formulated and tested in a simple setting in the hope that any problems in this formulation would be relatively easy to detect. After our first tests, we extended the theory, preserving, insofar as possible, validated assumptions and extending the definition of the relevant social situation as required. In part as a consequence of this strategy, it was possible to isolate the problem of contradictory sources, and to construct an empirical test between alternative formulations.

Finally, we would like to describe briefly several areas that clearly demand further theoretical and experimental attention. Our intent here is to facilitate reactions to this work, and also to encourage extensions of it by others. Some of these issues have arisen in the work reported here, and some are independent.

First, it seems worthwhile to investigate whether individuals in the situations we are interested in will make *inferences* about the ability of evaluators in the same way as they are known to make inferences about others in direct interaction. For example, if an individual is being evaluated by an other whose ability is unknown but who holds a high state of a diffuse status characteristic, will that evaluator be accepted? Previous versions of expectation theory have asserted that specific expectation states will be formed directly from diffuse status characteristics, but so far this research has not been applied to the problem of sources of expectations. Some experiments, not reported here, indicate that the status characteristic extension may be straightforward, but this is still a problem to be investigated.

Second, we have touched upon the question of *combining information* in the multiple-source and the two-source experiments. Individuals are faced daily with multiple inputs of information, and must come to some overall conclusion about it. Knowing how one task ability is used to make inferences about another task ability, or how information about a task ability and a diffuse status characteristic are combined to reach a conclusion about a second task ability would permit a significant extension of the theory to important real-life situations. Some work has been done in this area already (Berger and Fisek, 1970; Webster et al., 1972; Kervin, 1972; and see Berger and Fisek, chapter six, this volume), and suggests that relatively straightforward conceptualizations can adequately represent the combining process. However, the ideas have not as yet been incorporated into a version of source theory, nor have their implications for other theories such as the looking-glass self been spelled out.

Third, the idea often is expressed that individuals "prefer" or seek as favorable a self-image as possible. The idea often is implied in the self-evaluation literature, yet the empirical status of this argument is not clear. We are presently investigating this problem using our basic experimental situation, for we feel that this is not only a widespread concern, but an important theoretical issue. In our data, there is only slight evidence to support any hypothesized tendency toward self-maximization. Probably an even more fruitful question that might be posed concerning this issue is "*Under what conditions do individuals act or not act to maximize their self-concepts?*" It may be that individuals will try to enhance their self image when the task is relatively unimportant to them, or when the evaluative standards are unclear, for instance. Perhaps individuals will act upon a "maximized self" when there are few consequences from such behavior. At this point, however, a tentative answer to the early question is largely conjecture, and any specification of conditions surrounding self-maximization are entirely speculative.

Finally, we believe that an entire set of questions about conditions surrounding the stability or the change of an existing self-evaluation, or self-expectation state, deserves further study. Our work here has been limited to *formation* of ideas of ability, not to how or how long these ideas will persist if undisturbed; nor what sorts of interventions will produce what sorts of changes. In addition to the pure theoretical interest, stability and change of self-evaluation levels has numerous practical applications for children in school, adults at work, and a variety of therapeutic transactions.

APPENDIX 1

Sources of Evaluations and Expectation States

DEFINITION 1

An interaction situation is *task situation S* if and only if:
a. there are at least two actors, p and o, making performance outputs;
b. there are at least two actors, e_1 and e_2, who have the right to make evaluations of the performance outputs of p and o;
c. p and o have no prior expectations for their own or each other's performance at the task;
d. all actors are task-oriented;
e. all actors are collectively oriented.

DEFINITION 2

E is a *source* for p in S if and only if p believes that e is more capable of evaluating performances than p is.

ASSUMPTION 1

In S,
a. if *only one e* is a source for p, then p will make the same unit evaluations of any actor's performances as does that e;
b. if *both e_1 and e_2* are sources for p and both e_1 and e_2 make *the same* unit evaluations of any actor's performance, then p will make the same unit evaluations of performances as e_1 and e_2;
c. if *both e_1 and e_2* are sources for p and e_1 and e_2 make *different* unit evaluations of performance output of any actor, then p will distribute agreeing unit evaluations between e_1 and e_2.

ASSUMPTION 2

In S, if p evaluates a series of performances of any actor, then he will come to hold an expectation state for that actor that is consistent with those evaluations.

ASSUMPTION 3

In S, if p holds higher expectations for any actor o_1 than for another actor o_2:
a. p will be more likely to give o_1 action opportunities than o_2;
b. p will be more likely to evaluate positively o_1's future performance outputs than o_2's;
c.   in case of disagreement between o_1 and o_2, p will be more likely to agree with o_1;
d. p will be more likely to accept o_1 than o_2 as a source.

ASSUMPTION 4

In S, the higher the expectations an actor p holds for self relative to the expectations he holds for o:
a.   the more likely he is to accept a given action opportunity and make a performance output;
b.   in case of disagreement with o, the more likely he is to reject influence.

REFERENCES

BACKMAN, C. W., P. F. SECORD, and J. R. PIERCE. 1963. Resistance to change in the self-concept as a function of perceived consensus among significant others. *Sociometry* 26: 102–11.

BERGER, J., and M. H. FISEK. 1970. Consistent and inconsistent status characteristics and the determination of power and prestige orders. *Sociometry* 33: 327–47.

BERGER, J., B. P. COHEN, T. L. CONNER, and M. ZELDITCH, JR. 1966. Status characteristics and expectation states: a process model. In *Sociological theories in progress*, eds. J. Berger, M. Zelditch, Jr., and B. Anderson. Boston: Houghton Mifflin Company.

BERGER, J., T. L. CONNER, and W. L. MCKEOWN. 1969. Evaluations and the formation and maintenance of performance expectations. *Human relations* 22 (December): 481–502.

COOLEY, C. H. 1902. *Human nature and the social order*. New York: Charles Scribner's Sons. Reprinted by Schocken Books, 1964.

HAAS, H. L., and M. L. MEAHR. 1965. Two experiments on the concept of self and the reaction of others. *Journal of personality and social psychology* 1: 100–105.

HARARY, F., and D. CARTWRIGHT. 1965. *Structural models*. New York: John Wiley & Sons, Inc.

JAMES, W. 1890. *Principles of psychology*. New York: Holt, Rinehart & Winston.

JONCKHEERE, A. 1954. A distribution-free K-sample test against ordered alternatives. *Biometrika* 41:133–145.

JONES, S. C., and D. J. SCHNEIDER. 1968. Certainty of self-appraisal and reactions to evaluations from others. *Sociometry* 31: 395–403.

KERVIN, J. 1972. An information combining model for the formation of performance expectations in small groups. Unpublished Ph.D. thesis, The Johns Hopkins University.

KINCH, J. W. 1963. A formalized theory of the self-concept. *American journal of sociology* 67: 481–86.

MEAD, G. H. 1934. *Mind, self and society.* Chicago: The University of Chicago Press. Reprinted 1962.

MIYAMOTO, S. F., and S. M. DORNBUSCH. 1956. A test of interactionist hypotheses of self-conception. *American journal of sociology* 61: 399–403.

OFSHE, R. 1968. A theory of behavior under conditions of reference group conflict. Unpublished Ph.D. thesis, Stanford University.

REEDER, L. G., G. A. DONOHUE, and A. BIBLARZ. 1950. Conceptions of self and others. *American journal of sociology* 66: 153–59.

SAVAGE, I. R., and M. WEBSTER. 1972. Sources of evaluations reformulated and analyzed. *Proceedings of the sixth Berkeley symposium on mathematical statistics and probability.* Vol. IV: 317–27. Berkeley, Calif.: The University of California Press.

SOBIESZEK, B. 1972. Multiple sources and the formation of performance expectations. *Pacific sociological review* 15: 103–22.

SULLIVAN, H. S. 1947. *Conceptions of modern psychiatry.* Washington, D. C.: The William Alanson White Psychiatric Foundation.

WEBSTER, M., L. ROBERTS, and B. SOBIESZEK. 1972. Accepting significant others: six models. *American journal of sociology* 78: 576–98.

WEBSTER, M., and B. SOBIESZEK. 1973. *Sources of self-evaluation,* a research monograph to be published by John Wiley & Sons.

ZETTERBERG, H. L. 1957. Compliant actions. *Acta sociologica* 2: 179–201.

STATUS CHARACTERISTICS AND SOCIAL INTERACTION

INTRODUCTION TO PART FOUR

The research in this section is concerned with one of the "classical" problems in sociology: the effect of broadly defined, socially valued status categories on interpersonal behavior. That status characteristics such as age, sex, or race do affect in determinate ways the behavior of individuals in social situations has long been accepted by the sociologist and has become virtually an article of his faith that is frequently summarized by the statement: "status organizes interaction." However, the assertion that "status organizes interaction" at best provides the sociologist with an orientation to a set of research problems. It does not, however, provide him with either an adequate generalization or an explanation for what, in fact, is a common social phenomenon: the effect of status characteristics on the behavior of individuals. To increase our understanding of this phenomenon as well as to increase our capacity to explain it, this orienting assertion must be "unpacked." First, what is it about status characteristics, in terms of their features, properties, and constituents, that operate in organizing interaction and behavior? Second, which behaviors of the individual are or are not, in fact, organized and determined by status characteristics? Third, what is meant by the innocently sounding terms: "organizes" and "determines"? What are the mechanisms and processes involved that result in relating status characteristic differences to relevant behavior differences? And fourth, what are the social conditions in which status characteristics operate to organize and determine the individual's behavior? Much of the research presented in this section can be viewed as attempts to provide answers to these four questions.

The history of expectation states research on the status characteristic problem is reviewed in some detail in the following chapter by Berger and Fisek, so that it suffices for our purposes simply to delineate its major phases. The original work by Berger, Cohen, and Zelditch had two primary objectives. The first of these was to formulate an abstract empirical generalization (or generalizations), on the basis of a dozen or so empirical "small groups" investigations, that describes the relations between the distribution of participation, reactions, and influence in decision-making groups that are initially different in terms of age, sex, occupation, education, race, or similar social categories. The second objective was to construct a formulation, which eventually took the form of the Status Characteristics and Expectation States Theory that, among other things, explained the abstract empirical generalization that had been formulated (Berger, Cohen, and Zelditch, 1966; B. P. Cohen et al., 1972). Subsequent to this work, the second phase of the research in this problem area was

160

concerned: (a) with providing direct tests of the original Status Characteristics Theory, and (b) with providing empirical information that is relevant to extending and refining the theory (see Berger, Cohen, and Zelditch, 1972). The original Status Characteristics Theory restricted itself to task situations in which a single "diffuse status characteristic" was operating. As a consequence, the third phase of expectation states research on this problem has been concerned primarily with extending the theory so that it is possible to describe the status-organizing process in situations in which "multiple status characteristics" are operating simultaneously. The primary objective of the following chapter by Berger and Fisek is to develop, in fairly abstract terms, just such a generalization of the original theory.

For readers who are interested in examining additional work on this problem, we call their attention to two further lines of expectation states work. First is the applied research by E. G. Cohen and her students (1968, 1970, 1971) and Lohman (1972). Their research, based primarily on the original Status Characteristics Theory, has dealt with developing techniques to modify and eliminate the effects of diffuse status characteristic differences in on-going interpersonal situations. Second is the research by Thomas Fararo (1968, 1970, 1971, 1972), which has been concerned with constructing alternative theoretical formulations and models of the status characteristic process within the framework of Expectation States Theory.

REFERENCES

BERGER, J., B. P. COHEN, and M. ZELDITCH, JR. 1966. Status characteristics and expectation states. In *Sociological theories in progress*, vol. I, eds. J. Berger, M. Zelditch, Jr., and B. Anderson, pp. 29–46. Boston: Houghton Mifflin Company.

———. 1972. Status characteristics and social interaction. *American sociological review*, June.

COHEN, B. P., J. BERGER, and M. ZELDITCH, JR. 1972. Status conceptions and interaction: a case study of the problem of developing cumulative knowledge. In *Experimental social psychology*, pp. 449–83. New York: Holt, Rinehart & Winston.

COHEN, E. G. 1968. Interracial interaction disability. *Technical report no. 1*. School of Education, Stanford University, October.

COHEN, E. G., M. R. LOHMAN, K. HALL, D. LUCERO, and S. ROPER. 1970. Expectation training I: altering the effects of a racial status characteristic. *Technical report no. 2*. School of Education, Stanford University, January.

COHEN, E. G., S. ROPER, and D. LUCERO. 1971. Modification of interracial interaction disability through expectation training. Read at American Education Research Association meetings, New York, February.

FARARO, T. J. 1968. Theory of status. *General systems* 13: 177–88.

———. 1970. Theoretical studies in status and stratification. *General systems* 15: 71–101.

———. 1971. Macro-status and micro-status. Paper presented at American Sociological meetings.

———. 1972. Status and situation: a formulation of the structure theory of status characteristics and expectation states. *Quality and quantity: the European journal of methodology* 6: 37–98.

LOHMAN, M. R. 1972. Changing a racial status—implications for desegregation. *Journal of education and urban society* 4, August.

CHAPTER SIX

A Generalization of the Theory of Status Characteristics and Expectation States*

JOSEPH BERGER

M. HAMIT FISEK

I. BACKGROUND AND STATEMENT OF THE PROBLEM

The purpose of the present paper is to analyze the ways in which status characteristics organize social interaction. The problem with which we are concerned is one of the oldest problems in sociology. By 1908 Simmel was

*Research for this paper was supported by grants from the National Science Foundation (GS 1170; GS 34182), the Advanced Research Projects Agency, Department of Defense (DAHC15 68; C 0215), and a special research fellowship to Joseph Berger by the National Institutes of Health. This paper represents a revision and extension of two earlier unpublished theoretical papers that were concerned with formulating a generalization of the Status Characteristics Theory (Berger and Fisek, 1969, 1970). It also makes use, in its introduction and summary sections (I and IV), of material that appears in Berger, Cohen, and Zelditch (1972). We would like to acknowledge the advice and assistance of Bernard P. Cohen, Paul Crosbie, Karen Cook, and Lee Freese. We would also like to express our special indebtedness to Thomas L. Conner, Robert Z. Norman, and Morris Zelditch, Jr. for their advice and assistance.

163

already saying that, "The first condition of having to deal with somebody at all is to know with *whom* one has to deal" (Simmel, 1908; quoted from Wolff, 1950, 307, italics in the original). While one might know with whom one had to deal from direct knowledge of the particular individual, Simmel observed that one might also know with whom one had to deal from a knowledge of his status category (Simmel, 1908; in Wolff, 1959, 344–45). Twenty years after Simmel's *Soziologie*, Park already took for granted a conception of interaction in which an individual, on encountering another individual, classified him in terms of status categories such as age, sex, and race, attributed to him characteristics associated with his social type, and organized his conduct towards him on the basis of such stereotyped assumptions (Park, 1928).

A considerable number of investigations in what is conventionally regarded as the "small groups" literature deal with this problem; that is, there are a considerable number of investigations in which some interaction measure, such as participation or influence, is observed in groups the members of which differ in age, sex, race, occupation, or some similar status category. For example, Caudill finds that positions in the occupational hierarchy of a psychiatric hospital determine participation rates in ward rounds. The ward administrator participates more than the chief resident, the chief resident more than other residents, the most passive resident more than the most aggressive nurse (Caudill, 1958, Chap. 10). Or Torrance finds that positions in a B-26 air crew determine influence over decisions made by the group. Pilots are more able to influence decisions than navigators, navigators more than gunners; and this is true even when the pilot's opinion is by objective standards incorrect; true also, even when the task of the group has nothing much to do with the activities of B-26 air crews (Torrance, 1954). In juries, it is found that sex and occupation determine participation, election to foremanship, and evaluation of competence as a juror (Strodbeck, James and Hawkins, 1958; Strodbeck and Mann, 1956). In biracial work groups it is found that whites initiate more interactions than blacks, they talk more to other whites than to blacks, and even blacks talk more to whites than to other blacks (Katz, Goldston, and Benjamin, 1958; Katz and Benjamin, 1960). Similar findings are reported in over a dozen investigations between 1950 and 1965 alone. (In particular, see, in addition to the above references, Croog, 1956; Heiss, 1962; Hoffman, Festinger, and Lawrence, 1954; Hurwitz, Zander, and Hymovich, 1960; Leik, 1963; Mishler and Tropp, 1956; Zander and Cohen, 1955; and Ziller and Exline, 1958.)

The concrete details of these investigations are very diverse. They differ in the status characteristics used, the measures of the interaction effects, the task and interaction conditions. Nevertheless, they have a number of common elements. First, they all deal with *some* form of status difference. Furthermore, all the status categories employed, however different in concrete detail, have at least two properties in common: (1) Differences in status always appear to imply differential evaluations of individuals. (2) Differences in status always provide the basis for inferring differences in one or more other capacities or characteristics possessed by the individual. The assumptions made about the individual on the basis of his status category appear to be of two kinds. Specific expectations are formed about capacities relevant to performing in the situation of interaction itself; and, often more general expectations apparently are formed about capacities of the sort that might extend over many kinds of situations. For example, assumptions might be made, on the one hand, about the ability to solve a mathematical puzzle; on the other hand, about intelligence. For the time being we shall refer to a characteristic that has differentially evaluated states and implies possession of specific or general expectations as a *status characteristic*; and a status characteristic associated with general expectations about individuals is a *diffuse* status characteristic. These ideas will subsequently be developed in a more rigorous manner in section II of this chapter.

Second, almost all of the aspects of interaction important in these studies can be conceptualized in terms of four kinds of observable behavior: (1) Individuals either give or do not give *action opportunities* to others; that is, they either do or do not distribute chances to perform, as when one individual asks another for his opinion. (2) Given an action opportunity, individuals either do or do not contribute a *performance output* to the interaction of the group. (3) Given a performance output, others evaluate it positively or negatively; given that they evaluate it positively or negatively, they either communicate a positive or negative *reaction* to another or they do not. Finally, (4) as a consequence of exchanging views with respect to the task, it sometimes happens that one individual is *influenced* by another; that is, one individual changes his mind as a result of discovering a difference of opinion with another, or he does not. The properties of these behaviors, their relations to each other, and the interpretation that they can be regarded as different behavioral consequences of an underlying structure of expectation states have already been developed in part two of this book. Following the terminology introduced there, we shall continue to refer to these four kinds of interactions collectively as the *observable power and prestige order of the group*.[1]

Third, though the tasks, settings, and interaction conditions in these studies are concretely very different, in all cases the individuals in the group are collectively oriented to a common task. Usually, the task requires that the group make a decision; there is some belief that there is a right and a wrong deci-

---

[1] In some cases the dependent variable is not one of these four kinds of interactions, but is some behavior that can be shown to be dependent on them. For example, in Zander and Cohen (1955) the dependent variable is satisfaction with the group experience, which we interpret as due to differences in the rates of action opportunities and positive reactions received by high- as compared to low-status individuals.

sion; and the purpose of the group is to make the right decision. In coming to the right decision it is typically the case that it is legitimate to use another person's opinion as the basis of one's own opinion if one believes that the other is right. Hence, one may say that members of the group are looking for the right answer either from themselves or from others. Again following previously introduced usage: A task that is defined as having a right and a wrong answer, if the right answer is defined as "success" and the wrong answer as "failure," is a *valued* task; a task in which it is either necessary or legitimate to use *whatever* opinion one believes is right, whether it is the opinion of another or of oneself, is a *collective* task. A group oriented to a collective, valued task is a *task-oriented* group.

On the other hand, there are important ways in which these investigations differ: First, it appears to make no difference in the effect of a status characteristic whether it is embedded in a formal structure or not. Second, it appears to make no difference whether the status characteristic has any prior association with the task of the group or not. In all these groups there are status distinctions, sometimes formalized and sometimes not, and sometimes the status distinctions have a prior association with the group's task and sometimes not.

In general, then, if formulated sufficiently abstractly, this research adds up to the following empirical generalization:

> When a task-oriented group is differentiated with respect to some external status characteristic, this status difference determines the observable power and prestige order within the group whether or not the status characteristic is related to the group task.

The theory of status characteristics and expectation states was originally formulated by Berger, Cohen, and Zelditch (1966) to explain this empirical generalization. It assumed that a critical role is played by the underlying structure of *performance expectation states* that members of the group come to hold for self and others. The theory made the observable power and prestige order depend upon these expectation states and the formation of performance expectation states (their "assignment") depend on status characteristics. Among other things, what the Status Characteristics and Expectation States Theory sought to do was: (1) stipulate at least the sufficient conditions under which a status organizing process takes place;[2] (2) specify what it is about status characteristics that determines behavior; (3) specify what kinds

---

[2] The theory did not claim that the conditions it stipulated were the *necessary* conditions of the process. In their absence there may or may *not* be a status organizing process. For example, the theory assumed the process takes place in *task* situations; but this did not imply that it does not, under some conditions, take place in nontask situations. There has, however, been little work on this process in nontask situations, and it is not yet possible to stipulate the conditions under which status organization occurs in them.

of behavior are in fact determined by status characteristics; and (4) describe some of the mechanisms by which the process determines the observable power-prestige order.

The scope of the original theory was restricted to simplified social situations. The most important features of these social situations were that the members of the group were task oriented and they possessed different states of a *single* diffuse status characteristic. It is, of course, more common to deal with more complex situations, particularly situations in which there are several status characteristics operating. However, the strategy of our work has been to first describe and investigate how the status organizing process operates in simplified situations, and then extend our formulations to more general cases step by step.

The original theory claimed that, given the task conditions of such simplified social situations, the fact that individuals possess different states of a status characteristic is sufficient to activate it, that is, to lead individuals to attribute to the specific members of their group the evaluations and expectations associated with the status *classes* to which they belong (the "Activation" assumption). If the status characteristic is already associated in the minds of the individual members of the group with the task they are to perform—perhaps by cultural convention—this is sufficient to determine performance expectations for the specific situation. The only other assumption needed by the theory, in that case, is the assumption that performance expectations determine the distribution of action opportunities, performance outputs, positive and negative reactions, and influence (the "Basic Expectation" assumption). If the status characteristic is *not* initially associated with the group task, the status characteristic becomes relevant to the group's task even in wholly new situations, provided that there are no cultural beliefs that dissociate the status characteristic and the task (the "Burden of Proof" assumption). If this is the case, then new expectations will be formed that are consistent with the expectations already associated with activated status characteristics (the "Balanced Assignment" assumption). And by now applying the Basic Expectation assumption to this case, the theory explains how differences in a diffuse status characteristic determine the group's observable power and prestige order even when the status characteristic is not initially related to the group's task.

This status characteristic theory explained previous results. But it could be argued that the conditions stipulated by the theory were simpler than those found in any previous experiment, so that it required a good deal of interpretation to match the theory to the experiment. Furthermore, the theory implied that a status organizing process takes place in certain situations that had never been previously investigated. Therefore, the first step in investigating this theory required direct tests under conditions involving no more and no less than the conditions stipulated by the theory.

There have been two such tests. Both have taken place in a standardized experimental setting originally developed by Berger (see Berger and Snell, 1961, or Berger and Conner, 1969). The experimental situation was developed for the purpose of studying the emergence and effects of performance expectation states. The principal component of the observable power and prestige order that has been studied in this situation is a distribution of influence, as measured by the proportions of "stay-responses" (S-responses).

The first experiment that represented a test of the original Status Characteristics Theory was carried out by Moore (1968), using the standardized experimental situation developed by Berger. Moore found that subjects who believed that they had more education than their partner had a higher probability of an S-response, that is, they were less readily influenced than those who believed they had a lower educational status. Furthermore, and perhaps more important, Moore found no significant difference between subjects for whom the task ability was already associated with the status characteristic and those for whom it was not.

The logical structure of the original Status Characteristics Theory made it possible to obtain information on each of its basic assumptions. For example, the Burden of Proof assumption in that theory stated that status characteristics become relevant in *any* situation, unless accepted cultural beliefs specifically stand in the way of their doing so. Since this was one of the critical assumptions of the original theory, it was desirable, if possible, to isolate it for direct tests. This in fact could be accomplished, if (1) it was possible to experimentally induce subjects to attribute to self and other the (initially nonrelevant) specific and general expectations associated with their respective states of a diffuse status characteristic and (2) there was independent evidence confirming the assumptions that were being made about the assignment of performance expectation states and (3) there was independent evidence confirming the assumption that performance expectation states determined the observable power and prestige orders. If no differences were found in the probability of an S-response between subjects and it was known that expectations associated with the status characteristic had been "activated" (or made "salient") in the situation, then the failure could not be attributed to the assumption, which described how the status characteristic comes to be activated (or is made salient), nor to the Balanced Assignment and Basic Expectation assumptions of this theory (see Berger, Cohen, Zelditch, 1972).

The same reasoning could be applied to each assumption of the original theory in turn. This sort of reasoning led to an experiment in which 180 Air Force staff sergeants were informed either that one of the two subjects participating in the experiment was a staff sergeant and the other an airman third class, or else that one was a staff sergeant and the other a captain. (In all cases the partner was said to be from a unit sufficiently distant from the subject's own unit to eliminate direct command relations as a factor in the experiment.) Subjects were chosen on the basis of army general classification scores in such a way that their scores were about average; and 58 of them were told the supposed army general classification score of their partner, higher or lower than their own, whichever was consistent with their relative rank. The purpose of this treatment was to experimentally induce subjects to attribute to self and other the kind of expectations presumably associated with the status characteristic. Another 57 were told not only their partner's score, relative to their own, but also that previous work had shown that individuals with higher army classification scores performed better in "contrast sensitivity tests." The purpose of this treatment was to experimentally establish a consistent relation between army general classification scores and levels of the specific ability ("contrast sensitivity") that was relevant to their immediate task. The remaining 65 subjects were told nothing except the putative rank of their partner. No effort was made to directly induce differences in task-relevant performance expectations. Sufficient evidence existed from previous experiments to provide empirical support for the determination of influence by expectation states (see particularly Berger and Conner, 1969).

The results of this experiment revealed that the probability of an S-response is greater for subjects who believe their partner is an airman third class than for those who believe he is a captain, regardless of the amount of additional information the subject is given about himself and his partner. (See Berger, Cohen, and Zelditch, 1972.) In other words, the outcome was the same in all three conditions of the experiment. This result provided further independent support for the original theory.

Further research on the Status Characteristics and Expectation States Theory has been conditioned in large part by two purposes: First, to *refine* the theory, in the sense of increasing its precision; second, to *extend* the theory, in the sense of increasing its generality. Both go beyond what is conventionally called testing the theory. The theory, however, provides the *basis* for this research, in the sense that its problems come to be posed because of the theory, and the concepts and theoretical arguments employed to deal with these problems stem from the theory. Thus, the theory guided and organized this research and its results suggest modifications in the way the theory should be reformulated.

We shall describe seven experiments that fall into three basic groups: The first group of experiments is concerned with the effect of equating statuses, as well as of differentiating statuses, on the behavior of individuals in a group. The second is concerned with the conditions under which specific (as opposed to diffuse) status characteristics that are initially nonrelevant to the group's task become relevant to that task. And the third is concerned with the effect of multiple statuses, some of which are inconsistent, upon the individual's behavior.

1. *The effects of equating statuses.* The theory was originally formulated

to explain the consequences of differences in diffuse status characteristics on interaction. In formulating its scope, situations in which all individuals were alike with respect to diffuse status characteristics were ruled out. However, it was tacitly assumed that the presence of a diffuse status characteristic that did not discriminate between an individual, p, and his partner, o (such as sex in an all-male group), would not dampen the effect of one that did discriminate between an individual and his partner (such as education in an all-male group) in determining the observable power and prestige order.

This tacit assumption about the effect of equating diffuse status characteristics was called into question by the results of an experiment by Seashore (see Seashore, 1968). The original purpose of Seashore's experiment was to study situations involving incongruent diffuse status characteristics. For this purpose, Seashore had white female junior college students work on the contrast sensitivity task with what were said to be black female Stanford students. To isolate the effect of incongruent statuses, three control conditions were employed: Subjects were informed that (1) o was a white female Stanford student of the same age as the subject; (2) o was a white female junior college student of the same age as the subject; or (3) o was a black female junior college student of the same age as the subject. The relevant status information was communicated by allowing the subject to see, in filling out a form, the form previously filled out by o showing o's name, age, sex, race, and school. Subjects were equated on all status characteristics not intended to produce differences in the behavior of the subject in the situation; for the original theory could be interpreted as claiming that the effect of an initially discriminating status characteristic would be inhibited only if there existed an inconsistent second diffuse status characteristic that discriminated between p and o.

Seashore found no differences between treatments (Seashore, 1968). While there had been a number of departures in procedure in the Seashore experiment, any of which might have accounted for the difference between her results and previous results, Cohen, Kiker, and Kruse (1969) reasoned that Seashore had activated diffuse status characteristics that equated subjects, and the effect of equating subjects was to reduce the effect of the differentiating status characteristic on the probability of an S-response. They therefore replicated Seashore's experiment, using as conditions: White female junior college students (1) who were informed that o was black, but who were given no other information about o; or (2) who were informed that o was black and of the same age as the subject; or (3) who were informed that o was a Stanford student, but were given no other information about o; or (4) who were informed that o was a Stanford student of the same age as the subject. This experiment provided support for the hypothesis that equating subjects on diffuse status characteristics reduces the effect of a differentiating status characteristic on the probability of an S-response.

The result implies that for a particular discriminating diffuse status characteristic to be maximally effective not only must there be no other (inconsistent) status characteristic that also discriminates between p and o, there must also be no other activated status characteristic that equates p and o. It should be observed that it does not follow from this result that if subjects are left to *choose* for themselves from multiple sources of status information that they will activate equating diffuse status characteristics that produce a dampening effect. This question remains an open experimental and theoretical issue.

2. *Effect of other kinds of status elements.* In an effort to extend the scope of the status characteristics—expectations states formulation, Berger and Fisek (1969) constructed a generalization of it that sought to describe the operation of *specific* as well as diffuse status characteristics and the operation of *multiple* as well as single status characteristics in task situations. The experiments described in this and the next section [in (2) and (3)] arose out of attempts to refine the initial generalization and to answer questions it posed.

For present purposes we may regard a specific status characteristic as a status characteristic with states that are differentially evaluated and from which one believes it possible to infer some specific expectations for p and o. This concept will be more rigorously developed in section II of this chapter. A specific status characteristic differs from a diffuse status characteristic in not being associated with general expectation states. The original theory did not deal with such characteristics; it dealt only with diffuse status characteristics and, indeed, tacitly assumed that general expectation states were one of the principal mechanisms by which diffuse status characteristics become relevant in situations never previously defined by p. While there is no evidence to disprove this, there is evidence to show that, under certain circumstances, specific as well as diffuse status characteristics can be made relevant in situations to which they have no prior relevance.

Berger, Fisek, and Freese (1970) have shown that one can make a specific status characteristic relevant, even if it has no prior association with the characteristic instrumental to a task, if it is made the basis for allocating rewards to p and o. This happens even though allocation of rewards on the basis of the irrelevant characteristic is made to look quite arbitrary. The investigation required a two-experiment design: In the first experiment, subjects were tested for their *meaning insight* ability, an intuitive ability that makes it possible for some individuals to know which of two non-English words is the same in meaning as a comparison English word. (The ability, of course, is artificially created by the experimenter; for details, see Berger and Conner, 1969). In the second experiment, in which the same subjects participated, they were told that it was customary to give twenty-five cents per trial to subjects with high contrast sensitivity, the ability required by the experimental task, and ten cents a trial to subjects with low contrast sensitivity, as rewards for their respective contributions to the group effort. As the experimenters were very pressed for time, they could not test subjects for contrast sensitivity; but because they wanted to keep the conditions of this study fairly comparable to the conditions of their other studies, they would pay the subjects on the basis of the only information they did know, the meaning insight scores they knew subjects had been given from the previous experiment in which it was known they had participated. Thus, there is a characteristic, C_1, irrelevant to the task; a characteristic, C_2, instrumental to the task; and a reward that is supposed to be associated with the ability that is instrumental to the task. When the reward is instead given to subjects on the basis of the irrelevant characteristic, the irrelevant characteristic determines the probability of an S-response in the experiment.

A similar two-experiment design has been used by Freese (1970) to show that given three specific characteristics, say C_1, C_2, and C_3, if subjects believe that C_1 and C_2 are positively correlated, they make inferences about the task characteristic C_3 from C_1. On the other hand, if they believe C_1 and C_2 are inversely correlated, they do not make inferences about their task characteristic. Freese first tested subjects on their *meaning insight* ability, C_1. They were then informed either that one could also infer, if one had high meaning insight ability, that one also had high *social prediction* ability, C_2, or else that it was known that individuals with high meaning insight ability had low social prediction ability. (Social prediction ability was presented as the ability to predict behavior in complex social situations.) The experiment then ended, but subjects were asked to participate in a second experiment in which the contrast sensitivity ability, C_3, was used. Meaning insight ability, C_1, determined the probability of an S-response for subjects on a task involving contrast sensitivity ability, C_3, if they believed it was positively correlated with social prediction ability, C_2, but not if they believed it was negatively correlated.

These two experiments show that, under certain circumstances, other status elements of the situation as well as the diffuse status characteristic are capable of defining it; and they raise the question of what are the *different* mechanisms by which status characteristics come to determine behavior in totally new task situations.

3. *Multiple-characteristic status situations.* Where two or more status characteristics are activated (or made salient) in a situation, the possibility arises that they are inconsistent; it is about such situations that most theories of status characteristics have been written (see, for example, Hughes, 1945, or Homans, 1961).

Experiments by Berger et al., and Tress (1971) suggest that under certain conditions subjects "combine" inconsistent status information, and that their behavior is a function of this combined "resultant." These experiments involved constructing two equally-weighted specific status characteristics, each of which was made equally relevant to the group's task. When they are made inconsistent, subjects are found to have a probability of an S-response lower than those who are consistently high, but higher than those who are consistently low (see Berger and Fisek, 1970a; also Tress, 1971). Furthermore, a subject who was high on one characteristic and low on another had a lower probability of an S-response when his partner was high on both characteristics than when his partner was low on one but high on the other characteristic, and similarly for the obverse case (Berger, Fisek, and Crosbie, 1970.) These experiments provide significant clues as to how individuals process inconsistent status information in *specific types of task situations*.

The original Status Characteristics and Expectation States Theory generated (a) experiments that provide evidence supporting the principal derivations of that theory (see Moore, 1968 and Berger, Cohen, and Zelditch, 1972); and (b) formulations and experiments that suggest extensions and refinements of the original theory (see Seashore, 1968; Berger and Fisek, 1969; Cohen, Kiker, and Kruse, 1969; Freese, 1969; Berger and Fisek, 1970a; Berger, Fisek, and Crosbie, 1970; Berger, Fisek, and Freese, 1970; and Tress, 1971). Our task is now to "start over again": to construct from "first principles" a formulation that represents a generalization of the original theory, and in particular provides a theoretical explanation of those experiments that suggest extensions and refinements of the original formulation.

II. CONSTRUCTING A GENERALIZATION OF THE THEORY OF STATUS CHARACTERISTICS AND EXPECTATION STATES

A. OBJECTIVES

The present formulation has two primary objectives. Its first objective is to increase the generality of the original theory of status characteristics and expectation states. It will do this by extending the scope of the original formulation (1) so that we are able to describe the operation of *both diffuse* and *specific* status characteristics and (2) so that we are able to describe the simultaneous operation of *multiple* (specific and diffuse) status characteristics in organizing behavior. Its second objective is to increase the explanatory power of the original theory. This it will do by (1) trying to account for the experiments described in section I above as refinements and extensions of the original theory and by (2) providing a structure from which new consequences can be derived.

The scope of this more general formulation is described in section B below. Given the task and interaction conditions described in section B, our theoretical task involves three basic issues:

1. How and under what conditions are the status elements possessed by members of the group brought into play? This problem is dealt with in section C.
2. If they are brought into play in a given situation, how and under what conditions do the status elements possessed by members of the group become organized so as to define the situation for them? This problem is dealt with in section D.
3. If status elements become organized so as to define the situation for members of the group, how does this organization determine their behavior? More specifically, how does it determine the power and prestige positions of the members of the group? This problem is dealt with in Section E.

B. SCOPE CONDITIONS, STATUS ELEMENTS, AND RELATIONS

1. *Scope Conditions and Status Elements of the Theory*[3]

Our theory is formulated from the point of view of an actor, *p*, oriented to two or more social objects: The actor as an object to himself, *p'*, and to at least one other, *o*. The social objects, *p'* and *o*, are described in terms of *characteristics*, such as artistic ability, mathematical ability, sex, or race. The characteristics have distinct *states*, such as high or low mathematical ability, male or female. (For simplicity of exposition, all characteristics are treated as if they were dichotomies and no claim is made that all characteristics are in fact dichotomies.)

A *characteristic* is some aspect or property of an individual that might be used to describe him. For a characteristic to be a *status* characteristic we require that it consist of at least two states that are differentially evaluated in terms of honor, esteem, desirability. Since we shall deal only with dichotomies, the states of the characteristic will be said to be differentially evaluated if one is positively and one negatively evaluated. Further, for a characteristic to be a *status* characteristic we require that there be *distinct performance expectations* associated with each of these states. These are stabilized beliefs about how an individual possessing a given state of the characteristic will perform. Expectations are said to be *specific* if the stabilized beliefs about how an individual will perform are held with reference to clearly defined situations. Expectations are said to be *general* if the stabilized beliefs are not restricted to specified situations. In line with this, a status characteristic may be *specific* or *diffuse*. It is specific if it involves a single set of specific expectation states. That is,

---

[3] A number of important relational terms in our theory such as *possession, relevance*, and *direct task relevance* that are introduced in this section will be more explicitly formulated in the next section.

DEFINITION 1

(Specific Status Characteristic) A characteristic C is a *specific status characteristic* if and only if
1. The states of C are differentially evaluated.
2. To each state x of C there corresponds a distinct specific expectation state, SPE_x, having the same evaluation as the state C_x.

For example, mathematical ability may function as a specific status characteristic. We distinguish different levels of this characteristic; we associate differential social values with these levels (positive and negative); and we associate beliefs as to how individuals possessing the different states of the characteristic will perform in specified situations.

A status characteristic is diffuse if it involves more than one set of specific expectation states and, in addition, at least one set of general expectation states. That is,

DEFINITION 2

(Diffuse Status Characteristic) A characteristic D is a *diffuse status characteristic* if and only if
1. The states of D are differentially evaluated.
2. To each state x of D there corresponds a distinct set of states of specific, evaluated characteristics associated with D_x.
3. To each state x of D there corresponds a distinct general expectation state, GES_x, having the same evaluation as the state D_x.

For example, sex is a diffuse status characteristic for a given individual p if it is more highly valued to be male (or female) than to be female (or male); if males (or females) are assumed by p to be more mechanical or more mathematical than females (or males); and if males (or females) are assumed by p to be more intelligent than females (or males).[4]

In the present formulation, p' and o may possess any number of status characteristics, specific or diffuse. However it is assumed that they do possess at least one characteristic that discriminates between p' and o. That is, there is at least one characteristic such that p' possesses a different state of the characteristic than o possesses. Furthermore, it is assumed that the only in-

---

[4]The theory takes the status characteristics of the culture of p as given. It does not, of course, treat such characteristics as "natural" or given in nature. For example, it does not assume that males *are* more mechanical than females, even if in some particular situation they in fact happen to be so. That they are or are not is assumed to be due to the operation of the processes described by the theory, not to any natural differences between males and females, or blacks and whites, or adults and children, etc. While no status characteristic is in this sense taken for granted as "in nature," any status characteristic is taken as given in the *institutional* sense. In other words, the theory does not describe *how* a status characteristic comes to be one. It describes only what follows from the fact that a status characteristic *is* one.

formation that the members of the group have of each other is of the status characteristics that they may possess.

The social objects (p' and o) and the status characteristics (C and D) they possess form one essential component of the Status Characteristics and Expectation States Theory (sometimes referred to as the "actor component"); the other essential component is the *task*, T, and aspects of the situation associated with it. The theory assumes that p is oriented to a task, T, having the following properties:

1. T is *evaluated.* That is, there are outcome states of the task that are defined by members of the group as "success" and "failure." Equivalently, one outcome state is positively evaluated, one negatively evaluated.
2. p is assumed to believe that there exists at least one characteristic, C_i, that is *directly task relevant.* That is if p or o possesses one of the states of C_i, he expects or is expected to attain the "success" outcome of the task, T, while if either possesses the other state of C_i he expects or is expected to attain the failure outcome of the task.[5] Thus, p does not believe that success is merely a matter of luck or chance; rather he believes that it requires some ability to accomplish success.
3. T *is unitary.* Either there is only one explicitly defined characteristic directly relevant to T, or, if there is more than one, they form a consistent set. If these characteristics are not explicitly defined, it is still assumed that there exists either one or a consistent set of abilities, whatever they may be, directly relevant to T. Furthermore, if T consists of more than one subtask, as is often the case, we assume all the subtasks to be identical, in the sense that the same set of characteristics is directly relevant to each subtask.
4. T *is collective.* That is, it is both necessary and legitimate for each actor to take the behavior of the others into account in solving T.

In saying that p is *task-oriented,* or *oriented* to T, we mean that p is motivated to achieve the positively evaluated state of T and to avoid the negatively evaluated state of T.

It may be the case that one or more of the characteristics possessed by p' and o is known to be directly relevant to T. It may also be true that one or more of the diffuse status characteristics possessed by p' and o is culturally associated with T. However, neither of these conditions is required for the theory to apply. In fact, the theory's power must be assessed largely in terms of its capacity to predict status organizing processes in precisely those situations in which status characteristics possessed by p' and o initially are neither associated with nor directly relevant to the group task.

The present formulation may also apply to situations in which *goal-objects* with differentially evaluated states are associated with the task. That

---

[5]See footnote 3 on page 174.

is, it may deal with situations in which differential rewards (such as high and low rates of pay) are allocated for differential *contributions* in solving the task. Further, our theory may be applied to a situation in which goal-objects with differentially evaluated states are associated with the different states of the characteristic believed to be directly relevant to the task. In other words, it may deal with situations in which differential rewards (high and low rates of pay) are associated with differential *capacities* to solve the task. Goal-object states are, if they exist, regarded as part of the "task component" of the situation. Goal-object states often provide "paths" by which elements in the status situation become relevant to each other. In such situations goal-object states (where "state" may be "high" or "low" rate of pay) are treated in the same manner as states of characteristics and outcome states of the task.

We shall designate a situation satisfying the conditions given above as S^*. That is, S^* is any situation in which there is an evaluated, unitary, collective task T to which p is oriented, and there are two or more social objects, p' and o, who possess any number of status characteristics, either specific or diffuse, at least one of which discriminates between p' and o.

When it is necessary or convenient to make general reference to states of characteristics, task outcomes, or states of goal-objects in S^* we refer to them in general as "elements" or "status elements" of the situation, denoted by e_i, e_j, or e_k. To make general reference to the social objects p' or o, we use italic lower case letters y or z.

Before we can describe the conditions and properties of status organizing processes, we must first examine more closely the types of relations that can obtain between the elements of our system. This is the task we turn to next.

2. *Primitive and Defined Relations of the Theory*

Possession, expected possession, similarity, and relevance are the relations of particular interest to us. We shall treat possession, expected possession, and similarity as primitive terms. The meaning of these terms will accord in general with common understanding and common usage. The relation of relevance, however, will be explicitly defined, making use of primitive terms in our theory.

The relations "y possesses element e_i" and "y expects or is expected to possess element e_i" have certain special properties that should be noted. Within our system we assume that these relations must always involve a social object (such as p' or o) as the transmitter of the relation, while the receiver of the relation must always involve a nonsocial object: the state of a status characteristic or goal-object, or the outcome state of the task—those things that we have designated as "elements." Indeed these relations can be characterized by the fact that their sets are partitioned into two parts (social objects and elements) with the property that all transmitters are social objects and all

receivers are elements. It follows at once that possession and expected possession are asymmetric; and we assume that this is the operative property of
these relations in describing the behavior of the actors in S^*.[6]

Similarity is the third of our primitive relations. The similarity relation is
predicated to hold only between those things that we have designated as
"elements." Two elements are similar if an actor in the system perceives them
to have some commonality, to be in some sense alike. Obviously, similarity is
a symmetric relation; if an element e_i is similar to a second element e_j, then
e_j is similar to e_i. We assume that the actors in S^* behave as if this relation is
symmetric.

As we develop the theory it will become clear that the relation of relevance
plays a crucial role in this formulation. With the concept of relevance we want
to capture the idea that actors tend to establish "possession expectancies"
with respect to the elements in S^*. Given that they already possess or have
attained a particular element, e_i, this fact leads them to expect to attain or
possess some other element, say e_j, in S^*. The conditions that govern the
development of such "possession expectancies" are extremely important and
will have to be explicitly formulated, but for the moment we observe that
when a "possession expectancy" holds between two elements, e_i and e_j, for
any social object in our system, we say that e_i is relevant to e_j. We state this
idea in the definition below.

DEFINITION 3

(Relevance) Element e_i is *relevant* to element e_j if and only if when y possesses e_i, then y expects or is expected to possess e_j.

From the standpoint of its logical properties, relevance as defined is neither
symmetric nor transitive. However, we shall shortly argue that under certain
special conditions, that is, when a "path of task-relevance" exists (see below),
the actors in S^* behave *as if* the direction of the relation were irrelevant, and
as if the relation were transitive.

Within the general concept of relevance, we now formulate a special case
of this concept, which is of particular importance in our work: *direct task
relevance*. We say that an element e_i is *directly task relevant* to an element e_j
if when either p' or o possesses e_i he expects or is expected to possess e_j and
e_j is an outcome state of the task (see footnote 6). We shall be particularly
concerned with situations in which the element e_i is a state of status char-

---

[6]For our purposes the notion of "attainment" is regarded as a special case of possession,
and so shares the properties assumed for the comprehending relation. Normally, the
phrases "y has attained e_i" and "y expects or is expected to attain e_i" are used in the case
where e_i is an outcome state, that is, the "success" or "failure" state of T. Therefore, the
phrases "y possesses e_i" and "y expects to possess e_i" are to be understood as also cover-
ing those cases where e_i is an outcome state of a task.

acteristic and with questions of how such elements become directly task relevant if they are not initially so.

We are now ready to address ourselves to the principal theoretical problems of this paper: What are the conditions and processes that describe how status characteristics come to be significant and organized in task-situations that satisfy the properties of S^*?

C. SALIENCE OF STATUS ELEMENTS IN THE TASK SITUATION

That individuals possess states of status characteristics is not sufficient to account for the fact that these status characteristics are significant to them in their social interaction. Although surprisingly little research has been concerned with this issue, it is clear that status characteristics are *not* brought into play in all social situations. In some situations the information that the members of the group are of different sex, for example, may be of no significance to the evaluations they make and the expectations they form for each other; whereas in other situations, this information may be sufficient to provide the evaluational and performance cues that determine their behavior. When it is true that the members of the group use the evaluations and performance information associated with status characteristics as cues to organize and define their immediate social situation, we say that the status characteristics have become *salient* in that situation. Our first theoretical problem is to formulate a set of sufficient conditions under which status characteristics become salient and to describe a process by which these characteristics come to be admitted as usable cues in a social situation.

At this stage, the first part of the problem presents us with no new analytical issues. For we maintain that any social situation that has the properties we have stipulated for a situation S^*, is one in which status characteristics will become salient. Our reasoning here is straightforward. In a situation S^*, the actor is confronted with a valued task and he is committed to try to achieve the positively evaluated outcome state of that task. In addition, it is legitimate and necessary for him to take the behavior of the other into account in his task activities. By virtue of the fact that he is task-focused and collectively oriented, there is pressure on him to search for whatever information is available about the actors in the situation. If he cares to do well, he will want to profit by the suggestions of a high-ability other while not being misled by the suggestions of a low-ability other. Although he has had no prior interaction experience with the other, he may be made cognizant of the fact that he and the other possess states of diffuse and specific status characteristics. Given these conditions, he will come to use the evaluational and performance information associated with the available status characteristics as cues to organize and define his situation.

What is the process by which status elements possessed by p' and o come to be salient in situation S^*? We assume that the first set of status elements that become salient in S^* are those which, on the basis of cultural beliefs or special information, are normally associated with the task in S^*. Thus, we assert that if status elements, possessed by p' and o, are *known* or *believed* to be *directly task relevant*, they will become salient in S^*. Following the processing of elements of this first type, the search continues and we assume that the actors will focus on status elements, diffuse or specific, that (1) provide them bases of discrimination, and (2) have not been dissociated from T in S^*. It will be recalled that a status characteristic provides a basis of discrimination if it is *known* that p' and o possess different states of the characteristic. Two characteristics, or a characteristic and a task, are *dissociated* when actors believe them to be independent of each other. Athletic ability and intellectual ability, for example, in our society are usually dissociated in that actors will not try to predict the state of one ability possessed by an individual on the basis of the state of the other. These ideas regarding saliency are formally presented in the following assumptions.

ASSUMPTION 1.1: SALIENCE OF RELEVANT CHARACTERISTICS

If p' and o possess status characteristics that are directly task relevant, then these characteristics will become salient in S^*.

ASSUMPTION 1.2: SALIENCE OF DISCRIMINATING CHARACTERISTICS

If p' and o possess status characteristics that are bases of discrimination and not dissociated from T, then these characteristics will become salient in S^*.

These assumptions describe the operation of the saliency process in situation S^*. Essentially, they define a priority order whereby status elements become admissible social cues in the task situation. First, any characteristic that is directly relevant to the task will become salient, and this will occur whether or not the status characteristic equates or differentiates the members of the group. Following the search for such characteristics (which may not exist), the actors will then focus on just those characteristics which *do* discriminate between them, and, provided that these are not dissociated from the task, they become salient in S^*. Thus, given the conditions assumed for situation S^*, the saliency process is determinate for this situation.[7]

[7]It is easy to interpret these saliency assumptions as describing a process by which status characteristics are "automatically" brought into play. Such an interpretation is not correct. As already noted, there obviously exist social situations in which non-relevant status characteristics do not become usable cues for behavior. The substantive import of our assumptions (particularly 1.2) must be understood in conjunction with our definition of situation S^*. So understood, Assumption 1.2, for example, asserts that status characteristics are brought into play, at least in situations that are task situations, in which no prior interaction or affectual relations have been established among group members, and in which the status characteristics discriminate between members. In effect, this raises as problems for future empirical and theoretical work such issues as to whether initially non-relevant status

Before leaving this problem, it is of particular theoretical interest to consider the special problems that are involved in activating or making salient status characteristics in naturally occurring open interaction situations. Since we assume that at the outset of their interaction the members of the group have had no prior interaction experience with each other, how do individuals make each other aware of the fact that they possess (if they believe they do) different states of status characteristics? There does not seem to be any special difficulty in the case of some diffuse characteristics whose different states are identified with visually discriminable cues such as is true of sex, race, and age. But such visually discriminable cues are typically absent in the case of specific status characteristics and may also be absent or ambiguous in the case of some diffuse characteristics. We believe that individuals, in these circumstances, do engage in behavior that has as its intent activating, or making salient, discriminating states of specific status characteristics. The variability of such behavior in terms of subtlety and form is impressive. At one extreme it may involve open declarations of special competence, "I've worked on problems like this and have had a lot of experience in solving them." Typically their form is more subtle and indirect, "I just so happen to have read a book (or to have taken a course) that explained all about these kinds of problems." Whatever be the form of this behavior, from the standpoint of the status characteristic theory, its intent is clear. First, the individual engaging in such behavior is attempting to establish a claim that he possesses a special state (vis-à-vis the others in the group) of one or more specific status characteristics; and second, that the state or states of these characteristics are relevant to the group's task. If by this behavior the actor is successful, he has, in terms of status characteristic theory, activated or made salient one or more status characteristics that are now perceived to be directly relevant to the group's task.[8]

D. ACTOR-TASK CONNECTIVITY AND THE PROCESSING OF SALIENT ELEMENTS

Given that status elements have become salient, the question arises as to how these elements become organized. More specifically, what are the processes

---

characteristics become salient, for example, in purely "social-emotional" situations. Also on this problem, it is interesting to observe that Leik's research suggests that the effect of a diffuse status characteristic in a given situation is modified by the extent of prior acquaintance of the group members (Leik, 1963).

[8] The fact that such "presentation of self" behavior is often "indirect," and "non-offensive" in form is not difficult to understand. If the actor succeeds in establishing his claims, particularly at the outset of the group's interaction, he has taken significant steps (whether he is fully conscious of it or not) in determining the expectation structure of the group and its power and prestige ordering (see section II.E below).

and under what conditions do status elements come to be related to each other and related to the group's task? When status elements have come to be directly related to the group's task, the system has attained what we shall refer to as an actor-task connectivity state. More precisely, we say an *actor-task connectivity state* (or simply actor-connectivity state) exists when status elements possessed by p' and o that are salient in S^* have come to be *directly relevant* to the outcome states of the group's task.

For one class of status elements that we have considered there is no problem. These are the status elements, possessed by p' and o, that become salient because the actors in S^* already believe that they are directly relevant to the group's task. For these elements an actor-connectivity state already exists and there is no further issue of relating them to the group's task. However, our salience assumptions allow for the possibility that there may exist elements salient in S^* that initially are not directly task relevant and we face the problem of how such elements are processed. To deal with this problem we first distinguish two different situations that may in fact obtain in S^*, and then describe the organizational process that occurs in each situation.

In the first situation, some relations are assumed to exist between the elements in the actor component and the elements in the task component in the situation but there is no direct relation between an element possessed by p' and o and their task. There may be, for example, a salient characteristic whose states are possessed by p' and o that is relevant to a goal-object, whose states are related to the task, while the states of the characteristic are not *directly relevant* to the task. We shall analyze such cases under the heading of "Paths of Relevance." The second type of situation obtains when no connection exists between the task component and the actor component, when no diffuse or specific characteristic, possessed by p' and o and salient in S^*, has been associated previously with the task nor with any element that is connected to the task. For reasons that will become clear later, we will treat this case under the title of "Burden of Proof." It may be useful to think of the paths of relevance process as the formation of direct relevance relations on the basis of already existing relations, and the Burden of Proof process as the formation of direct relevance relations in the absence of any other connecting relations.

1. Paths of Relevance and the Induction of Direct Task Relevance

Given that p' and o possess status elements that are related to the task component in S^*, but are not directly related to their task, how does the actor deal with this situation? Fundamentally, we assume that the actor, in this situation, engages in what might be considered a form of search behavior. By search behavior he seeks to determine relational linkages between the status elements he and his partner possess and elements that are associated with the task component of the situation. If such relational linkages exist, he will then act to complete the structure by directly relating the elements he and the other possess to the outcome states of their task, *on the basis of these relational linkages.* Furthermore, we assume that the greater the number of such relational linkages, the greater the "strength" of the completed structure (or the greater the likelihood that he will complete the structure). We refer to the process of establishing actor-connectivity as the *spread of task relevance,* and to the "relational linkages" involved in this process as *paths of task relevance.* In order to describe the process precisely, we need to define the concepts of (1) paths of task relevance and (2) degree of direct task relevance.

With the concept "path of task relevance" we want to represent the idea of an *indirect* relational linkage between elements possessed by p' and o and task outcomes in S^*. Further, the "points" of this relational linkage are *elements* that in a given linkage may even be of a different type (states of status characteristics, states of goal-objects, and task outcomes). And finally, similarity and relevance are the principal relations that hold between the elements of such a linkage. The features of a relational linkage are expressed in the following definition of a "path of task relevance."

DEFINITION 4

(Path of Task Relevance) A *path of task relevance* from e_1 to e_n is a collection of distinct elements $e_1, e_2, e_3, \ldots, e_n$ $(n \geq 3)$ together with $n-1$ relations, such that

1. A similarity or relevance relation holds between each pair $e_1 e_2$ or $e_2 e_1$, $e_2 e_3$ or $e_3 e_2, \ldots, e_{n-1} e_n$ or $e_n e_{n-1}$, with at least one of the relations being that of relevance.
2. The element e_1 is possessed by y, and is salient in S^* and the element e_n represents an outcome state of the task T.[9]

Two things should be noted in connection with this definition and its usage in our formulation. First, that the relation between any two adjacent points can be defined in either direction, $e_k e_{k+1}$ or $e_{k+1} e_k$, is intended to cover the substantive idea that in a path of relevance the effect of a relevance relation is independent of its direction.[10] Second, in employing the concept of path of relevance, we assume that if there is a path of relevance, for example, from p' to the task, then there is also a corresponding path from o to the task. Nothing in the definition of this concept requires this application, but it is

---

[9]For the case where a path consists of two elements linked by a relevance bond, the path of relevance and the direct task relevance bond are the same units. Further, it should be noted that in developing this idea of a "path of task relevance," we have made implicit use of the concepts of "semi-path" and "semi-cycle" as these concepts have been formulated by Harary, Norman, and Cartwright (1965).

[10]No special assumption on this count is necessary for the similarity relation, since we have already assumed that this relation *in general* is symmetric.

consistent with our general simplifying tactic of treating the social objects in S^* in a symmetric fashion.

As defined, the concept of path of relevance allows us to deal with a large number of cases in which elements possessed by p' and o are indirectly related to the group's task. The following are some common examples of such paths:

1. An actor knows that some element (e_i) that he possesses is relevant to some nonpossessed element (e_j) that is in turn relevant to an outcome state (e_k) of the group's task, (T).

2. An actor knows that a possessed element (e_i) is relevant to a goal-object state (e_j) while an outcome state of the group's task (e_k) is relevant to (e_j).

3. An actor knows that some possessed element (e_i) is relevant to the outcome-state (e_j) of some *second* task (T'), which is in turn similar to an outcome state (e_k) of the group's task, (T). All such cases represent paths of task relevance as the concept is here defined.

Given the existence of such a path, and the basic motive-force of the actor's task-orientation in S^*, a new relevance bond will be induced in the situation, one that directly links e_1 to e_n. In other words, we assert that on the basis of a path of relevance the actor will "perceive" or come to behave as if the element he possesses, e_1, is itself *directly relevant* to e_n,—a task outcome state.

It is clear that the induction of direct task relevance bonds will be affected by a number of features in the situation. For example, if there exist a number of paths inducing the same direct task relevance bond, it is reasonable to expect that the "strength" of this induced bond (or the likelihood that this bond will be induced) will be greater than it would be if it was being induced by a single path. In order to show how different features of the status situation affect this relation, we must refine our general notion of relevance *when dealing with the special case of direct task relevance bonds*. We do this by introducing the concept of *degree of direct task relevance*.

Degree of task relevance, as a variable, has a highly intuitive meaning. The concept can be made clearer, however, by recalling the general definition of relevance. An element e_i is relevant to e_j if when an actor possesses e_i he expects or is expected to possess e_j. Expectation in this context can be given a probabilistic interpretation, and we can say that an element e_i is relevant to an element e_j if when an actor possesses e_i he expects to possess e_j with a probability greater than or equal to some number α. Then the greater the value of α, the probability with which the actor who possesses e_i expects to possess e_j, the greater the degree of direct task relevance of e_i to e_j, although the degree of direct task relevance is not necessarily equal to this probability measure. We designate the degree of direct task relevance for the states of characteristic i as r_i, and assume its values to be scalable in the interval $[0, 1]$. The maximum value of degree of direct task relevance is equal to one, and in general we assume that in experimental situations direct task relevance bonds established by the experimenter have this maximum value. While at present we have no means of directly measuring degrees of direct task relevance, it is possible for us to use this concept (with subsidiary assumptions) to make distinctive ordering predictions (for example, see section III.)[11]

We are now in a position to formulate the spread of task relevance assumption.

ASSUMPTION 2: SPREAD OF TASK RELEVANCE

Given a path of task relevance in S^*, relevance will spread such that the initial element of the path e_1 possessed by p' or o will become directly relevant to e_n, where e_n represents an outcome state of the group's task, T.

The greater the number of paths of a fixed type inducing a specific direct task relevance relation, the greater the degree of the induced relation.

Several comments are in order with respect to Assumption 2. First, it is to be noted that nothing in Assumption 2 restricts the operation of the process to consistent task relevance bonds, that is, bonds in which the possessed status element and the task outcome are of the same evaluation signs. Thus, the Spread of Task Relevance process may give rise to "consistent" as well as "inconsistent" bonds in the status situation.

Second, in assessing the effect of the number of paths inducing a direct task relevance bond, comparable paths are to be considered. In the first instance two paths are comparable if they consist of the same number of elements, and have a similar pattern of relations between elements. This is the import of the phrase "of a fixed type." So understood, this part of the assumption claims that the greater the status support (in terms of indirect linkages) for a given direct task relevance bond, the greater the "strength" of the established bond. It is clear that other features of the path of relevance situation may affect the degree of relevance of the task bond as, for example, the length of one path compared to a second path inducing a given bond. However, given our present stage of knowledge concerning the process, it appears to be advisable to leave further specifications of Assumption 2 for the future. Be that as it may, Assumption 2 as it stands describes what we believe to be a crucial process in the status determining phenomenon; namely, how direct status-task bonds come to be determined by the structure of indirectly related status elements.

---

[11]We also believe that it is possible to construct models based on this formulation which allow us to get a secondary measure of r and in some situations actually determine its value. It should also be observed that an alternative approach to this quantity, r, is to regard it as representing the "probability that a direct task relevance bond is established." Given further theoretical and experimental research with this formulation it should be possible to determine which of the two possible conceptions of r, interpreting it as a measure of the "degree of the direct task relevance bond," or as "the probability that a direct task relevance bond has been established" is the more fruitful approach.

2. Burden of Proof and the Establishment of Direct Task Relevance

We now consider the situation in which we have status elements, possessed by p' and o and salient, that are neither directly nor indirectly related to the task in S^*. How are these elements organized, and what are the principles that govern the manner in which they come to be related to the group's task? Once again our basic argument rests on the fact that the actors in S^* are task oriented. Given that they are oriented to achieve the success outcome state of their task, and that it is both legitimate and necessary to take each other's behavior into account, they are motivated to attempt to infer, from whatever information is available to them, the relative task capacities of the members of the group. What is available is the information contained in the status elements they and their partner possess; namely that they and their partner possess differentially evaluated performance capacities. Although the capacities have not been related to the group's immediate task, neither have they been defined as dissociated from that task. We assume that the actors will come to establish direct task relevance bonds between the elements they possess and the outcome states of their task. In this situation, the actors act as if the *burden of proof* is on showing that these elements are not relevant to their task, rather than the other way around. Although this is a strong assumption, we believe it delineates one of the basic processes in the evolution of status structures.

What are the principles governing the Burden of Proof process? How do salient but nonrelated status elements become related to the group's task, and what factors affect this process? Briefly, we argue that this process is determined and affected by the evaluational significance of the states of status characteristics. Our argument has two parts. First we assume that elements that have *similar evaluations* and are neither directly nor indirectly related will become relevant to each other. That is, given a characteristic with differentially evaluated states and salient in the situation, the positively evaluated state will become relevant to the "success" outcome of the task, while the negatively evaluated state will become relevant to the "failure" outcome.[12] And second, we argue that where an individual possesses the states of a number of *different* characteristics the evaluational consistency of the characteristics will affect the outcome of the Burden of Proof process. Specifically, we reason that where an individual possesses consistent states of several characteristics, this consistency increases the evaluational signifi-

---

[12]This argument does not make a judgment as to *which* component of a salient status characteristic does in fact become initially relevant to the task outcome state. Each of the components of a status characteristic, the state of the characteristic, and its associated specific or general performance states are evaluated units. Further, these components are related to each other in a consistent manner, that is, related components have similar evaluations (see Definitions 1 and 2). Consequently, our argument admits the possibility that one or all of the components of a status characteristic become related to the task outcome states.

cance of each of the possessed states, and as a consequence increases, by some amount, the degree of relevance of established task bonds. Thus, if p', for example, possesses two positively or two negatively evaluated status elements, the evaluational significance of each of these elements is enhanced (compared to what it would be if he simply possessed a single evaluated element), and the degree of direct relevance of the bond linking these elements to either the positively or negatively evaluated task outcome is correspondingly increased. Once again, our problem is to construct a precise formulation of these ideas.

In order to formulate these ideas, we must first introduce the concept of a *maximally consistent subset* of possessed status elements. A maximally consistent subset is a subset of those status elements possessed by p' and o that satisfies three properties:

1. Its elements are salient in S^* and are neither directly nor indirectly related to T, nor dissociated from T.
2. It is consistent in the sense that its elements are status elements that have similar evaluations; they are either all positive or all negative.
3. It contains all the elements of similar evaluations that are under consideration (those neither directly nor indirectly related to T nor dissociated from T, that are possessed by p' and o and are salient in S^*).

We need one more concept to capture the idea that increases in the number of consistent states of characteristics increase the evaluational significance of each of the states possessed by p' and o and, as a consequence, increase by some amount the degree of relevance of established task bonds. This concept is that of the *relative comprehensiveness* of any two maximally consistent subsets. Simply put, we shall say that a maximally consistent subset s_i is *more comprehensive* than a subset s_j if and only if it is the case that all the elements in s_j are also elements in s_i, and there exists at least one element in s_i that is not in s_j. Under these conditions s_j, of course, can also be referred to as *less comprehensive* than (or included in) s_i.

We can now formulate the principles governing the Burden of Proof process.

ASSUMPTION 3: BURDEN OF PROOF

Given maximally consistent subsets of status elements possessed by p' and o in S^*, the elements of these subsets will become directly relevant to the outcome states of task T in a consistent manner.

The more comprehensive the subset s_i compared to subset s_j, the greater the common degree of direct task relevance between each of the elements in s_i and the outcome states of the task, T.[13]

[13]If we could assume that in terms of their evaluational significance different status elements were equal, then we could formulate the simpler and more general assertion that "the greater the number of status elements in a maximally consistent subset, the greater the

Before leaving the Burden of Proof process, there are two features of this process, as described by Assumption 3, that require comment. First, unlike the Spread of Task Relevance process, through the operation of the Burden of Proof process established task relevance bonds are stipulated to occur *only* between consistent elements (elements with similar evaluation signs). Thus, a positively evaluated status element is seen as becoming relevant to the positively evaluated task outcome state, while the negatively evaluated status element becomes relevant to the negatively evaluated outcome state. This is the meaning of the phrase "will become relevant . . . in a consistent manner," and is basic to our conception of how this process operates. A second feature of this process, formulated in Assumption 3, is the idea that *all* status elements possessed by p' and o that are members of maximally consistent subsets and are salient will become directly relevant to task outcome states. Thus, if an actor possessed inconsistent subsets, the claim of Assumption 3 is that *both* the negative and positive elements in these subsets will become relevant to appropriate outcome states with a degree of task relevance that is *common* to the elements of the subsets. Although there are alternative conceptions of this aspect of the Burden of Proof process, it is the case that this implication of our assumption is consistent with our general argument that the actor seeks to use whatever status elements are available to him to organize and interpret his status situation.[14]

---

common degree of task relevance between each of the elements in the subset and the outcome states of task T." But it is clear that different status elements may differ markedly in their evaluational significance.

Perhaps one of the most obvious reasons for such differences, in the case of diffuse characteristics, arises from differences in the γ sets associated with these characteristics (see Definition 2). The γ sets associated with the states of different diffuse characteristics may, in themselves, differ in terms of their evaluational consistency. That is, a γ_i set, for example, may be composed of a greater number of similarly evaluated states than some γ_j set. If this is the case, and the γ_i set is associated with D_i and the γ_j set is associated with D_j then the magnitude of evaluational significance attached to the states of D_i would be greater than that embodied in the states of D_j.

In any event, one of the unsolved theoretical tasks in this area is to construct a more general version of the Burden of Proof assumption that takes into account the fact that the different elements in maximally consistent subsets may differ in their evaluational significance.

[14]A reasonable alternative conception of this process is one that argues that Burden of Proof has both an inconsistency-reducing component and a relevance-establishing component. In this conception, if an actor possesses inconsistent sets of status elements, he is expected to first select one of these sets and then to relate only the elements of the selected set to the appropriate outcome state of the task. Such a conception of the Burden of Proof process can be readily constructed in terms of the concepts developed in this section. On theoretical grounds, such a conception of the Burden of Proof process cannot be easily dismissed. Fortunately, it is the case that an inconsistency reducing formulation of the Burden of Proof process taken in conjunction with the other assumptions in our theory will, under certain conditions, yield predictions differing from those based on Assumption 3. Thus, as is true in other cases, it should be possible to refine our formulation of Assumption 3 if appropriate empirical tests demonstrate that inconsistency reduction is, indeed, an aspect of the Burden of Proof process.

E.   PERFORMANCE EXPECTATIONS AND THE OBSERVABLE POWER
AND PRESTIGE ORDER

Through the operation of the processes we have been considering an actor-task connectivity state is attained in situation S^*. That is, states of specific and diffuse status characteristics possessed by p' and o have come to be significant cues to the actors in the situation and these states have come to be directly related to outcome states of the group's task. Our task now is to describe how actor-connectivity states are related to the power and prestige order that develops in the group. For purposes of analysis, we distinguish two aspects of this problem. The first of these concerns the process by which actors in the group form *combined or aggregated expectation states* for self and other given that an actor-connectivity state exists. The second of these concerns the process by which particular self-other expectation states are related to the power and prestige positions that develop in the group.

1.   Formation of Aggregated Expectation States

With the existence of an actor-connectivity state, status elements possessed by p' and o are directly related to the task in situation S^*. These status elements may differ in the degree of direct relevance that links them to the task. Further, each of the status elements carries evaluational and performance information about the actors who possess it. That is, the status elements provide "units" of information about the differentially evaluated performance capacities of the actors—information that is now related to outcome states of their task. Our concern at this stage is to describe how the evaluational and performance information contained in these status units come to be organized for the actors in the system.

Basically, we assume that given status elements that are directly related to the task in S^*, the actor uses these status elements to form performance expectations for self and other. These performance expectations are "stabilized conceptions" that the actor constructs of the performance capacities of the members of the group with respect to their immediate task. As such these conceptions are seen to embody the evaluational and performance information contained in each of the status elements directly related to the task. Our basic idea is that the actor functions like a mechanism that processes all the task relevant status information and combines this information in forming an overall expectation structure. Further, in "combining these status elements," their nature and relevance to the task are significant in determining the resultant structure. Thus the sign and the degree of direct task relevance are the properties of an element that determines its relation to the stabilized task expectations that are developed.[15]

[15]In spite of the fact that we describe the formation of aggregated expectation states in such phenomenological terms as "stabilized conceptions," and "combining status elements,"

On a general level we shall assume that: the greater the combined relevance of those positively evaluated status elements, possessed by an actor, that are directly related to the task, the higher will be the performance expectations formed for the actor. Within this general assumption it is possible to construct more precise versions that adequately represent our substantive ideas concerning this process. With precise versions, we are able to derive specific predictions concerning the power and prestige positions of actors in an experimental situation. Since this will be of interest to us in examining some of the empirical consequences of our theory, we present one such version (of several that are possible) as the form of the Aggregated Expectation States assumption that we shall employ.

Let E_y represent the "value" of an aggregated expectation state, where y stands for either p' or o.

ASSUMPTION 4: AGGREGATED EXPECTATION STATES

The actor will develop aggregated expectation states for self and other such that these states, E_y, are equal to the ratio of the sum of the positively evaluated elements y possesses weighted by their degree of direct relevance to the task, to the sum of all elements y possesses directly relevant to T. That is:

$$E_y = \frac{\sum_{i=1}^{m} r_i^{(+)} \hat{e}_i^{(+)}}{\sum_{i=1}^{n} \hat{e}_i}$$

In this expression, n is the total number of elements possessed by y and m is the total number of elements possessed by y that are positive; $\hat{e}_i$ is 1 if the ith element possessed by y is directly relevant to the task, T, and 0 if it is not; and r_i, a number between 0 and 1, is the degree of direct task relevance of $\hat{e}_i$ to T. The plus signs in parentheses that are superscripts to r_i and $\hat{e}_i$ in the numerator indicate that the sum is to be taken over the positive elements alone.

It is clear from an examination of this expression that the value of the aggregated expectation state, E_y, ranges over the interval [0,1]. The value of unity corresponds to the highest expectations and the value of zero to the

---

this, as we have noted in other chapters, is primarily a heuristic device. Such entities as aggregated expectations and the processes involved in their formation are unobservable states and processes in our theory, and no assumptions are being made as to how these processes and states do in fact relate to the structure of an individual's conscious and verbalizable cognitions. Inferences about how aggregated expectation states emerge or change *during* the course of interaction are made on the basis of conditions and behaviors that are postulated to lead to such states or behaviors that are postulated to be consequences of such states.

lowest. The highest expectation value is obtained when the actor possesses the positively evaluated state of every directly relevant characteristic in the system and when all these characteristics are maximally relevant to the task. The lowest expectation value is obtained when the actor possesses none of these positively evaluated states. This form of the Aggregated Expectation States assumption allows us to calculate values for the expectation states developed for each actor when we are in a position to estimate or make assumptions about the number and the degrees of relevance of the characteristics in the situation.

2.   The Basic Expectation Process

Given that actors in S^* have formed aggregated expectation states for self and other, how are the expectation values associated with these states related to the actor's power and prestige position in the group? In order to deal with this problem we must first clarify what is meant by "position" in an observable power and prestige order and more importantly what is meant by the idea that "position A is higher than position B" in such an order.

By "an observable power and prestige order" we refer to a set of task relevant behaviors that tend to be differentially distributed among the members of a group. These behaviors include: chances to perform or action opportunities; performance outputs or problem-solving attempts; reactions or communicated unit-evaluations; and exercised influence. It should be observed that not only are these behaviors unequally distributed among the members of the group but that these distributions tend to be highly correlated with each other in an established power and prestige order. Within this framework we can characterize and *compare* any two positions, A and B, in such an order, in terms of the relative likelihoods that an occupant of these positions will engage in or be the object of these related task behaviors. Thus we shall say that position A is higher than position B in the observable power and prestige order if an actor occupying position A, as compared to position B, is: (a) more likely to receive action opportunities; (b) more likely to make performance outputs with or without being given action opportunities; (c) more likely to have his performance outputs positively evaluated; and (d) less likely to be influenced in the case of a disagreement with another. Further, the greater the distance between positions A and B, the greater the difference in the likelihoods of initiating and receiving these behaviors.

We now relate self and other expectation values to the actor's power and prestige position in the group. We do this by assuming that p's power and prestige position relative to o is related to his *expectation advantage* over o. Expectation advantage is defined as a quantity equal to the value of the aggregated expectation state p holds for self minus that which he holds for other. Thus, p's expectation advantage is a determinable quantity that can range from $+1$ (maximum expectation advantage of self relative to other) to -1 (the least expectation advantage for self, or maximum "expectation disadvantage").

Substantively, the notion of expectation advantage embodies the idea that it is the *relative* expectation position of an actor that is significant in determining his power and prestige position. More exactly, we assume that the greater p's expectation advantage relative to o, the higher will be p's power and prestige compared to o.

ASSUMPTION 5: BASIC EXPECTATION ASSUMPTION

Given that p has formed aggregated expectation states for self and other, p's power and prestige position relative to o will be a direct function of p's expectation advantage over o.

This assumption describes the fundamental mechanism of the basic expectation process. Taken together with the other assumptions of our theory, it enables us to specify the observable consequences of those processes which organize status elements and make them relevant to outcome states of the task. More precisely, this assumption allows us to make specific *ordering* predictions with regard to the power and prestige positions that will emerge in a given status situation.

Assumption 5 has been formulated in general terms and can be satisfied by a number of different specifications. Further, if we are interested in making predictions that are more exact than those involved in power and prestige orderings, it is necessary to be more specific about the relation between expectation advantage and power and prestige position. To see exactly what is involved in this task, we consider one of the possible specifications that can be constructed for Assumption 5. The relation we shall examine is applicable to the specific standardized experimental situation developed by Berger. It will be recalled that in this experimental situation we are able to obtain exact information on the acceptance of influence component of power and prestige orders. Subjects are asked to perform a series of binary choice task problems. On each problem both subjects make an initial choice and exchange this information with each other. After the exchange of information, both subjects make private final choices. The dependent variable is the proportion of times the subject will make identical initial and final choices after disagreeing with his partner on the initial choice. The actor's probability of making "stay-choices" $P(s)$, is then taken as a measure of his power and prestige position. Within the context of this situation, we can provide a more precise version of Assumption 5:

ASSUMPTION 5*: BASIC EXPECTATION ASSUMPTION: A SPECIFIC FUNCTION

Given that p has formed aggregated expectation states for self and other, p's power and prestige position as measured by $P(s)$ will be given by the following function:

$$P(s) = \begin{cases} m + q_1(E_{p'} - E_o)^2 & \text{if } E_{p'} > E_o \\ m - q_2(E_{p'} - E_o)^2 & \text{if } E_{p'} < E_o \end{cases}$$

where m, q_1, q_2 are empirical constants.

m is an empirical constant that is equivalent to the stay-response probability $P(s)$ that is characteristic of status-equal interaction; and q_1 and q_2 are constants of proportionality whose values will vary as a function of the specific operationalizations employed for the task conditions in our formulation. Thus, the values of these constants will be affected by the particular experimental techniques that are used, for example, to induce the "collective orientation" condition required for situation S^*. $E_{p'}$ and E_o are the aggregated expectations that p has formed for self and other, respectively. It is asserted that the power and prestige position varies as the square of the expectation advantage. This reflects the idea that while small expectation differences have negligible effects on power and prestige differences, these effects accelerate with increasing expectation differences. Furthermore, by the form of 5^*, differences in expectation advantage are seen to vary the actor's power and prestige position around a value that is characteristic of peer interaction.

With all this said, we must be careful about attaching special priority to this specific function. It is one of a number of possible functions that can be constructed that will embody the ideas we have just discussed. We have selected it, in the first instance, because of its simplicity, and because it enables us to illustrate an important idea; namely, that by using such a function in conjunction with the other assumptions of the theory, it is possible to derive exact predictions with regard to the power and prestige order of groups studied in a specific experimental situation.

We have now completed our theoretical task. With these assumptions we have constructed a formulation that enables us to describe how status elements come to organize behavior in specific social situations. The overall structure of our formulation is summarized in Figure 6–1 in the form of a flow chart: the rectangular boxes represent the states of the system and the hexagonal boxes represent specific conditions and processes. Thus, the task givens and the operation of the salience process in conjunction with the available status characteristics determine the inputs into the system. The processing of status characteristics that are initially directly task relevant, and the

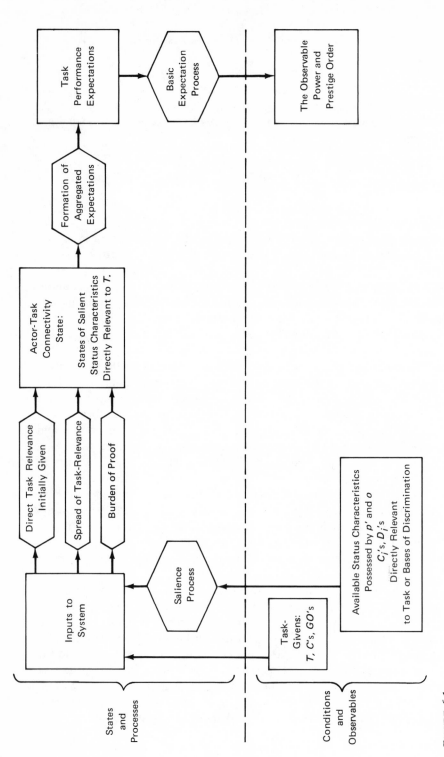

FIGURE 6-1

The status organizing process.

operation of Spread of Task Relevance and Burden of Proof processes establish actor-connectivity states. By the formation of aggregated expectations these processes result in task expectations being ascribed to the actors in the group. And finally, task expectations in conjunction with the basic expectation process determine the observable power and prestige order.

III.   EMPIRICAL APPLICATIONS

In this section we shall examine two experiments that are concerned with investigating the effects of status elements on the behavior of individuals in task-oriented situations. These experiments (briefly described in Section I) were originally conducted to provide information that is relevant to the assumptions in our theory. The primary reason for examining these studies is that they illustrate the type of derivations that can be made for specified social situations by using the formulation we have developed.

A.   THE OPERATION OF MULTIPLE STATUS CHARACTERISTICS[16]

If discriminating multiple status characteristics are allocated in a consistent manner among the members of the group, it is reasonable to expect that the power and prestige order of the group will coincide with the states of these characteristics. However, it is not clear just what the effects of multiple status characteristics will be on power and prestige orderings if these characteristics are *inconsistently* allocated among the members of a group. This is the case, for example, when in a two-characteristic situation one of the actors has the positively evaluated state of one characteristic and the negatively evaluated state of the second while the other has the negatively evaluated state of the first and the positively evaluated state of the second characteristic. Our theoretical formulation enables us to describe in general terms the effects of multiple characteristics under conditions of both consistent and inconsistent allocations, and it also enables us to derive specific predictions concerning these effects.

In order to satisfy the scope conditions of our theory we constituted two-person, task-focused groups whose members were collectively oriented. Our experiment consisted of two phases. In the first phase we established two specific status characteristics, C_1 and C_2, and assigned states of these characteristics to the two subjects. The specific characteristics we used were two fictional abilities, "Meaning Insight Ability" and "Relational Insight Abil-

---

[16]Although for simplicity of presentation the results of this research are reported as a single study, they represent the combined findings from two separate experiments (See Berger and Fisek, 1970; and Berger, Fisek, and Crosbie, 1970).

ity," both of which we knew, on the basis of previous experience, to be believable and yet ambiguous enough to allow us to assign any state of these characteristics to a subject without arousing his disbelief. Both characteristics were presented as important, or *socially valued*, and both were presented as *relevant* to the group's task. We took care to ensure that both characteristics were perceived as *equally* relevant to the group's task.

The subjects were administered tests ostensibly measuring the amount of these abilities they possessed and their scores were reported to them. We assigned them specific states of the characteristics by telling a subject that he had obtained a high score if we wanted him to perceive that he possessed the positively evaluated state, and a low score was reported to indicate the negatively evaluated state. The distribution of the states of the two characteristics among the two group members constitutes the "independent variable" of the experiment. Specifically, we created five different conditions in the experiment by assigning the states of C_1 and C_2. The first paired an actor (p) possessing the high states of both characteristics with an actor (o) possessing the low states of both characteristics. We designate this condition as the *HH-LL* condition, with the first two letters symbolizing the states of C_1 and C_2 possessed by p, and the last two letters, the states possessed by o. The second case paired p possessing the high states of both characteristics with o possessing the high state of one characteristic and the low state of the other, *HH–HL*. The third condition had both p and o possessing one high state and one low state, though of different characteristics, *HL–LH*. The fourth and fifth conditions were mirror images of the second and first conditions, respectively, with condition four the *HL–HH* case and condition five the *LL–HH* case.

The second phase of the experiment was the group's task part of the study and was conducted in the standardized experimental situation developed by Berger. The subjects were asked to perform a task, T, consisting of a series of binary decisions. The actual task, called *Contrast Sensitivity*, required the subjects to select the one of two black and white geometric patterns that contained the greatest amount of white area. These patterns were presented on slides. The stimuli were previously standardized so that the probability of picking either pattern was approximately 0.5. For each slide, or trial, the group members were asked to make an initial choice, communicate these choices to each other, and then make a private final choice. The initial choices were communicated through a system of buttons and lights that we controlled so that the subjects were led to believe they were disagreeing on their initial choices on twenty of the twenty-five trials of the study. The proportion of the number of times subjects stayed with their initial choices when making their final decisions to the total number of critical trials, which we call the stay-response rate, $P(s)$, is the "dependent" variable of the experiment. The stay-response rate is an indication of the actor's power and prestige position.

Since this experimental situation satisfies the scope conditions of our formulation, what predictions can we derive from the formulation? By Assumption 1.1 (Salience of Relevant Characteristics) the two characteristics C_1 and C_2 established in the first phase of the study will be *salient* in the second phase since they are defined as directly relevant to the task. Since they are already directly relevant, neither the Burden of Proof nor the Spread of Task Relevance assumptions are involved in our analysis and we can proceed directly to the Formation of Expectation States phase of the process. The Aggregated Expectation States assumption (4) allows us to assign numerical values to the expectation states that will be formed for each actor, based on the states of C_1 and C_2 that he possesses. Here it is of importance to bear in mind two facts. First, we attempted to define C_1 and C_2 as being of equal social value. Second, we assume that the degree of task relevance of both characteristics is equal to the maximum value of unity since this relevance is established by the experimenter. We can now directly determine the value of the aggregated expectation states for p' and o in each of the five conditions of the experiment. These values are given below in the fourth and fifth columns of Table 6–1. From these values we determine the expectation advantage for p, which is simply the difference between the expectation values for p and o. These are given in the sixth column of Table 6–1. By applying Assumption 5, the Basic Expectation assumption, we derive the ordering of the power and

TABLE 6-1

Condition	Distribution of states of C_1 and C_2	Number of Subjects	Aggregated Expectation States		Expectation Advantage of p	Derived Order of Power and Prestige Positions	Observed Values of $P(s)$
			P	o			
1	HH–LL	26	1	0	1	1	0.821
2	HH–HL	27	1	0.5	0.5	2	0.718
3	HL–LH	26	0.5	0.5	0	3	0.661
4	HL–HH	22	0.5	1	-0.5	4	0.620
5	LL–HH	24	0	1	-1	5	0.533

prestige positions of p across the experimental conditions (see column 7). The observed values of the proportion of stay-responses for each condition, based on the total of 125 subjects, is given in the eighth and final column of Table 6–1. It is clear that the observed values are in agreement with the derived order.

We can now consider how close we can come to deriving the actual values of the proportion of stay-responses for each condition by using the Basic Expectation assumption (5*). The mathematical form of this assumption involves three empirical constants, m, q_1 and q_2, which have to be estimated from the data. As a simplification we shall assume that in this experiment $q_1 =$

$q_2 = q$. Since the constant m is the proportion of stay-responses character-istic of peer interaction, we can assign an *a priori* value to it on the basis of previous experimental results (Berger and Conner, 1969). These results indi-cate that a value of 0.665 is a reasonable estimate of m. We are now left with only one empirical parameter to estimate. In order to do this we can choose any one of the experimental conditions, substitute the observed value of the proportion of stay-responses in the equation of Assumption 5*, and solve for q. For this purpose, we arbitrarily choose Condition 1. Solving for q, we obtain a value of 0.156. We can now derive the proportion of stay-responses for Conditions 2 through 5. Table 6–2 presents the derived as well as the observed values for each condition.

TABLE 6-2.   Observed and Derived Proportions of Stay-Responses for Each Condition in the Consistent and Inconsistent Characteristics Study

Condition	Number of Subjects	Derived $P(s)$	Observed $P(s)$
HH–LL	26	0.821*	0.821
HH–HL	27	0.704	0.718
HL–LH	26	0.665	0.661
HL–HH	22	0.626	0.620
LL–HH	24	0.509	0.533

*This condition used for parameter estimation.

It is clear that for these experiments the derived and observed proportions of S-responses (using the specific function given in Assumption 5*) are in reasonable agreement.

On a more general level what does our formulation say about the operation of multiple status characteristics? First, that for the kind of situation we have considered, a single unitary performance expectation states structure will be developed in the group. Second, that an actor's position on this structure will be a combined resultant of the performance information associated with the states of the characteristic he possesses. And finally, that these expectation positions will be directly translated into power and prestige positions in the group.

B. STATUS EFFECTS OF SPREAD OF RELEVANCE

It is generally recognized that under certain conditions, indirectly related status elements come to be directly related, but important theoretical ques-tions remain. What is the process by which this occurs? Under what con-ditions does it occur? And what are its effects? Our generalization describes a process by which indirectly related status elements come to be directly related to the group's task. It stipulates conditions in which this process takes place, and it also describes the effects of the process on the power and prestige order of the group. As in the case of the operation of multiple status characteristics, our theory enables us to describe general features of this process, and in specified social situations, to make exact predictions about the effects of the process. The experiment reported here was designed to test our assumptions concerning this process.[17]

In structure this experiment is similar to the one described in III. A., with two-person task groups working within the Berger standardized experimental situation. This experiment also consisted of two phases, which were, however, represented to the subjects as *two different* studies.

In the first phase, we established a specific status characteristic. Using one of the two fictional characteristics from the first experiment, Meaning Insight Ability, we assigned states of this characteristic to the two subjects in the experimental group. In each group one subject was assigned the high state of the characteristic and the other subject was assigned the low state. We designate these conditions as *HL* and *LH*, with the first letter representing the state of p' and the second the state of o.

The second phase of the experiment was presented to the subjects as a separate study; and was similar to the second phase of the experiment described in section III. A. It involved the same collective task situation using the *Contrast Sensitivity* task and the standardized decision-making sequence. Before starting the decision-making sequence, the subjects were told that it was customary to pay participants in the study according to the amount of Contrast Sensitivity they possessed, this amount being determined by a special test administered before the participants took part in the study. The subjects were told that due to special circumstances this test could not be administered that day and their rates of pay would be determined on the basis of the results of the study they took part in earlier. We, therefore, allocated the positively evaluated goal object—the high rate of pay—to the subject who was given the high state of the characteristic in the first study, and the negatively evaluated goal-object—the low rate of pay—to the subject who had been assigned the low state.

When we allocated goal-objects we created two additional experimental conditions: A direct relevance condition and a path of task relevance condition. In the direct relevance condition the subjects were told that the rationale for allocating the goal-objects on the basis of the results of the previous study was that the Meaning Insight characteristic was actually relevant to their task, contrast sensitivity. In the path of task relevance condition the

[17]This experiment was conducted by J. Berger, H. Fisek, and L. Freese, "Paths of Relevance and the Determination of Power and Prestige Orders," unpublished manuscript (Stanford, California) 1970.

subjects were told that the reason for using the results of the first study, which was a *separate* study, was that this was the only information about the subjects available to the experimenter, and nothing more. Thus we have four experimental conditions: Direct Relevance *HL* and *LH* and Path of Task Relevance *HL* and *LH*. In the direct relevance conditions, a direct relevance bond has been established between *C*, the specific status characteristic in the first study and the group's task, *T*. In the path of task relevance conditions, a direct relevance bond between *C* and *T* was *not* established, but a path of task relevance does exist. The states of the characteristics are relevant to the goal-objects since the goal-objects are allocated on the basis of these states; and the goal-objects are relevant to the task because an actor, for example, who possesses the positive goal-object would expect to achieve the positively evaluated outcome of the task and vice-versa.

What derivations can be made from our theory for these experimental conditions? First, we consider the direct relevance cases. From the fact that *C* is directly relevant to *T* and Assumption 1.1, it follows that meaning insight is salient in the contrast sensitivity situation. Because this characteristic is already relevant to the task we can immediately apply Assumption 4, and infer that the actor with the high state of meaning insight will have high performance expectations on the contrast sensitivity task, while the actor with the low meaning insight state will have low performance expectations. From this fact and Assumption 5, we derive that the first actor will have a higher power and prestige position (indicated by a higher rate of stay-responses) than will the second actor. Table 6–3 gives the observed results from this study, based on a total of eighty-five subjects. An inspection of rows one and two shows that this derivation is clearly supported.

TABLE 6-3. The Observed Proportions of Stay-Responses in the Paths of Relevance Study

Conditions	Number of Subjects	Observed $P(s)$
Direct Relevance: High-Low	21	0.802
Direct Relevance: Low-High	21	0.472
Path of Relevance: High-Low	22	0.752
Path of Relevance: Low-High	21	0.602

Next we consider the path of task relevance conditions. From the fact that *C* is a characteristic that discriminates between *p'* and *o* and Assumption 1.2, it again follows that Meaning Insight is salient in these contrast sensitivity situations. Unlike the previous cases, *C* is not directly relevant to the contrast sensitivity task and it cannot become a basis for the formation of performance expectations until it is further processed in this situation. However, paths of task relevance do exist, and given this fact in conjunction with

Assumption 3, we infer that the members of these groups will come to establish, with some degree of task relevance, direct links between the states of C and the outcome states of T. Given that such direct links are established, Assumption 4 enables us to predict that performance expectations on the contrast sensitivity task will be formed on the basis of the states of the meaning insight characteristic possessed by each individual. Applying Assumption 5 to this result, we are able to predict that the power and prestige orders in the path of task relevance groups will be similar to those which emerge in the direct relevance groups; namely, that the actor who possesses the high state on the meaning insight characteristic will have a higher power and prestige position than the actor who possesses the low state. An examination of rows three and four of Table 6–3 shows that this derivation is borne out by our experimental results.

Finally, it should be noted that with our formulation and certain subsidiary assumptions, we can derive the fact that the power and prestige order of these groups, operating under different relevance conditions, will also differ in certain respects. In the direct relevance groups the relevance of the characteristic to the task was established by the experimenter as a given status condition. We assume that in such a situation the degree of task relevance assumes a maximum value of unity. In the path of task relevance groups, however, the relevance bond is brought about by the operation of the spread of task relevance process. In this case it is reasonable to assume that the degree of task relevance that is established is some value less than unity. These considerations, taken in conjunction with Assumptions 4 and 5, enable us to derive the consequence that the magnitude of differentiation of power and prestige positions in the direct relevance groups will be greater than that to be found in the path of task relevance groups. The observed values in Table 6–3 accord with this result.

As with the study described in III. A., we can now illustrate how we can derive the actual values of the stay-response rates for each condition by employing Assumption 5*. Once again, we need to estimate the empirical parameters of the system. We can, in this case as well, use the *a priori* value of .665 for the value of the parameter m, which leaves us with the parameter q to estimate. However, we need to estimate one further quantity from the data, the degree of task relevance condition, since it is not possible to assign an *a priori* value to it. We arbitrarily choose to estimate the parameter q from the direct relevance high self–low other condition. Substituting the value of the stay-response rate in our equation and solving for the single unknown, q, we obtain the value of 0.136, which is similar to that obtained for q for the first study. Using this value of q and arbitrarily choosing the path of relevance high self–low other condition, we can estimate the value of r. The equation again contains a single unknown, r, and the value yielded is 0.80. Using these values of m, q, and r, we can derive the remaining two conditions. Table 6–4 presents the derived values as well as the observed values for each condition.

TABLE 6-4. Observed and Derived Proportions of Stay-Responses for Each Condition in the Paths of Relevance Study

Condition	Number of Subjects	Derived $P(s)$	Observed $P(s)$
Direct Relevance			
High–Low	21	0.802*	0.802
Path of Relevance			
High–Low	21	0.752*	0.752
Path of Relevance			
Low–High	22	0.578	0.602
Direct Relevance			
Low–High	21	0.528	0.472

*These conditions used for parameter estimation.

While these derived values are reasonable, clearly they do not agree with the observed values as well as they did in the first study. Since our *general predictions* have accorded well with the results of this study, it suggests that the problem lies with the specific function we have selected for Assumption 5*. It is clear that further empirical and theoretical research is necessary to develop a more satisfactory function within the specifications of Assumption 5.

IV.   SUMMARY

The theoretical and empirical research described in this chapter can be summarized in terms of the following stages:

1. The first stage was one in which an abstractly formulated empirical generalization was constructed from an analysis of the dozen or so investigations reported between 1950 and 1965 of the distribution of participation, prestige, and influence in decision-making groups that are initially different in age, sex, occupation, education, race, or similar social categories. When task-oriented groups are differentiated with respect to some external status characteristic, the differences in status between individuals determine the observable power and prestige order of the groups, whether or not the status characteristic is previously associated with the task.

2. In the second stage of this research, a theory was formulated that explained this generalization. The theory explained it by attributing to status

characteristics differential evaluations, differential specific expectations, and differential general expectations. These three properties are called into play when two or more individuals are committed to some outcome, must take each other into account in bringing this outcome about, and have no other or no prior basis for inferring who is better able to achieve this outcome. They are called into play even if no prior association exists between status characteristics and instrumental task characteristics, just so long as nothing positively stands in the way of making a connection between the two. Becoming in this way relevant to the immediate task situation, expectations for performance in the particular situation are formed that are consistent with the components of the status characteristic. Once formed, such performance expectations are assumed to determine the distribution of opportunities to perform, the rate of performance outputs, the likelihood that a performance output is positively rewarded, and the exercise of influence.

3. The third stage involved direct experimental tests of the assumptions made by this original theory. Direct experimental tests provided support for the basic derivations of the original Status Characteristics Theory.

4. The fourth stage has been concerned with the refinement and extension of the theory. Further experiments revealed that: (a) under certain circumstances, other status elements can become the basis for organizing the distribution of power and prestige in the group; (b) given information about two relevant characteristics, subjects combine this information, even if it is inconsistent, thus creating a hierarchy of power and prestige that places inconsistent individuals between those who are consistently high and those who are consistently low; (c) information that equates the status of subjects is combined with other information in the same manner, so that under certain circumstances, if subjects are equal in status this reduces the effect on the power and prestige order of status characteristics that discriminate between them.

5. The fifth stage, which has been the primary concern of this chapter, has involved constructing a generalization of the original theory that can account, in theoretical terms, for the results of experiments that have been designed to refine and extend the original status characteristics formulation.

The tasks that now face us are clear. First, they involve direct experimental tests of those consequences of the generalized theory that have, up to now, not been subject to thorough empirical investigation. The results of such experiments will provide us with independent tests of our generalization and with information that should enable us to refine the assumptions of the generalized theory. Second, we must do research to enable us to still further increase the scope and determinacy of this theory—a theory that seeks to describe and explain what is clearly a fundamental phenomenon: the processes by which status characteristics organize social interaction.

REFERENCES

BERGER, J., B. P. COHEN, and M. ZELDITCH, JR. 1972. Status characteristics and social interaction. *American sociological review* 37 (June): 241–55.

BERGER, J., and T. CONNER. 1969. Performance-expectations and behavior in small groups. *Acta sociologica* 12: 186–98.

BERGER, J., T. CONNER, and W. McKEOWN. 1969. Evaluations and the formation and maintenance of performance expectations. *Human relations* 22: 481–582.

BERGER, J., and M. H. FISEK. 1969. An extended theory of status characteristics and expectation states, unpublished manuscript.

————. 1970a. Consistent and inconsistent status characteristics and the determination of power and prestige orders. *Sociometry* 33: 287–304.

————. 1970b. Status characteristics and expectation states: an extended formulation, unpublished paper.

BERGER, J., M. H. FISEK, and L. FREESE. 1970. Paths of relevance and the determination of power and prestige orders, unpublished manuscript, Stanford University.

BERGER, J., M. H. FISEK, and P. CROSBIE. 1970. Multi-characteristic status situations and the determination of power and prestige orders. *Technical report no. 35.* Laboratory for Social Research, Stanford University.

BERGER, J., and J. L. SNELL. 1961. A stochastic theory for self-other expectations. *Technical report no. 1.* Laboratory for Social Research, Stanford University.

CAUDILL, W. 1958. *The psychiatric hospital as a small society*, chapter 10. Cambridge, Mass.: Harvard University Press.

COHEN, B. P., J. BERGER, and M. ZELDITCH, JR. Forthcoming. Research monograph. In preparation.

COHEN, B. P., J. KIKER, and R. KRUSE. 1969. The formation of performance expectations based on race and education: a replication. *Technical report no. 30.* Laboratory for Social Research, Stanford University.

CROOG, S. H. 1956. Patient government: some aspects of participation and social background on two psychiatric wards. *Psychiatry* 19: 203–7.

FREESE, L. 1970. The generalization of specific performance expectations, unpublished Ph. D. dissertation, Stanford University.

HARARY, F., R. NORMAN, and D. CARTWRIGHT. 1965. *Structural models: an introduction to the theory of directed graphs.* New York: John Wiley & Sons.

HEISS, J. S. 1962. Degree of intimacy and male-female interaction. *Sociometry* 25: 197–208.

HOFFMAN, P. J., L. FESTINGER, and D. H. LAWRENCE. 1954. Tendencies toward group comparability in competitive bargaining. *Human relations* 7: 141–59.

HOMANS, G. C. 1961. *Social behavior: its elementary forms.* New York: Harcourt Brace Jovanovich.

HUGHES, E. C. 1945. Dilemmas and contradictions of status. *American journal of sociology* 50: 353–59.

HURWITZ, J. I., A. F. ZANDER, and B. HYMOVITCH. 1960. Some effects of power on the relations among group members. In *Group dynamics*, eds. D. Cartwright and A. Zander, pp. 448–56. New York: Harper & Row, Publishers.

KATZ, I., J. GOLDSTON, and L. BENJAMIN. 1958. Behavior and productivity in bi-racial work groups. *Human relations* 11: 123–41.

KATZ, I., and L. BENJAMIN. 1960. Effects of white authoritarianism in bi-racial work groups. *Journal of abnormal social psychology* 61: 448–56.

LEIK, ROBERT K. 1963. Instrumentality and emotionality in family interaction. *Sociometry* 26: 131–45.

MISHLER, E.G., and A. TROPP. 1956. Status and interaction in a psychiatric hospital. *Human relations* 9: 187–205.

MOORE, J. 1968. Status and influence in small group interactions. *Sociometry* 31: 47–63.

PARK, R. E. 1928. Bases of race prejudice. *The annals* 140: 11–20.

SEASHORE, M. 1968. The formation of performance expectations for self and other in an incongruent status situation. Unpublished Ph. D. dissertation, Stanford University.

SIMMEL, GEORG. 1908. The secret and the secret society. In *The sociology of Georg Simmel*, ed. Kurt H. Wolff, pp. 306–75. Glencoe, Ill.: The Free Press, 1950. This is a translation of chapter 5 "Das Geheimnis und die geheime Gesellschaft" in *Soziologie* by Georg Simmel, Leipzig, Germany: Verlag von Duncker & Humblot, 1908.

———. 1908. How is society possible? In *Georg Simmel, 1858–1918: a collection of essays*. Columbus, Ohio: The Ohio State University Press, 1959. This is a translation of the passage entitled "Exkurs über das problem: wie ist Gesellschaft möglich?" in *Soziologie* by Georg Simmel, Leipzig, Germany: Verlag von Duncker & Humblot, 1908.

STRODTBECK, F. L., and R. D. MANN. 1956. Sex role differentiation in jury deliberations. *Sociometry* 19: 3–11.

STRODTBECK, F. L., R. M. JAMES, and C. HAWKINS. 1958. Social status in jury deliberations. In *Readings in social psychology*, 3d ed., eds. E. E. Maccoby, T. M. Newcomb, and E. L. Hartley, pp. 379–88. New York: Henry Holt and Company.

TRESS, P.H. 1971. Inconsistent status characteristics and influence processes: a replication and reformulation. *Technical report no. 6*. Department of Sociology, Michigan State University.

TORRANCE, E. P. 1954. Some consequences of power differences on decision-making in permanent and temporary three-man groups. *Research studies* 22: 130–40, State College of Washington.

ZANDER, A., and A.R. COHEN. 1955. Attributed social power and group acceptance: a classroom experimental demonstration. *Journal of abnormal social psychology* 51: 490–92.

ZILLER, R. C., and R. V. EXLINE. 1958. Some consequences of age heterogeneity in decision-making groups. *Sociometry* 21: 198–201.

Part Five

APPLICATIONS OF EXPECTATION STATES THEORY

INTRODUCTION TO PART FIVE

To apply a formal, general theory such as Expectation States Theory to natural settings for the purpose of producing useful results entails numerous problems. Theoretical concepts must be embodied in terms of concrete variables important to the applied field; techniques must be developed that permit a degree of precise control and measurement in a natural situation and that do not simultaneously destroy its naturalness and complexity; and results must stand up to tests derived from two sets of criteria—the theoretical criteria of logic and empirical success, and the applied criteria of the significance of the effects and their relation to the concrete goals of the applied field. Furthermore, there is no guarantee that the ranking of importance of variables predicted by the theory will be reflected in the "impure" natural setting where a variety of other factors and processes operate.

At the same time, the potential rewards from this approach are great. The theory offers a way to simplify and analyze complex natural phenomena. It enables the comparison of many diverse empirical studies from the perspective of a single vantage point and encourages the development of cumulative findings. It may point the way to effective practical intervention in a situation by directing attention to causal variables. In addition a theory will often aid in explaining both successful and unsuccessful attempts to produce practical results.

Entwisle and Webster have undertaken a systematic and sequential research program to apply some of the concepts and propositions of Expectation States Theory to the classroom. The purpose is to study the effects of various social structures and interpersonal processes upon the development of children's conceptions of their own and each other's abilities. For a long time both professional educators and interested laymen have believed on intuitive grounds that the child's beliefs about his own likely success at classroom tasks act like a self-fulfilling prophecy: children who expect to do well at something will usually do better than children who do not think they can master the new field. In addition, several recent studies have shown that teachers' beliefs about children's abilities will sometimes show up later in children's grades and test performance. Like any natural setting, however, the classroom has produced results that are far from simple, clear, or uniformly successful in producing the expected findings.

The first task of this program is analytic. The classroom is shown to resemble in important respects the task-oriented groups to which

Expectation States Theory has been applied. Previous classroom studies are analyzed in terms of Expectation States Theory, and a circular process involving teachers' expectations for students, students' expectations for themselves and other students, and classroom behavioral consequences of expectation states is isolated.

Of particular importance, the analysis indicates that it is the *children's* expectations for their own performance that are crucial. Some earlier studies (the "teacher expectancy" studies) had pointed to the *teacher's* expectations as somehow determining students' performance and ability conceptions. Entwisle and Webster argue that what these earlier studies probably did was to cause teachers to treat students differentially, and thus sometimes to affect students' self-expectations. Only when the students' expectations are altered in the manner specified by the theory will the interaction changes and improved learning take place.

The second task of this research is to test and apply this analysis. This involved developing a procedure to raise children's self-expectations, which the theory asserts are the crucial links in the circular process of expectations. The version of Expectation States Theory developed in chapter five is selected both because of its relatively straightforward relation to the classroom situation and because the laboratory confirmation of the theory enables Entwisle and Webster to concentrate here on developing effective procedures in the natural setting, rather than upon theory testing. The initial classroom experiments indicate success; expectations are raised by a simple procedure that does not rely heavily upon false information, and the expectations affect a significant behavior— the willingness to engage in classroom interaction.

The third step is to assess the generality of the procedure and the results across various sociological subgroups based on race, residence, sex, and age. Results of a second series of experiments show that the procedure is successful with a wide sample of children.

A fourth step involves some methodological refinements in the experimental procedures: (a) some experiments are reported that study more precisely the effect of racial match between evaluator and children, and (b) some more elaborate experiments involve an additional control group. Finally, the question of alternative interpretations of the experiments are considered, and an experiment designed to rule out a "behavior reinforcement" interpretation is described.

This constitutes the first major report of the Classroom Applications Expectation Program. Data from the initial experiments have been published (Entwisle and Webster, 1972), and partial results of the sociological subgroups analyses have been published (Entwisle and Webster, 1973), but linkages between the source theory and the classroom, crucial issues of task and procedure development, and the analysis of classroom interaction in terms of Expectation States Theory have not previously been presented. A technical report describing early stages of the program is available (Entwisle and Webster, 1970) as are a series of unpublished working papers and reports presented at professional meetings.

Though this program is still in relatively early stages, initial successes are encouraging, and suggest that the approach of applying a well-confirmed explicit theory for practical purposes in a natural setting is promising. A parallel program under the direction of Elizabeth G. Cohen at Stanford (Cohen, 1968; Cohen et al., 1970; Lohman, 1970) is currently applying a different version of Expectation States Theory to analyze the effect of racial status characteristics in determining children's interaction, and to develop techniques to modify the effect of these characteristics in certain circumstances. Clearly there is opportunity for work by additional investigators in educational and other applied settings.

Long-range goals of the Entwisle-Webster program at Johns Hopkins are a systematic study of the "natural history" of expectation states development in young children, effects of the social comparison process, and the structure of competition in schools. Some topics currently under investigation are: the effect of expectation states in determining allocation of performance chances and evaluations, the relation between other measures of self-esteem and variables of Expectation States Theory, development of procedures in nonintellectual tasks (such as athletic ability), analysis of the long-term effects of expectation states upon the structure of competition throughout school years, and isolation of variables connected with parents' and peers' effects on expectation development longitudinally.

REFERENCES

Cohen, E. 1968. Interracial interaction disability. Unpublished research report. School of Education, Stanford University.

Cohen, E., M. Lohman, K. Hall, D. Lucero, and S. Roper. 1970. Expectation training I: altering the effects of a racial status characteristic. *Technical report no. 2*. School of Education, Stanford University.

Entwisle, D. R., and M. Webster, Jr. 1972. Raising children's performance expectations. *Social science research* 1: 147–58.

———. 1973. Research note: status factors in expectation raising. *Sociology of education* 46: 115–126.

Lohman, M. R. 1970. Changing a racial status ordering by means of role modeling. *Technical report no. 3*. School of Education, Stanford University.

CHAPTER SEVEN

Raising Children's Expectations for Their Own Performance: A Classroom Application*

DORIS R. ENTWISLE

MURRAY WEBSTER, JR.

In this chapter we are concerned primarily with *consequences* of expectations; that is, with examining the behavioral effects produced by the expectation states actors already hold for each other. We are interested both in specifying more completely the types of effects that may result from these expectation states and in enumerating more of the empirical interpretations of

*Early work was supported partly by the Center for the Social Organization of Schools, The Johns Hopkins University, Grant No. OEG-2-7–061610–0207 and by Grant MH 18183–01 from the National Institute of Mental Health. Later work has been supported by the Office of Education, Grant OEG-3-71–0122. We would like to thank Margaret Boeckmann for her work devising the experimental procedure and Ellen Dickstein, Judy Kennedy, and Barbara Bricks for their help with the field work. Special thanks are due to Jack Epstein and Dr. George Gabriel for arranging for this research in schools. Principals who cooperated in the research helped in many ways. They are: Lyman Huff, William J. Maczis, Daniel Richowiak, Samuel Sharrow, Elliott Epstein, Ralph Thompson, Dr. Evart Cornell, Frank Tondrick, and George Fanshaw. We want to thank the teachers and students in the several schools who participated in the pilot studies and experiments.

specified consequences. To state the distinction somewhat differently, in preceding chapters one of the main interests has been specifying processes that would generate a particular pattern of expectations; in this chapter, a particular pattern of expectations is taken as the independent variable, and the interest is in specifying additional consequences, dependent variables, that will be produced by the expectations.

A second way in which the work reported in this chapter differs from that of previous chapters is that the interest here is primarily in *application* of the theory to empirical situations, rather than in theory development. Thus for this work we take propositions of Expectation States Theory that have received some verification in the highly controlled environment of the social psychological laboratory and attempt to use them to produce desired results in a naturalistic situation. This work may help reduce the gap between the precise but artificial laboratory setting, and the imprecise but naturalistic classroom setting in which educational research is often conducted.

Earlier chapters in this book have dealt primarily with problems of elaborating interactional and structural *determinants* of performance expectations; that is, with extending the basic propositions of expectation theory so as to predict the specific performance expectations formed from various combinations of initial status relations, agreement or disagreement interactions, unit evaluations of performances, or activating or making salient status characteristics. Most versions of the theory presented so far have included a statement of what has been called the "basic expectation assumption": the structure of expectations held by the group members will determine the distribution of the components of the observable power and prestige structure in the group. In chapter five, the source version of the theory was extended to include explication of the concept of a *source* of expectations, an actor whose evaluations are accepted and are used by others as the basis of the expectations they hold for their own and each others' performances. The basic expectation assumptions—Assumptions 3 and 4 in that chapter—were not problematic in this task, for they were assumed to have received adequate confirmation in earlier research.

In most (although not all) of the theory development research reported earlier the effect of expectation states produced by the various independent variables has been assessed using the single consequence *rejection of influence* under conditions of disagreement. For purposes of developing the theory by specifying additional determinants of expectations, this uniform measurement operation is an advantage, for it often permits direct comparisons of results across experiments. The basic expectation assumptions, however, actually predict a variety of behaviors (including rejection of influence) that result from expectation states, and these are important components of interaction as well. These other components of interaction are important both for explaining frequently reported results and for identifying variables that are important to processes outside the immediate group participating in an experiment. For example, likelihood of acceptance of an action opportunity, a component of observable interaction that is predicted to vary according to the level of expectations held, is important not only as a component of interaction in a given group, but additionally because it is related to such other problems as learning in the classroom, assertiveness, and the impression of competence given to teachers and to other students.

Several investigators working with grade school children have reported results that in a general way are related to the variables of Expectation States Theory research. Rosenthal and Jacobson (1968), for example, report that when teachers are told that some randomly selected children were "potential academic bloomers," the selected children sometimes showed gains in academic achievement, both by teachers' ratings and by more objective measures such as intelligence test scores. Meichenbaum, Bowers, and Ross (1969) report similar results, and also show that teachers' behaviors toward the selected children differ from their behavior toward unselected children. By contrast, other investigators have reported clearly negative results from similar attempts to produce these effects (Claiborn, 1969; Jacobs, 1969). Using similar procedures in similar settings, they have been unable to produce similar effects. In this research, often called the "teacher expectancy" field, there are both successful instances and unsuccessful instances. This is perplexing. But even more perplexing from our viewpoint is that no matter what the outcome, there is no single, clear, convincing rationale to support the choice of techniques, the selection of the sample, the success of an experimental maneuver, or, in the cases where it applies, the failure to observe predicted effects.

The classroom research in expectancy concerns important phenomena, both in practical terms of children's learning and in theoretical terms of improving our understanding of educational institutions and the learning process, even though the findings have been sometimes inconsistent and contradictory. A major cause of the inconsistent results, we feel, is the lack of a sociological or social-psychological context. To our knowledge, work in the "teacher expectancy" field has not been guided in any systematic way by a theory that explicitly specifies the determinants, the definition, or the consequences of the "expectancies." We feel that Expectation States Theory, with appropriate interpretation, can specify the determinants, the definition, and the consequences of "expectancies," in this new research area.

The work reported in this chapter is intended to be a direct application of Expectation States Theory to problems of interest in educational research. Many ordinary classroom interaction situations meet the task orientation and collective orientation conditions of Expectation States Theory. Also, many of the "observable components of the power and prestige structure" specified in the basic expectation assumptions are similar to variables studied by educators.

Allocation of action opportunities, for example, can be seen when a teacher calls upon students.

I. THE TEACHER EXPECTANCY STUDIES; ANALYSIS AND INTERPRETATION

Studies in teacher expectancy research usually include the following features. First, the investigator describes his research to participating teachers as being involved with academic achievement of students and with predicting and assessing achievement. Students are tested, using one or more of the common standardized psychological tests. Test scores of students are not revealed to the teachers. At some later time, usually after a few days, the teacher is told that some students (typically around 20 percent of the class) have unusual academic potential, and that the teacher will probably observe unusual intellectual growth in those students during the coming months. The selected students are picked either at random, or in ways independent of their actual scores at the testing. Several months later, students are retested. In a recent reassessment of this research (Rosenthal and Rubin, 1971) about 39 percent of such studies show positive results: selected students show greater gains on retest than their unselected classmates (see, for example, Rosenthal and Jacobson, 1968; Meichenbaum et al., 1969). Positive findings have also been noted when the objective tests used to measure expectancy effects were administered by the schools rather than by experimenters.

Expectation States Theory suggests the following chain of events. The researcher enters a social institution where ability and evaluations of ability are central, and he presents himself as a capable judge of ability. The initial testing tends to legitimate his claims. The researcher, by stating that certain students possess unusually high academic potential, gives teachers information that should raise the expectations they hold for the chosen students.

If the teacher's expectations for a given student are raised, the basic expectation assumption predicts teacher behavior will be altered. The student will receive more action opportunities than other students, or than he received prior to the manipulation; for example, he will be called on more often in class. More importantly, this student will be more likely to receive positive evaluations from the teacher for any given performance output; that is, whatever the student says in class will be more apt to be positively evaluated. This student will be more likely to have his opinion agreed with by the teacher and by other students, especially in cases where the teacher and others have not yet decided upon the "correct" answer.

The effect upon a student's expectations of raising the teacher's expectations for him may also be predicted from the theory: his expectations for his own performance should be raised. The theory sees one of the immediate determinants of any individual's expectations as the positive and negative unit evaluations of individual problem-solving attempts.

This analysis of the changes in teacher behavior points to selected students' receiving more positive evaluations, and as a consequence, coming to hold higher expectations for their own performance. Then according to the basic expectation assumption, the selected students will be more likely to emit performances. They will raise their hands more, and will speak out more in class. They will also be more likely to think their ideas are good ones, that their solutions to problems are the correct ones—in general they will be more self-confident and less likely to accept influence from others when their opinions are disagreed with. The process is circular, once set in motion, for these changes in students' behavior are of precisely the sort that are likely to lead teachers, even teachers who have forgotten the experimenter's initial revelations about test scores or other teachers who did not receive the score information, to convey high expectations.

Successful teacher expectancy studies are simply explained: students' higher grades on both standardized tests and classroom tests are the consequences of the expectation raising manipulation triggering the circular process described above. Higher scores on objective tests, for example, could stem from an improved mobilization of the student's resources in his now more responsive environment, from actual improved learning by greater class participation and involvement, or even from added increments of extra-school learning because improved self-confidence and positive expectations generalized outside school. First of all, learning should be improved by the increased interaction with the teacher and with other students, which would be directly predicted from the basic expectation assumption. Second, the behaviors associated with holding high self-expectations are probably important motivational amplifiers, perhaps leading to increased attention, curiosity, self-confidence, and interest in independent study.

The processes involved in the teacher expectancy research are important, both in practical terms and in terms of application of formal Expectation States Theory. We therefore designed several classroom studies in which the work to be reported was guided by two interrelated goals: (1) to apply some of the basic terms and assumptions of Expectation States Theory as a tool for analyzing a naturalistic situation, and (2) to use the theory to suggest simple procedures and tasks that will produce useful results in the field.

II. APPLICATION OF THEORY AND TASK DEVELOPMENT

For guiding the field studies in expectation raising, we decided to apply a version of Expectation States Theory that had previously received laboratory test and support. We are concerned here with ability and evaluations of ability, expecially as they are affected by opinions of a "significant other" such as a teacher or a parent. Therefore, it seemed appropriate to adapt the single-source version of the source theory developed in chapter five. For reference, the explicit definitions and assumptions are presented in the appendix to this chapter.

All versions of Expectation States Theory assume the initial conditions of *task orientation* (interest in solving some problem) and *collective orientation* (willingness to consider answers from any individual in the group). These conditions are frequently met in classroom interaction: by definition, much learning activity is directed towards problem solution, and except for written testing situations, ideas and advice from many individuals are actively sought. The source theory speaks of a *source of evaluations*—an individual accepted as more competent to evaluate performances than the subject of interest, *p*. In the classroom, the teacher fills this role, both by virtue of his or her greater knowledge, and, usually, by access to objective information such as an answer key. For our experiments, we decided to fix acceptance of the experimenter as a source; we *told* children that we were competent to evaluate their performances at the task to be described below (information that they were willing to believe).

Given an accepted source, Assumptions 1 and 2 lead to the derivation that if the source (e) evaluates a series of performances by any individual (p), p will come to believe that his ability is consistent with the evaluations received. High ability conception (or self-expectation state) is the direct consequence of receiving positive evaluations from a source. Adding Assumption 4a enables us to predict an observable consequence of the expectation state p comes to hold; the higher the self-expectation state, the more likely is he to accept an action opportunity and to make a performance output.

Because we are interested in improving children's self-conceptions, we decided to attempt only to *raise* expectation states, not to lower them. (The latter would be desirable for theory testing purposes, not for our goal of practical application.) Thus, our experimental design calls for giving heavy doses of positive unit evaluations to selected children and predicting that this will raise their self-expectation states, and, consequently, increase their likelihoods of accepting action opportunities. In the classroom, teachers distribute action opportunities to the entire class when they ask something like "Who knows the answer to this question?" Children who think they know the answer—that is, children who hold high self-expectations for that task—accept the action opportunity by raising their hands or speaking out. Our experiment, described in detail below, was designed to be analogous to this sequence of behaviors. In general, we predict that we can increase the rate at which a child raises his hand in response to group-directed questions as a direct function of the self-expectations that he holds, and that we can increase the child's self-expectation state by giving him a large number of positive unit evaluations of past performances. More precisely, we formulate for testing the following two derivations, using Assumptions 1, 2, and 4a from the single source theory:

DERIVATION 1

If an individual (p) has received no unit evaluations of his performances at time t_1 and receives a large proportion of positive unit evaluations from a source at time t_2, then the likelihood that p will accept a given action opportunity and make a performance output will be greater at time t_3 than at t_1.

DERIVATION 2

If an individual (p_1) has received a large proportion of positive evaluations at time t_2, then as compared to a second individual (p_2) who has not received any performance evaluations, the likelihood at t_3 that p_1 will accept a given action opportunity and make a performance output is greater than the likelihood that p_2 will do so.

A large part of our initial work was devoted to development of an appropriate experimental task that had to meet different requirements from those met by previous laboratory tasks. Laboratory studies usually alter expectations by giving subjects false information. For example, subjects are given fictitious test scores or are led to believe that other subjects are disagreeing with them by means of apparatus that alters communications. All previous laboratory work and all teacher-expectancy studies mentioned earlier rely heavily upon the use of false information to alter expectations.

Using false information may be very effective and consequently useful for research purposes (especially in laboratory studies where the deception involved may be explained immediately afterward), but for repeated use in applied research false information is clearly not desirable. In studies where expectation states are raised, there are both practical and moral difficulties associated with the continued use of false information. For example, one would not wish to tell a child that he is bound to do much better than he has been because if the prediction fails he may suffer an impaired self-image. As for giving teachers false information, the Rosenthal and Jacobson studies have already received sufficient notice in the press so that teachers and principals nod smilingly if an investigation reports "new high test scores." In studies where expectation states are relatively lowered, as in some tracking studies, there are moral difficulties. No one would care to tell a child that he is likely to fail in the next semester or that he will not do as well as he hopes. Research in a naturalistic setting thus demands modification of the main experimental maneuver used in the previous laboratory work with the need to alter expectation states in some way *other* than the giving of false information.

After some pilot studies we decided upon the procedure described in what follows, a modification of a story-telling task previously used in research on cognitive development of children (Entwisle, Grafstein, Kervin, and Rivkin, 1970). One adult interacting with one child gives consistent positive evaluations of performance in a task where the child's actual ability is almost irrelevant. The evaluations are therefore not inconsistent with anything known about the child or with his potential. The aim of the maneuver is to raise the child's expectations. In addition to meeting the major criteria listed above, the pilot studies demonstrated that the task met practical criteria: (1) it provided discrete, easily observable performance outputs that permit clear evaluations, and (2) it was interesting enough to capture children's attention.

The experiment has three phases, corresponding to the three "times" referred to in the derivations. Phase I determines the "baseline" level of acceptance of action opportunities for both the "experimental" and the "control" groups. Children fill in words in a story skeleton and the experimenter is neutral. The experimenter notes who raises his hand as each word is called for. (The experimental and control groups correspond to individuals p_1 and p_2, respectively, in Derivation 2.) In Phase II, the attempt is made to manipulate upwards the self-expectations of children in the experimental group. One child (experimental group child) fills in words in a second story skeleton and is praised and encouraged by the experimenter after every word. The other children (control group) participate in a neutral procedure. Then the group of children (experimental and controls) is reassembled for Phase III and fills in a third story skeleton, with the experimenter again neutral and noting who raises hands.

To tie this back to the theory: the validity of Derivation 1 can be assessed by comparing the results of Phase I to Phase III for children in the experimental group. How well Derivation 2 is confirmed can be assessed by comparing results of Phase III for children in the experimental group with results of Phase III for children in the control group.

The basic experiment just described serves as the foundation for all empirical studies to be reported in this chapter, although modifications are introduced where necessary for purposes of studying the effects of new variables. Experiments have been classified into three "series," according to chronology and according to issues that emerged during the course of the research.

For the First Experimental Series, work is concerned with testing the task and experiment designed: would they work in the way we expected on the basis of the theory and laboratory studies? Would the children understand and be willing to participate in the research? Is the procedure simple enough that we could show others who have little interest in abstract theory or experimental design how to raise expectations? In order to gain information on these and other basic questions, we applied the procedure to as wide a range of subjects (white rural children; black inner city children) as initially possible, in the age range of some interest in expectation development (third and fourth grades).

The Second Experimental Series was conducted to expand downwards the age range to study earlier effects upon expectation state development, and white middle class children were the subject sample. This extension permits comparison with data from the First Series to assess the relative effects of status, race, age, and sex factors upon the processes.

The Third Experimental Series is addressed to "special problem" issues that arose in the earlier work: the effect of racial mismatch between source and child, the "debilitating effect of school" in forming low self-expectation states, the "contrast effect" in our expectation raising experiment, and an alternative "behavioral modification" interpretation of our experimental results.

III. FIRST EXPERIMENTAL SERIES

A. SUBJECTS

For the first set of studies, children were drawn from four schools in the Baltimore area, two inner city schools with nearly 100 percent black students, and two rural schools with nearly 100 percent white students. The rural schools are located in a farming district 30 miles north of Baltimore, near the Pennsylvania line.

For the two inner city schools, only students whose school records showed tested IQ scores between 90 and 110 were selected for the study. The IQ range for rural students is considerably larger, from 76 to 141, but the mean IQ is 105 for rural third graders and 108 for rural fourth graders. Experimenters were middle class white persons in the 20–30 age range, both sexes.

B. PROCEDURE

At the beginning of an experimental session, children were brought together and told that the researchers were looking for people who could tell good stories. They were to be divided into "teams" and were told that the team that made the best stories would win a prize. Then one experimenter took the members of each team to a separate room and described the story-telling task to them. Members of a team were chosen so that children on one team came from different classrooms.

Children were told that the "game" consisted of making up a story. The experimenter would help by starting sentences, but then the children should try to make interesting stories by supplying "good" words when asked for words for the story. In every phase the same story skeleton (see Figure 7-1) was used, and the skeleton contained twelve blanks. Children filled these blanks with twelve words or phrases.

THERE WAS ONCE A VERY TALL PRINCE WHO HAD A   (castle)

THAT (HE, SHE)   (lived in)

ONE DAY (HE, SHE) HAD TO GO TO   (the dungeon to see his prisoners)

(HE, SHE) DID THIS VERY   (angrily)

BECAUSE (HE, SHE) WANTED TO   (make sure they were there)

THIS WAS VERY DANGEROUS BECAUSE OF THE   (strong prisoners)

WHO (WHICH) WAS (WERE) VERY   (mean)

IN ORDER TO FOOL THE (FILL IN) THE (FILL IN) DRESSED UP AS   (another prisoner)

IN SUCH A DISGUISE THE (FILL IN) LOOKED   (mean)

AND WHEN THE (FILL IN) SAW THE (FILL IN), THEY   (welcomed him)

THIS MADE THE (FILL IN)   (feel pretty good)

AND   /COMPLETE STORY/   (he let his new friends go).

The experimenter chooses from alternatives in parentheses the item consistent with the story line. For example, in this story the pronoun "he" is chosen because it refers to "prince."

FIGURE 7-1
Story Skeleton with Sample Entries from a Rural Group

Children were told to listen carefully while the sentence was being read, then when the blank was reached, to try to think of a good word. Anyone who thought of a good word was to raise his hand, and the experimenter would select one child to give the "team's word" for that sentence. Children were cautioned not to raise their hands unless they thought they had a good word, for if they were called on and gave a bad word, this would hurt the team's score. The purpose of this instruction was to help maintain the task orientation and collective orientation required by the scope conditions of the theory. The experimenter allowed 30 seconds to elapse after reading a sentence before calling upon a child.

Before calling on a child, the experimenter recorded privately which children were holding up their hands (the measure used to determine the expectation state—acceptance of an action opportunity). The experimenter held a clipboard so that children could not see what was on it. The clipboard was used for recording words given by the children. During the 30-second waiting period, he made small marks indicating which children had volunteered without the students being aware of this.

Phase I consists of an initial story being produced as just described. The experimenter (E) does not evaluate any of the words given during Phase I. He calls upon each child in Phase I approximately the same number of times. With twelve blanks to fill in and with four children playing, each child can be called upon three times. In only a few instances did any child volunteer fewer than three times altogether and so unbalance the selection of respondents.

At the end of Phase I children are asked to return to the room where they initially assembled. After they begin to move out, E quietly tells one child (chosen because his level of hand-raising was near the median for the group) to stay in the experimental room and wait there a minute. After E makes sure that the control children are on their way to the proper destination, he returns to the room and to the selected (experimental group) child. E then tells the experimental child that he will have an opportunity to make up a story all by himself; also that E has played with many children making up stories and that E thinks he/she (the experimental child) is really good at the task. Then a story skeleton with a new lead word is filled in orally by the child, just as before, but of course with only one child producing the story there is *no* volunteering. The child merely supplies a word for the blank when the sentence is read by E. After each blank is filled, E indicates approval vigorously —by smiling, by nodding, by commenting "a very good word"—"good"— "that's interesting!", etc., that is, he indicates approval in every possible way consistent with sincerity.

Several experimental groups (four or five) were run simultaneously with an E for each group. A single coordinator for all the groups managed the initial explanation, story-reading for the Phase II control groups, and prize award sessions. When Phase II for the experimental child was complete, he went and joined the control children in their Phase II. Phase II for control group children is a story-reading session, and control children from several game groups gather in a central room as they finish Phase I to listen to the coordinator read a story. Children from the several experimental groups join the story-reading group (control groups, Phase II) as they finish their Phase II activities. The experimental children thus listen to the end of the story being read to the control groups. The experimental children's entrance is not noticeable because they join the story-reading group while the children's attention is directed toward the story teller. The story-reading prevents communication among the children during Phase II. At the end of the story-reading the children are asked to "go back to the room where you were before." *All* children thus return together. At this point E's are rotated among rooms so each E has a new group and is unaware of the identity of the experimental child. Phase III consists of a repetition of Phase I with the experimenter noting how many times each child volunteers to supply a word. The length of each phase varies, as would be expected, but the Phase II control procedure can adjust its length to the time requirements of each set of experiments.

At the conclusion of Phase III, the children are again brought together in a large group. One team is selected at random as having constructed the best team stories, and each member of the winning team is given a prize of a regular size candy bar. All other children are given a miniature candy bar, thanked for their help, and escorted back to their classrooms. Figure 7-2 summarizes the experimental design for all this research.

Results

Table 7-1 presents the gain in the number of times children in the control groups and in the experimental groups volunteered by raising their hands from Phase I to Phase III. (The mean *number* of times children raise hands in all groups is about 6.7 in Phase I.) A *t*-test of the mean gain of the experimental groups vs. the mean gain of the control groups is highly significant $(P(t_{270} \geq 3.17) < 0.01)$. Other *t*-values are displayed in the table for various subdivisions of the sample. It is noteworthy that in each stratum the gain for the experimental group exceeds the gain for the control group, even though not every individual comparison is statistically significant on *t*-test.

TABLE 7-1. Gains in Rate of Volunteering from Phase I to Phase III. (*N*'s in parentheses)

	Experimental Subjects		Control Subjects		Probability level, One-sided *t*-test of Differences between Experimental and Control Groups
All Black	(36)	+1.22	(108)	+0.64	N.S.
3rd Grade	(20)	+1.85	(60)	+0.88	N.S.
4th Grade	(16)	+0.44	(48)	+0.33	N.S.
All White	(32)	+2.28	(96)	+0.36	0.001
3rd Grade	(22)	+2.45	(66)	+0.56	0.001
4th Grade	(10)	+1.90	(30)	−0.07	0.025
Grand Total	(68)	+1.72	(204)	+0.51	0.001

The success of the story-telling task may also be assessed by noting the proportion of children in the experimental groups whose rate of hand-raising increased from Phase I to Phase III compared to the proportion in the control group (Table 7-2).

The *t*-tests assess the magnitude of the gain but this increase could come about because some children's rates increased markedly even though others did not. By examining the proportion of children who gain, one has information on the consistency of the effect. Proportions in the experimental groups consistently exceed proportions in the control groups. The overall proportion

TABLE 7-2.   Percentage of Persons Showing Gains from Phase I to Phase III.

	Experimental Subjects	Control Subjects
All Black	68	53
3rd Grade	78	68
4th Grade	56	33
All White	86	55
3rd Grade	89	61
4th Grade	80	43
Grand Total	76	54

of children gaining in the experimental groups is 76 percent, compared to 54 percent, just about chance level, in the control groups.

Thus the predictions of Derivations 1 and 2 are in general borne out by the results of the research. The data of Tables 7-1 and 7-2 show that the procedure apparently produced increases in expectation states, as measured by acceptance of action opportunities, although success was much greater with white children than with black children.

C. ASSESSMENT OF FIRST EXPERIMENTAL SERIES

In the First Experimental Series, 76 percent of the children who received the experimental treatment showed the desired increase, a significant gain when compared with that made by control students. Operationally the experimental procedure was a success. From a practical standpoint, the procedures were simple and easy to use. Field notes indicate that the children found the task involving and enjoyable and were highly motivated to succeed at it.

Variability in gains resulting from using this experimental procedure deserves some comment. (The black children have already been commented upon.) As a child grows older, his expectations for his general performance level at most tasks probably crystallize. Thus a greater increase for third graders than for fourth graders in both the control and experimental groups is not surprising. In fact such considerations led us to select third and fourth graders initially rather than older children who might have been preferable as subjects on other grounds. It also led to our extending the age range downward as reported in the next section (Second Experimental Series).

As mentioned earlier, maneuvers that give fictitious results to students or to teachers have drawbacks. Such maneuvers may be defended when they are one-shot procedures to demonstrate self-fulfilling prophecies, placebo effects, and the like, or when they are needed to allow quick and sizeable manipulation of variables in the laboratory. But such maneuvers are not defensible over the long term. They are not even viable when the goal is to change children's long-range expectations for themselves or others' expectations for children in classroom settings. If one goal of education is expectation alteration, then ways of altering expectations must be found that are compatible with other educational goals and that are suitable over the long term. The procedure described here has achieved modest success along these lines.

Besides the practical and educational criteria considered above, one must also evaluate the procedure in terms of its ability to operationalize the variables of the theory. Probably both "experimenter effects" and unintended biasing arise. Third, and perhaps most important, the question of alternative interpretations may be raised. Does Expectation States Theory provide the best context for interpreting the present results? We will now analyze these three questions in turn, and in the section on "Special Control" experiments we will reconsider them in the light of additional data.

(1) *Experimenter effects* were equalized insofar as possible. First, E's were trained to treat the children as equally as possible in Phase I and to refrain from evaluating any performances. The child selected as the "experimental" child at the end of Phase I was chosen on the basis of his having responded close to the median for his group. To choose a child with too *low* a response rate in Phase I might have biased results in favor of predictions through a "regression to the mean" phenomenon in Phase III. To choose a child with too *high* a response rate in Phase I would have biased results against predictions, because of a "ceiling effect."

To avoid drawing attention to the child selected to participate in Phase II, E did not say anything to that child until the children were on their way to the other room for Phase II; nor did the E explain at all to the others why this child was asked to remain behind. In most cases the fact that one child remained behind was apparently not noticed.

In addition, the control children were occupied at similar tasks in Phase II. *All* children were with an experimenter during Phase II, because control children were with the research coordinator in a story-reading session. The experimental group children participated in at least part of the control treatment because they joined the story-reading group as they finished the Phase II experimental treatment.

(2) *The issue of biasing* is troublesome, for even a slight change in a teacher's manner will change a child's disposition to raise his hand. Therefore, a number of steps were regularly taken to minimize bias from E. The major danger of biasing would come in Phase III, however, when E might respond more warmly or more positively to the "experimental child" than to the others. This child might also feel that because of the individual session with E in Phase II he (the child) had some "special" relationship with E. In order to minimize problems of this nature, E's were rotated before the beginning of Phase III. Thus the E was new to the entire group in Phase III, unfamiliar to both the experimental and control children. Furthermore, the *E did not know at this point which child had been given the Phase II "treatment"* and thus was

unlikely to treat the children differentially. In Phase III, as in Phase I, E's are trained to call on every child the same number of times insofar as this is possible.

(3) *Alternative interpretations* of experimental results are relatively easy to invent. Certainly we cannot rule out all competing interpretations for the results reported here. It seems difficult, however, to contrive an explanation that accounts for *all* our results, as well as for work by others mentioned earlier, as satisfactorily as Expectation States Theory. Suppose, for example, the effect of the treatment of the experimental group child in Phase II was to offer additional practice in story telling, and that practice *per se* increased the child's confidence in his ability to tell stories. This would imply that the strongly positive Phase II evaluations were unimportant, and possibly that the level of expectations in Phase III was irrelevant to behavior (hand raising) as well. But the task was selected partly because it calls for no special ability; it certainly is not one that can be "improved" through practice. Without evaluations from E, children have trouble deciding whether their words are "good ones"; children's remarks in the "unevaluated" Phase I point to this. So practice as an explanation is not appealing.

The results, by way of another example, might be accounted for by seeing the Phase II procedure as *reinforcement of behavior* rather than *positive evaluation*. The experiment might be seen as demonstrating that children will increase the rate of emission of behaviors that have been rewarded in the past. In assessing the reinforcement explanation, the reader should note carefully that our measure of expectation states in Phase I and Phase III was rate of volunteering, or *hand raising*. What were positively evaluated in Phase II were *words spoken* by the children. At no time during the experiment was anyone positively evaluated (or reinforced) for hand raising, the measured behavior. Positive evaluation (or reinforcement) was *never* given for hand raising because during the Phase II experimental treatment the child did not raise his hand. In the other phases when hand raising was occurring no evaluation (or reinforcement) was given. Furthermore, the specific words evaluated in Phase II were seldom the words volunteered in Phase III. Thus, a reinforcement explanation lacks force on analytic grounds; it requires making several tenuous interpretations of experimental variables, and making some rather complex assumptions about stimulus and response generalization.

Other research that explicitly measures children's expectations by using a kind of self-rating scale is consistent with our results. Expectations are seen to increase following approval and positive evaluation by an adult, but are unchanged when an adult maintains a neutral role (Hill and Dusek, 1969; Crandall, 1963; Crandall, Good and Crandall, 1964). The actual procedure used by Hill and Dusek was very similar to our own, for an adult responded "That's good. Fine. Very good. You're doing well" for positive evaluations following attempts at an angle-matching task. The adult was neutral and nonresponsive for the nonevaluative condition (like our Phase I and Phase III procedure). Other studies, also consistent with the conclusion, show that if an individual gets approving reactions from others with respect to some specified attribute, he will improve his self-rating on that attribute (Maehr, Mensing, and Nafzger, 1962; Videbeck, 1960).

IV. SECOND EXPERIMENTAL SERIES

The overview of the first set of classroom studies is encouraging, both in terms of procedure development and theory application. The Second Experimental Series aimed to extend the age range and dealt with middle class children. We wished to determine the age limits within which experiments would be robust and wished to see whether sex and race subgroups responded differentially to the procedure (hinted at by the apparently lower susceptibility of black children). Also, of course, further experiments provide replication of earlier work.

A. SUBJECTS

The experimental procedure already described was used with a sample of children from a white middle class suburb of Baltimore. There were approximately equal numbers of boys and girls, with 79 first graders, 84 second graders, 112 third graders, and 103 fourth graders. Insofar as possible, the four members of each experimental group were chosen from different classrooms. Some of the grades were distributed among four classrooms, some among only three. In the latter case, two children were taken from a single classroom, and the remaining two from two other classrooms.

B. RESULTS

For this and later experiments, we now change the method of reporting results and report results of analyses of variance. With a factorial design where treatment (experimental vs. control), grade, and sometimes residential locus are considered to be three fixed-effect factors, the data can be revised to yield proportional subclass numbers by randomly discarding some experimental groups. One second-grade group, eight third-grade groups and six fourth-grade groups were therefore eliminated using a random process before analyzing the data shown in Table 7-3.

TABLE 7-3.   Average Gain in Rate of Volunteering From Phase I to Phase III, White Middle Class Students (N's in parentheses)

	1	2	3	4	Av.
Experimental Group	1.20	2.55	1.85	1.85	1.86
	(20)	(20)	(20)	(20)	(80)
Control Group	0.67*	0.67	1.20	1.38*	0.98
	(59)	(60)	(60)	(59)	(238)
Difference Between Groups	0.53	1.88	0.65	0.37	0.88

*This mean is based on 59 rather than 60 observations.

Table 7-3 shows the mean gain in rate of volunteering from Phase I to Phase III by grade and sex for treated (experimental group) and untreated (control group) middle class children. Groups are approximately balanced for sex. Three sorts of changes in the dependent variable are reflected in this table. First, all experimental and control groups show some increase in rate of volunteering. Second, for all grades the increase is greater for children in the experimental group than for those in the control group. Third, second graders show the greatest difference between the experimental and control conditions. These results all are consistent with results of the First Experimental Series.

The analysis of variance in Table 7-4 based on gains in rate of volunteering from Phase I to Phase III reveals a significant treatment effect ($p < 0.05$), no significant grade differences, and no significant grade x treatment interaction.

TABLE 7-4.   Analysis of Variance for Gain in Rate of Volunteering, White Middle Class Students. (Approximately balanced for sex)

Source	d.f.	Sum of Squares	Mean Square	F-value
Experimental vs. Control Treatment	1	46.81	46.81	6.02*
Grade	3	22.42	7.47	0.96
Treatment × Grade	3	20.27	6.76	0.87
Within Treatment × Grade Groups	310†	2409.70	7.77	

*Beyond the 5 percent level
†Two observations are missing, estimated by subclass means.

It is of interest to combine data from third- and fourth-grade white middle class subjects of this experiment with the rural and inner city data discussed in the First Experimental Series. To do this, the earlier data have also been reduced by randomly discarding six black inner city fourth-grade groups and two white rural third-grade groups (see the data summarized in Table 7-2 vs. data of Table 7-6). Some of the fourth-grade subjects included in Tables 7-3 and 7-4 have also been eliminated randomly.

For the combined subjects of the First and Second Experimental Series, the treatment effect is again judged highly significant ($p < 0.01$). There is no evidence here that the effect of the treatment is different by grade or residential locus, since none of the interactions of treatment with any other factor is significant.

TABLE 7-5. Average Gain in Rate of Volunteering From Phase I to Phase III, for Children from Three Residential Loci, Grades 3 and 4 (N's in parentheses)

Residential Locus	Suburban		Inner City		Rural	
Grade	3	4	3	4	3	4
Experimental Group	1.85	2.20	1.85	1.90	2.60	1.90
	(20)	(10)	(20)	(10)	(20)	(10)
Control Group	1.20	2.07	0.97	0.20	0.57	−0.07
	(60)	(30)	(60)	(30)	(60)	(30)
Difference Between Groups	0.65	0.13	0.88	1.70	2.03	1.97

The combined data show that expectations were raised significantly in experimental children compared to control children, and as shown in the other analyses (Entwisle and Webster, 1973a), residential locus probably does not affect susceptibility to treatment (no $T \times R$ interaction).

TABLE 7-6. Analysis of Variance for Gain in Rate of Volunteering; Three Residential Loci; Two Grades

Source	d.f.	Sum of Squares	Mean Square	F-value
Treatment (T)	1	110.21	110.21	14.75*
Residential Locus (R)	2	43.62	21.81	2.92
Grade (G)	1	0.87	0.87	0.12
$T \times R$	2	22.21	11.10	1.49
$T \times G$	1	0.50	0.50	0.07
$R \times G$	2	35.77	17.88	2.39
$T \times R \times G$	2	2.27	1.14	0.15
Within T, R, G Subgroups	347†	2593.15	7.47	

*Beyond the 1 percent level
†Two observations are missing; estimated by subclass means.

C. DISCUSSION

The results of the Second Experimental Series extend the positive findings of the First, since white middle class children also respond to the experimental procedure by increasing their rate of hand raising. Although there are other groups that could be studied (for instance black middle class), the range of children already included suggests that the phenomenon is replicable and fairly general. The parallels are clear between the experimental task, completion of a story under the experimenter's direction, and many tasks overseen by teachers in classrooms. Expectation States Theory has, then, at least some relevance to elementary education.

The significance of social status in this study differs from its significance in earlier Expectation States Theory work. Generally, previous status characteristics research has been concerned with the effect of *differential status in assignment of power and prestige within a small group.* E. G. Cohen (1968, 1970), for example, has studied mixed groups of black and white boys attempting to solve a problem together, to see who makes more performance outputs. In the laboratory, Webster (1970) has studied the effect of status characteristics on the effectiveness of evaluators; performances were monitored by evaluators of high status (college students) or of low status (eighth graders). In both E. G. Cohen's and Webster's studies, it has been shown that the status characteristic will, under certain circumstances, lead to differential conceptions of ability in accord with the different states of the diffuse status characteristics.

The focus of the present work differs. Here we have groups, all of whose members are *equal* with respect to a status characteristic (such as sex, age, and race). The question is whether expectations will be raised to the same extent for members of each status group. Can expectations of rural children be increased as easily as expectations of inner city children, for instance? The intent is thus to look at the "demography" of expectation raising, particularly for the kinds of children—rural or inner city—who are often classed as low achievers. This experimental treatment for modifying children's expectations has worked with children from three very different residential settings and no significant differences by residential locus have appeared. The effect has been greatest for rural students and the suburban second graders, but not significantly greater (no significant treatment $\times$ locus interaction). So far age does not appear to be important in expectation raising, although only for one group (middle class) has age been sampled over any sizeable range.

More work is needed, however, to increase confidence that groups are as homogeneous as suggested here. For one thing, over the grade school years there are rapid shifts in children's interests and capabilities, so that a task suitable at one level may be inappropriate, or relatively ineffective, at other levels. The present research assumes that the group is collectively oriented and seriously motivated towards high performance of the task at hand. Partial failure to meet these conditions would attenuate any observable effects of expectations, or of our attempted experimental manipulations.

V. THIRD EXPERIMENTAL SERIES

The focus of concern in the First Experimental Series was task development and general feasibility of the research program. The Second Experimental

Series focused upon determining the generality of the effect across societal status groups. In the Third Series we were concerned with pursuing some suggestions, and also possibly problems, that grew out of the earlier experiments. Some instances of possible refractoriness to the expectation-raising treatment had occurred and these deserved more study. In addition, alternative interpretations of the results could be investigated with further work.

In studies reported to this point two kinds of children are not very responsive to the treatment: inner city black children and white middle class girls of third and fourth grades. The results for inner city children have already been discussed at some length. The lack of response in middle class girls has not been obvious to the reader because it was not possible to include sex as a factor in the analysis. The reader will note, however, in Table 7-7 where the full set of data for third- and fourth-grade suburban children is presented and tabulated by sex, that boys show sizeable increases and girls actually show decreases.

TABLE 7-7. Average Gain in Rate of Volunteering From Phase I to Phase III for White Suburban Children, Third and Fourth Grade. (N's in parentheses)

| | Girls | | | Boys | |
Experimental	Control	E-C	Experimental	Control	E-C
		Grade 3			
0.36	0.86	−0.50	2.29	0.71	1.58
(14)	(42)		(14)	(42)	
		Grade 4			
1.08	1.46	−0.38	1.86	0.52	1.34
(12)	(35)		(14)	(42)	

Also, during the experiments the experimenters observed that the white middle class girls were particularly withdrawn and unresponsive. We therefore performed two replications.

1. In the first replication we returned, exactly one year later, to the inner city schools where we had conducted the first experimental series with black children. On the return visit we employed only black female experimenters. Everything else in the replication including time in the school year, was the same as in the First Series.
2. The second replication study consisted of experiments with only girls of the third and fourth grades in a white middle class suburban school. The school where the replication was carried out was different from the school in the Second Series, but was very much like the Second Series school in social class and other characteristics. (Further work could not be done in the first school because all students had already participated.)

A.   BLACK INNER CITY REPLICATION

Two general lines of thinking seem to be consistent with the relatively lower efficacy of the experimental treatment for inner city black students. The first, which we may call the "debilitating effect of school hypothesis," holds that an important outcome of school for black children is to lower their self-confidence and self-evaluation. We speculate that as black children go through the grades, they receive predominantly negative evaluations of performances, and consequently become progressively more certain that they will fail at anything they attempt. They come, in other words, to hold self-expectation states that are fixed and low. If such effects have been building up over several years in school, our experimental procedure may be just too weak or too short in duration to produce any marked expectation raising with these children. The fact that effects of the procedure vary inversely with school grade for all three status group samples in the First and Second Experimental Series is consistent with the idea that expectation states become more difficult to modify as children become older.

An entirely different explanation is suggested by the work of Katz and his associates (1968, 1970), who present indications that white adults are perceived as hostile by some black children, and that when white examiners test black children, the children often assume that they are being compared to white children. In the former case, our white experimenters may not have been accepted as "sources" by the children; that is, as "significant others," whose evaluative opinions are accepted by them. In the latter case, we would expect that children would form low self-expectations because of the inferred comparision to white children who possess higher diffuse status, in the manner described theoretically by Berger et al. (1966), and documented with grade school children by E. G. Cohen and her associates (1970).

One way to distinguish between these competing explanations is to repeat the earlier research using black experimenters. If the "debilitating effect of school" is the explanation, then black experimenters should also be ineffective in raising expectations of black children. If racial mismatch was the problem, then black experimenters should be effective.

For this series, black women, students at a nearby college, served as the E's. As already mentioned, the schools selected for the experiments were the same inner city schools as those used the previous year. Students were all black fourth graders, the most resistant group in the earlier study, and also the group best suited for distinguishing between the competing explanations. Of course they were not the same students as those who had previously participated.

Table 7-8 shows the gain scores for children using this sample and the black experimenters. Control group children show an average gain of 1.82, and the average gain in the experimental group is 3.37. A *t*-test of the difference in gains is significant beyond the 5 percent level.

TABLE 7-8.   Average Gains in Volunteering ; Black Ss ; Black Es

Group	n	Gain
Experimental	57	+3.27
Control	19	+1.82

Black experimenters were thus successful in producing a gain in the rate of volunteering of black children. In previous data for inner city blacks with white experimenters, gains were not significant (see Table 7-1).

A number of reasons could account for the discrepant results of the two experiments with black inner city children. The most appealing reason is the racial difference in experimenters from the first experiment to the second, but a much more tightly controlled set of experiments is required to rule out other explanations. The experimental procedures, for example, were considerably refined by the time of the repeat experiments. Also, the black E's were probably more alike and more uniformly skillful than the E's used in the First Experimental Series. Nonetheless, significant differential gains are seen in a subgroup that previously had not manifested significant gains, and this argues once more for the general effectiveness of the experimental procedure.

Temporarily being less cautious, we note some suggestions based upon these results and the ideas mentioned earlier from Katz's work. This work indicates that some E's may not possess the necessary attributes to serve as effective sources. Attributes of a source, besides higher status (white skin color and/or age) or higher ability, reflect on that source's effectiveness as a purveyor of expectations, no doubt. Perhaps some sources can never achieve complete credibility for some subjects even though the status or ability criteria are met. An example will make this clearer. Suppose two social scientists are colleagues, and one is highly eminent and nationally known, whereas the other has only a local reputation. The eminent colleague is disposed never to criticize and always makes favorable comments about the work of his local colleagues. In this situation the less widely known social scientist will not weigh very heavily any favorable remarks from his eminent colleague because he sees very little variation in the tenor of the eminent colleague's remarks; no matter what occasions them, they are always positive. The eminent colleague does not possess credibility in the sense we have used the term even though his status and other attributes, as well as his positive remarks, meet the surface conditions of serving as a source. In the same vein, if black children interact mostly with adults (white teachers who elect to work in the ghetto) whose strong tendency may be to remain pleasant and to refrain generally from negative evaluations, such adults may lose credibility as sources for raising expectations.

The issues here are undoubtedly complex. Studies by Katz and his associates (see Katz, 1970) suggest that a black examinee's perceived probability of a successful performance on a test is apparently determined by his beliefs about the reference group he is being compared with—if black comparison groups are explicitly mentioned, the black examinee does best with a white administrator. In our use of white E's with black S's in the First Experimental Series, the children might have assumed they were being compared with other children (mostly white) whom the white E had dealt with in the past. In this case, following the line of reasoning suggested by Katz's work, the probability of success perceived by black children may have been low.

In applied work the characteristics of a source that makes him effective at raising expectations may be a research issue of high priority. Teachers, for example, of the same ability (educational level) and status are notoriously variable in their influence on students. One thing making a teacher effective may be ability of the teacher to hold and to convey high expectations about students. A teacher's high expectations for a student may be a powerful inducement for the student to enter a high expectation state for his own performance.

B. SUBURBAN FEMALE REPLICATION

At the beginning of this section (see Table 7-7) it was noted that third- and fourth-grade suburban girls actually decrease their rate of volunteering from Phase I to Phase III. When these data are pooled with other suburban data and sex is not included as a factor in the design, increases in other groups are sufficient to mask this finding. Overall there is a significantly larger gain score for experimental subjects versus control subjects in spite of the negative gains observed for these girls. Since research in an early stage, like the exploratory studies presented in this chapter, cannot be entirely insensitive to patterns in the data, we obtained permission to run an additional fifteen experiments ($n = 60$) with third and fourth grade *girls only* at a suburban school much like the one enrolling the suburban children of the Second Experimental Series. These results are shown in Table 7-9.

TABLE 7-9.   Average Gains in Volunteering; White Suburban Female Subjects; Grades 3 and 4

Group	n	Gain
Experimental	15	+1.80
Control	45	+1.49

For experimental group girls in this replicating experiment, the mean gain in rate of volunteering from Phase I to Phase III is 1.80; for control group girls it is 1.49. The difference, 0.31, is not significant on t-test. Our tentative conclusion is, therefore, that the present procedure has not been effective for third and fourth grade white suburban girls, although we now believe it is probably effective for all other groups, if races of experimenters and subjects are matched.

What factors could account for the sex difference in effectiveness? It is thought that boys, more often than girls, are blamed or criticized by teachers of elementary school (Brophy and Good, 1969, 1970). Because of this, the expectation-raising procedure of Phase II may be considerably more effective for boys than for girls. Boys who hear consistent praise during the experiment may be contrasting it with a background before the experiment of little positive evaluation. Girls, on the other hand, who apparently are seldom subjected to blame or criticism, could interpret the expectation raising maneuver of Phase II as a continuation of positive evaluations they have been receiving all along. Or, since girls generally do well in elementary school compared to boys, their expectations for performance at verbal tasks may already be at an asymptote so that attempts to raise expectations further are fruitless. Our data do not allow a choice between these explanations.

C. SPECIAL CONTROL EXPERIMENTS

In assessing the basic experimental procedure tested in the First Experimental Series, we concluded that the Expectation States Theory interpretation of the results was more plausible than alternative interpretations. The most reasonable alternative interpretation seems to be one that asserts that the experimental procedure produces increases in hand raising, not because of any improvement of the child's expectation state, but rather because of rewarding features of the Phase II situation. The alternative interpretation consists of one or both of two basic arguments: (1) experimental group children are responding to the situational rewards of receiving extra attention from an adult during Phase II; (2) experimental group children gain confidence through the additional practice of constructing an additional story during Phase II. Either or both of these elements can then be combined with implicit assumptions about behavior reinforcement to explain the increased hand raising observed for experimental group children, *without* any reference to expectation states or any change in the child's cognitions about his ability.

To provide empirical information relevant to the behavioral reinforcement interpretation of all these experiments we decided to conduct a set of experiments for which special controls were devised. In this set of experiments, two of the four children in each group were treated separately during Phase II. One child made up a story and received positive evaluations, exactly as the experimental group child had in all previous experiments. The other child, whom we shall call the "special control group" child, made up a story alone with an experimenter, but did not receive the positive unit evaluations of words. The experimenter for this group was neutral, nonevaluative; the child's words were received and written down silently, and the experimenter attempted to avoid any verbal or facial expressions of either approval or disapproval. Experimenters rotated among phases of the experiment so the experimenter effects would be balanced. Experimenters were unaware of the identity of either the experimental or special control child in Phase III.

Treatment of the special control group children thus incorporates the "special attention" and "practice" features of the experimental group treatment, but omits the positive unit evaluations that the theory asserts are essential in this situation for producing expectation state changes.

Subjects for this set of experiments were third graders at the white, suburban school used for the Second Experimental Series. Table 7-10 presents the mean gain scores from the control, special control, and experimental group children.

TABLE 7-10.   Average Gains in Volunteering; Special Control
Group Experiments

Group	n	Gain
Experimental	22	1.36
Special Control	22	0.00
Control	44	−0.18

$P_{(exp>special\ control)} < 0.05$

The control and special control groups both show essentially zero changes. The experimental group shows a gain in hand raising whereas the special control group does not ($p < 0.05$).[1] The data support the predictions of Expectation States Theory and do not support an explanation based on "special attention" and "practice" arguments. It may also be noted that the special control group children did not show a marked drop in rate of volunteering, as would be expected if they had interpreted the experimenter's behavior as hostile, negatively reinforcing, or negatively evaluative. As mentioned, experimenters for this set were carefully trained to be nonevaluative in Phase II. We conclude, both on the basis of theoretical analysis and empirical evidence, that the Expectation States Theory interpretation of the results of our experiments is most satisfactory.

[1] Recent work by Professor Barbara Sobieszek at the University of Rochester has produced results consistent with the results of this experiment. Subjects receiving differential amounts of action opportunities randomly allocated by the experimenter did *not* use this to form differential expectations for ability, even though this was the only differentiating information available to them under laboratory conditions. This result, obtained under conditions more highly controlled than ours, increases confidence in the results of the special control group experiments. We thank Professor Sobieszek for making these results available to us prior to publication.

VI. EDUCATIONAL IMPLICATIONS OF RESEARCH TO DATE AND FUTURE WORK

To place in perspective the work reported in this chapter, it must be seen for what it is intended to be: a *first step* towards applying some of the basic concepts and assumptions of the propositions of Expectation States Theory to naturalistic settings. Such attempts involve a large number of operational and procedural difficulties. To our knowledge, the only other sustained attempt to apply concepts and assumptions from Expectation States Theory for practical ends in educational research is represented by the work of E. G. Cohen and her colleagues (1968, 1970). These investigators also report difficulties with task development and experimental design like those encountered in our research program.

Despite some difficulties, it does seem possible, using relatively simple techniques, to intervene in a natural situation and to change the expectations of children so as to affect their subsequent behaviors in ways that should further educational goals. (See also Entwisle & Webster 1972, 1973*a*, 1973*b*.) Work of the Cohen group similarly suggests that it may be possible to overcome the negative effects of being black in producing differential performance expectations in mixed racial groups of grade school children.

A. RELATION TO TEACHER EXPECTANCY RESEARCH

Results of teacher expectancy studies have been disputed in some cases (see Barber and Silver, 1968) and unequivocally negative in others (Claiborn, 1969; Jacobs, 1969). The range of results of our own experiments points to possible sources of difficulty in the teacher expectancy work. First, while most children show slight increases in performance outputs even without much encouragement (the control groups), some children fail to manifest increases in performance even with extensive positive evaluations. Earlier we pointed out that white experimenters may not be able to provide very effective evaluations for black children. More recent work (Entwisle & Webster, 1973*b*) suggests that racial mismatch between adults and children is complex in its effect, interacting with social class as well.

Second, Expectation States Theory assumes a task orientation on the part of students and our experiment assumes a task where ability is equal or irrelevant. Both assumptions may be violated often in the teacher expectancy work, for many school children have little ego involvement in academic pursuits, and many already have firm ideas about their own level of ability. To the extent that children have access to objective standards or to alternative others for evaluating their performances, we would expect that the teachers' expectation for them would decrease in importance.

A third point, made by Claiborn (1969), is that there may be no changes in teacher–pupil interaction—no classroom analogue of our Phase II treatment. If teachers perceive pupils to be of high potential, teachers may alter their behavior, but teachers vary in how they change their behavior to suit children's ability (Kranz, Weber, and Fishell, 1970). For example, Kranz et al., show that some teachers behave similarly towards high- and average-ability children but differently towards low-ability children. If, as in most teacher expectancy experiments, a teacher is given false reports about students' potential, she might or might not change her behaviors toward the designated children depending upon how her own behavior pattern is expressed. Also, of course, since expectations typically flow from evaluations, which in most classrooms are expressed by peers as well as by teachers, changing expectations of only the teacher may not be sufficient to produce changes in children's self-expectations. Recent work by Cohen and Katz (1972) shows that expectations of both white children and black children of a work group must be molded if black children are to improve performance.

Perhaps what is needed most at this point is more fine-grained analysis of exactly what behaviors accompany changed expectations. Our own work is one approach to this. Other approaches besides those already mentioned include Meichenbaum et al.'s observations that expectancy instructions (identification of "late bloomers") cause some teachers to increase positive interactions with students, or to decrease negative interactions.[2] Positive interactions included conveying encouragement, praise, or any attitude of satisfaction. Also Brophy and Good (1970) observe that teachers tend to praise more those children for whom they hold high expectations, and to demand more in the way of performance from them.

One of the major results of this work is the experimental task itself. It offers a means of manipulating (raising) young children's expectations without the drawbacks that affected ways of manipulating expectations used previously. The behavior influenced—frequency of hand raising—is generally considered to be important educationally. Hand raising leads to greater participation. The importance of active participation to learning is too well known to require documentation. In future reports, we hope to study further how this procedure affects racial, age, and SES subgroups of the population. Further work will extend the basic experimental design to examine the relation between expectation change and structural variables like sociometric standing.

Also, further work will study students' expectations for academic performance as a function of their own feedback over time. What happens, for

---

[2] In other instances when expectancy or teacher expectancy experiments have failed to achieve results that were anticipated (Goldsmith, 1970; Fleming and Anttonen, 1970) an analysis of findings in terms of Expectation States Theory may be helpful. For example, it may be that the teacher does not alter expectancy because the students do not accept the validity of the teacher's expectations.

example, to a child's high expectations for himself when he gets a low evaluation (bad report card) from a teacher? If a child has low expectations for
himself, and his parents have high expectations for him, how does his classroom behavior evolve?

What is the potential of this kind of research for educational purposes?
There is value first of all, in making explicit parallels between social psychological research and research in classrooms. As has been so frequently noted,
there is a surprising gap between these two fields of research that hinders both.
By linking classroom research to a body of pre-existing theory, one gains
coherence and explanatory leverage on a whole body of research findings.

The experimental maneuver reported here may not be potent, by way of
long-term educational effects, however. The present procedure, as earlier
pointed out, does have the distinct advantage of avoiding the use of false test
scores or of any form of outright deception. It also has the advantage of
working directly on a child's expectations rather than on the expectations of
some other person for the child. It is difficult, however, to imagine using a
maneuver like the one described here over and over to obtain broad effects in
raising children's expectations. This procedure may nevertheless have useful-
ness over the short term in two ways:

1. The procedure may act as a pump primer. If a child's expectations for
    himself are suddenly raised, as in the experiment, he may alter his actions
    for a short time in ways consistent with his increased expectations for
    himself. Any intervention within the circular series of events—improved
    self-expectations leading to better performance leading to improved
    teacher evaluations—may be effective. The short-term change in a child's
    actions induced by an expectation raising procedure might thus fire a
    chain reaction that would tend to continue once started.
2. This procedure and others that could be invented may give precise sug-
    gestions as to how teachers can convey positive expectations. Some teach-
    ers may wish to convey positive expectations but not be very adept at
    it. The suggestion here is that praise for one activity (word giving) leads
    to an increased level of another activity (hand raising) at a later date. In
    classrooms where many activities occur, then, the teacher need not wait,
    perhaps in vain, for a praiseworthy performance in arithmetic to improve
    a child's expectations for himself in the area of arithmetic. If the child
    can be encouraged for one sort of performance this may generalize to
    yield increased participation across the board. In fact, some situations
    may be used primarily to improve expectations rather than for learning
    per se.

The results of the Special Control Group experiments indicate quite clearly
that it is the unit evaluations that determine children's expectations, or at
least that by comparison with other features of the situations, such as being
given action opportunities and special attention, the unit evaluations are far
more important. An important extension from this is that one means that

might be thought to raise children's expectations—calling upon them more often—probably is ineffective. This conclusion may be counterintuitive in some cases, for it might be thought that if the teacher calls upon certain children more frequently this would indicate to them that she thinks highly of their answers.

However, as was shown in the Special Control Group experiment, this "special attention" or differential allocation of action opportunities is probably ineffective in changing expectations. Thus, in order to apply the results of our experiments to raising children's expectations, it is important to bear in mind that calling on the selected children more frequently will not by itself improve their expectations greatly. What is probably required is to *praise* their responses, to give them extensive positive evaluations of their performances.

To summarize results at this stage of our research, we review the three general goals adopted at the outset. First, we hoped to apply a formal theory to analyze interaction in classrooms, particularly what has been called the "teacher expectancy effect," and to show that some of the previous results in this area could be incorporated into the scope of Expectation States Theory. Second, we hoped to develop techniques of intervention that would induce specific changes in classroom interaction to improve children's learning. Third, we needed to develop a task—the story telling game—that could be used easily and effectively. The overall results of our experiments indicate some success in meeting these goals.

More specifically, the experimental results showed increases in expectations for all groups except white, middle class female third and fourth graders, and, initially, black third and fourth graders. In the case of the black children, an additional set of experiments suggested that the earlier failure to produce results may have stemmed from racial mismatch between experimenters and children (white experimenter, black children). Preliminary experiments suggest that another kind of racial mismatch (black experimenters, white children) will *not* vitiate the procedure—black experimenters may turn out to be more generally effective across all kinds of subgroups of children than white experimenters. Research with black experimenters and white children and with racially mixed (black-white) groups is now commencing. We are also observing teachers in classrooms to get information about how teachers "naturally" convey expectations, and about how other students convey expectations. The effect of the treatment was greatest for rural children, perhaps because they attend schools where few breaks in the routine occur. The schools are in remote areas, and so are seldom included in research studies or special programs. Other schools where this research was carried out are almost continually involved in activities initiated by persons not on the regular staff. Thus the urban and suburban children may be more "sophisticated" in terms of serving as research subjects and less susceptible to any attempted treatment.

Further work in this program may be organized into three general categories. First, we are working to develop additional tasks that may be used in the research. It seems desirable to develop tasks unrelated to academic activity, for example, athletic tasks and social or leisure-time tasks such as hobbies. Second, we hope to be able to study factors that govern how successful the intervention is. For example, sex of the experimenters may have a differential effect, and probably operates in rather complex ways involving cross-sex and same-sex combinations. Factors of a different kind such as the centrality of sociometric ranking of the children and their average level of performance in school may also be related to expectation raising. Third, we hope to design studies based upon other aspects of the theory. One such study springs from Assumption 3, which asserts that action opportunities and evaluations will be *distributed* in accordance with expectations held for *others*. In some cases, perhaps when children are interacting together in the absence of an adult, the assignment of an action opportunity may be equivalent to the voicing of a positive evaluation.

	Phase I	Phase II	Phase III
Control *S*'s	one story is produced (12 words); no evaluations; level of volunteering observed	control *S*'s have story read to them by another adult, from 12 to 15 control *S*'s join in one group	repeat Phase I, with same control *S*'s and experimental *S*'s as in Phase I; experimenters are rotated so the experimenter is unaware of identity of experimental *S*'s
Experimental *S*'s	one story is produced (12 words); no evaluations; level of volunteering observed	experimental *S*'s make up story individually with the same experimenter they have seen in Phase I; receive all positive evaluations; experimental *S*'s join control *S*'s at end of this phase	repeat Phase I, with same control *S*'s and experimental *S*'s as in Phase I; experimenters are rotated so the experimenter is unaware of identity of experimental *S*'s

FIGURE 7-2
Summary of experimental procedure

Formal Statement of Propositions

DEFINITION 1

A situation is task-situation S if and only if it contains:

a. at least two actors, p and o, making performance outputs;
b. an actor, e, making unit evaluations of those performance outputs;
c. no previous expectations held by p and o of their own or each other's abilities at the task;
d. task orientation of all actors;
e. collective orientation of all actors.

DEFINITION 2

e is a *source* for p in task-situation S if and only if p believes that e is more capable than p of evaluating performances.

ASSUMPTION 1

In task-situation S, if e is a source for p, then p will agree with e's unit evaluations of any actor's performances.

ASSUMPTION 2

In task-situation S, if p evaluates a series of performances of any actor, then he will come to hold an expectation state for that actor which is consistent with those evaluations.

ASSUMPTION 3

In task-situation S, if p holds higher expectations for any actor o_1 than for another actor o_2:

a. p will be more likely to give o_1 action opportunities than o_2;
b. p will be more likely to evaluate positively o_1's future performance outputs than o_2's;
c. in case of disagreement between o_1 and o_2, p will be more likely to agree with o_1;
d. p will be more likely to accept o_1 than o_2 as a source.

ASSUMPTION 4

In task-situation S, the higher the expectations an actor, p, holds for self relative to the expectations he holds for o:

a. the more likely is he to accept a given action opportunity and make a performance output;
b. in case of disagreement with o, the more likely is he to reject influence.

REFERENCES

BARBER, J. and M. SILVER. 1968. Fact, fiction and the experimenter bias effect. *Psychological bulletin* 70: part 2.

BROPHY, J. E., and T. L. GOOD. 1969. Teachers' communication of differential expectations for children's classroom performance: some behavioral data. *Report no. 25*. The Research and Development Center for Teacher Education, The University of Texas at Austin.

BROPHY, J. E., and T. L. GOOD. 1970. Teachers' communication of differential expectations for children's classroom performance. *Journal of educational psychology* 61: 367–74.

CLAIBORN, W. L. 1969. Expectancy effects in the classroom: A failure to replicate. *Journal of educational psychology* 60: 377–83.

COHEN, E. 1968. Interracial interaction disability. Unpublished research report, School of Education, Stanford University.

COHEN, E. G., M. LOHMAN, K. HALL, D. LUCERO, and S. ROPER. 1970. Expectation training I: Altering the effects of a racial status characteristic. *Technical report no. 2*. School of Education, Stanford University.

COHEN, E. and M. KATZ. 1972. Personal communication.

CRANDALL, V. C. 1963. *National society for study of education yearbook*.

CRANDALL, V. C., S. GOOD, and V. J. CRANDALL. 1964. Reinforcing effects of adult reactions and nonreactions on children's achievement expectations: a replication study. *Child development* 35: 485–97.

ENTWISLE, D. R., and M. WEBSTER. 1972. Raising children's performance expectations. *Social science research* 1:147–58.

ENTWISLE, D. R., and M. WEBSTER. 1973a. Status factors in expectation raising. *Sociology of education* 46:115–126.

ENTWISLE, D. R., and M. WEBSTER. 1973b. Expectations in mixed racial groups. *Sociology of education,* in press.

ENTWISLE, D. R., D. GRAFSTEIN, J. KERVIN, and M. RIVKIN. 1970. Giant steps: a game to enhance semantic development of verbs. *Report no. 81*. Center for Study of Social Organization of Schools, Baltimore, Md.: The Johns Hopkins University.

FLEMING, E. S. and R. G. ANTTONEN. 1970. Teacher expectancy or my fair lady. Unpublished paper presented at the annual meetings of the American Educational Research Association.

GOLDSMITH, J. S. 1970. The effect of a high expectancy prediction on reading achievement and IQ of students in grade 10. Unpublished M. Ed. thesis, Rutgers University, New Brunswick, N. J.

HILL, K. T. and J. B. DUSEK. 1969. Children's achievement expectations as a function of social reinforcement, sex of S and test anxiety. *Child development* 40: 547–57.

JACOBS, J. F. 1969. Teacher expectancies: their effect upon peer acceptance. Mimeograph. University of Florida, Gainesville, Florida.

KATZ, I. 1968. Factors influencing Negro performance in the desegregated school. In *Social class, race, and psychological development*, eds. M. Deutsch, I. Katz, and A. Jensen, pp. 254–89. New York: Holt, Rinehart and Winston.

———. 1970. Experimental studies of Negro-White relationships. In *Advances in experimental social psychology*, vol. 5, ed. L. Berkowitz. New York: Academic Press.

KRANZ, P. L., W. A. WEBER, and K. N. FISHELL. 1970. The relationship between teacher perception of pupils and teacher behavior toward those pupils. Paper presented at American Educational Research Association meetings, Minneapolis, Minn.

MAEHR, M. L., J. MENSING, and S. E. HAFZGER. 1962. Concept of self and the reactions of others. *Sociometry* 25: 353–57.

MEICHENBAUM, D. H., K. S. BOWERS, and R. R. ROSS. 1969. A behavioral analysis of teachers expectancy effect. *Journal of personality and social psychology* 13: 306–16.

ROSENTHAL, R. and L. JACOBSON. 1968. *Pygmalion in the classroom.* New York: Holt, Rinehart and Winston.

ROSENTHAL, R., and D. RUBIN. 1971. Pygmalion reaffirmed. Mimeograph. Department of Social Relations, Harvard University (July). Prepublication version of an invited contribution to the volume *Pygmalion reconsidered.* National Society for the Study of Education.

VIDEBECK, R. 1960. Self-conception and the reaction of others. *Sociometry* 23: 351–59.

WEBSTER, M. 1970. Status characteristics and sources of expectations. *Report no. 82.* Center for Study of Social Organization of Schools, Baltimore, Maryland: The Johns Hopkins University.

APPENDIX

A Bibliography of Expectation States Research

This is a specially prepared, *selected* bibliography on expectation states research. It includes published and unpublished research papers and manuscripts that have either arisen out of or are directly relevant to the expectation states research program.

ASKINAS, B. E. 1971. The impact of coeducational living on peer interaction. Unpublished Ph. D. dissertation, Department of Sociology, Stanford University.

BALKWELL, J. W. 1969. A structural theory of self-esteem maintenance. *Sociometry* 32 (December): 458–73.

BERGER, J. 1958. Relations between performance, rewards, and action-opportunities in small groups. Unpublished Ph. D. dissertation, Department of Social Relations, Harvard University.

———. 1960. An investigation of processes of role-specialization in small problem-solving groups. Proposal funded by The National Science Foundation (July).

BERGER, J., and J. L. SNELL. 1961. A stochastic theory for self-other expectations. *Technical report no. 1*. Laboratory for Social Research, Stanford University.

BERGER, J. and M. ZELDITCH, JR. 1962. Authority and performance-expectations. Mimeograph. Department of Sociology, Stanford University.

BERGER, J., B. P. COHEN, and M. ZELDITCH, JR. 1966. Status characteristics and expectation states. In *Sociological theories in progress*, vol. I, eds. J. Berger, M. Zelditch, Jr., and B. Anderson, pp. 29–46. Boston: Houghton Mifflin Company.

BERGER, J., B. P. COHEN, T. L. CONNER, and M. ZELDITCH, JR. 1966. Status characteristics and expectation states: a process model. In *Sociological theories in progress*, vol. I, eds. J. Berger, M. Zelditch, Jr., and B. Anderson, pp. 47–73. Boston: Houghton Mifflin Company.

BERGER, J., and T. L. CONNER. 1966. Performance expectations and behavior in small groups. *Technical report no. 18*. Laboratory for Social Research, Stanford University.

BERGER, J., M. ZELDITCH, JR., B. ANDERSON, and B. P. COHEN. 1967. Status conditions of self-evaluation. *Technical report no. 24*. Laboratory for Social Research, Stanford University. Revised version is *Technical report no. 27*, February, 1968.

BERGER, J., and T. L. CONNER. 1969. Performance expectations and behavior in small groups. *Acta sociologica* 12: 186–97.

BERGER, J., T. L. CONNER, and W. L. MCKEOWN. 1969. Evaluations and the formation and maintenance of performance expectations. *Human relations* 22 (December): 481–502.

BERGER, J., and M. H. FISEK. 1969a. An extended theory of status-characteristics and expectation-states. Mimeograph. Department of Sociology, Stanford University.

———. 1969b. The structure of the extended theory of status characteristics and expectation states. Paper presented at the 15th Annual meeting of the Small Groups Conference. Seattle, Washington, April 23.

244

————. 1970. Consistent and inconsistent status characteristics and the determination of power and prestige orders. *Sociometry* 33 (September): 278–304.

BERGER, J., M. H. FISEK, and P. V. CROSBIE. 1970. Multi-characteristic status situations and the determinations of power and prestige orders. *Technical report no. 35.* Laboratory for Social Research, Stanford University.

BERGER, J., M.H. FISEK, and L. FREESE. 1970. Paths of relevance and the determination of power and prestige orders. Mimeograph. Department of Sociology, Stanford University.

BERGER, J., B. P. COHEN, and M. ZELDITCH, JR. 1972. Status characteristics and social interaction. *American sociological review* 37 (June): 241–55.

CAMILLERI, S. F., and J. BERGER. 1967. Decision-making and social influence: a model and an experimental test. *Sociometry* 30 (December): 367–78.

CAMILLERI, S. F., J. BERGER, and T. L. CONNER. 1972. A formal theory of decision-making. In *Sociological theories in progress*, vol. II, eds. J. Berger, M. Zelditch, Jr., and B. Anderson. Boston: Houghton Mifflin Company.

COHEN, B. P. 1968. Status and conflict: a sociological perspective on the urban race problem. *Stanford today* (Summer/Autumn), series I, no. 24, pp. 10–14, Stanford University.

COHEN, B. P., J. E. KIKER, and R. J. KRUSE. 1969a. The use of closed circuit television in expectation experiments. *Technical report no. 29.* Laboratory for Social Research, Stanford University.

————. 1969b. The formation of performance expectations based on race and education: a replication. *Technical report no. 30.* Laboratory for Social Research, Stanford University.

COHEN, B. P., J. BERGER, and M. ZELDITCH, JR. 1972. Status conceptions and interaction: a case study of the problem of developing cumulative knowledge. In *Experimental social psychology*, ed. Charles G. McClintock, pp. 449–83. New York: Holt, Rinehart and Winston.

COHEN, B. P., J. BERGER, and M. ZELDITCH, JR. *Status conceptions and power and prestige.* Research monograph. In preparation.

COHEN, B. P., and HANS E. LEE. Forthcoming. The effects of social status upon conflict resolution. Research monograph.

COHEN, E. G. 1968. Interracial interaction disability. *Technical report no. 1.* School of Education, Stanford University.

————. 1970. Interracial interaction disability. In *A new approach to applied research: race and education*, pp. 98–117. Columbus, Ohio: Charles E. Merrill.

COHEN, E. G., M. LOHMAN, K. HALL, D. LUCERO, and S. ROPER. 1970. Expectation training I: altering the effects of a racial status characteristic. *Technical report no. 2.* School of Education, Stanford University.

COHEN, E. G. 1971. Interracial interaction disability: a problem for integrated education. *Urban education*, January, pp. 336–56.

COHEN, E. G., S. ROPER, and D. LUCERO. 1971. Modification of interracial interaction disability through expectation training. Read at American Education Research Association Meeting, New York, February.

COHEN, E. G. 1972. Interracial interaction disability. *Human relations* 25, no. 1, pp. 9–24.

CONNER, T. L. 1965. Continual disagreement and the assignment of self-other performance expectations. Unpublished Ph. D. dissertation, Department of Sociology, Stanford University.

————. 1972*a*. A continuous time, discrete state Markov model of performance expectations and behavior in small groups. *Technical report no. 8.* Department of Sociology, Michigan State University.

————. 1972*b*. Performance expectations and initiation and receipt of task related behavior in open interaction settings. *Technical report no. 9.* Department of Sociology, Michigan State University.

COOK, K. 1970. *Training manual for conducting expectation states experiments.* Laboratory for Social Research, Stanford University.

DEAL, T. E. 1971. An experimental attempt to offset the effects of a diffuse status characteristic in decision-making groups. Unpublished Ph. D. dissertation, School of Education, Stanford University.

ENTWISLE, D. R., and M. WEBSTER, JR. 1970. Raising children's expectations for their own performance. *Report no. 87.* Center for Social Organization of Schools, The Johns Hopkins University.

ENTWISLE, D. R., L. CORNELL, and J. EPSTEIN. 1971*a*. The principal as the S. O. B. Mimeograph. Department of Social Relations, The Johns Hopkins University.

————. 1971*b*. The effect of a principal's expectations on test performance of elementary-school children. Mimeograph. Department of Social Relations, The Johns Hopkins University.

ENTWISLE, D. R., and M. WEBSTER, JR. 1972*a*. Raising children's performance expectations. *Social science research* 1 (June): 147–58.

————. 1972*b*. Raising expectations in the classroom. Paper presented at the 1972 Eastern Sociological Society meetings, Boston, Mass.

————. 1972*c*. Teacher expectancies and student expectation states. Paper presented at the 1972 Pacific Sociological Association meetings, Portland, Oregon.

————. 1972*d*. Status factors in expectation raising. Paper presented at the 1972 meetings of the American Sociological Association, New Orleans.

————. 1973. Research note: status factors in expectation raising. *Sociology of education* 46 (Winter): 115–26.

EVAN, W. M., and M. ZELDITCH, JR. 1961. A laboratory experiment on bureaucratic authority. *American sociological review* 26 (December): 883–93.

FARARO, T. J. 1968. Theory of status. *General systems* 13: 177–88.

————. 1970. Theoretical studies in status and stratification. *General systems* 15: 71–101.

————. 1971. Macro-status and micro-status. Paper presented at American Sociological Association meetings, Denver, Colo.

————. 1972. Status and situation: a formulation of the structure theory of status characteristics and expectation states. *Quality and quantity: the European journal of methodology* 6: 37–98.

————. 1973. An expectation-states process model. In *Introduction to mathematical sociology.* New York: Wiley-Interscience. (forthcoming).

FISEK, M. H. 1968. The evolution of status structures and interaction in task oriented discussion groups. Unpublished Ph. D. dissertation, Department of Sociology, Stanford University.

FISEK, M. H., and R. OFSHE. 1970. The evolution of status structures. *Sociometry* 33 (September): 327–46.

FOSCHI, M. 1968. Imbalance between expectations and evaluations. Paper presented at the Canadian Sociology and Anthropology Association meetings, Calgary, Canada.

———. 1970. Contradiction of specific performance expectations: an experimental study. Unpublished Ph. D. dissertation, Department of Sociology, Stanford University.

———. 1971. Contradiction and change of performance expectations. *Canadian review of sociology and anthropology* 8: 205–22.

———. 1972. On the concept of "expectations." *Acta sociologica* 15: 124–31.

———. 1972. The formation of performance expectations: a test of a conceptualization. Presented at the West Coast Conference for Small Group Research, Portland, Oregon, April.

FOSCHI, M., and R. FOSCHI. 1972. Expectations, contradictions, and the revision of subjective probabilities. Paper presented at the Canadian Sociology and Anthropology Association meetings, Montreal, Canada.

FREESE, L., 1970. The generalization of specific performance expectations. Unpublished Ph. D. dissertation, Department of Sociology, Stanford University.

KERVIN, J. B. 1972. An information processing model for the formation of performance expectations in small groups. Unpublished Ph. D. dissertation, The Johns Hopkins University.

LEE, H. E. 1967. A mathematical study of decision processes. Unpublished Ph. D. dissertation, Stanford University.

LEWIS, G. H. 1966. Performances, evaluations and expectations: an experimental study. Unpublished Ph. D. dissertation, Department of Sociology, Stanford University.

———. 1971. Performances, evaluations and expectations. Read at the West Coast Conference for Small Group Research, Honolulu, Hawaii.

LOHMAN, M. R. 1971. Changing a racial status ordering by means of role modeling. Unpublished Ph. D. dissertation, School of Education, Stanford University.

———. 1972. Changing a racial status ordering—implications for desegregation. *Journal of education and urban society* 4 (August).

MAYER, T. F. 1967. A continuous model for influence processes in small groups. Unpublished Ph. D. dissertation, Department of Sociology, Stanford University.

MCKEOWN, W. L. 1971. Development of conceptions of relative ability in task performing groups. Unpublished Ph. D. dissertation, Department of Sociology, Stanford University.

MOORE, J. C., JR. 1967. General status characteristics and specific performance expectations. Unpublished Ph. D. dissertation, Department of Sociology, Stanford University.

———. 1968. Status and influence in small group interactions. *Sociometry* 31 (March): 47–63.

———. 1969. Social status and social influence: process considerations. *Sociometry* 32 (June): 145–68.

OLIN, W. A. 1972. Decision-making, gain-loss theory, and the utility of self consistency. Unpublished Ph. D. dissertation, Department of Sociology, Michigan State University.

RAYMOND, P. H. 1971. Status and personality factors in inservice training groups. Project No. 141, General Research Support Grants Program, State of California Department of Public Health.

REIMER, F. 1972. The contradiction of expectations based on specific and diffuse information. M. A. thesis, Department of Anthropology and Sociology, University of British Columbia.

ROPER, S. S. 1971. The effect of race on assertive behavior and responses to assertive behavior in small groups. *Technical report no. 6.* School of Education, Stanford University.

SAVAGE, I. R., and M. WEBSTER. 1971. Source of evaluations reformulated and analyzed. *Proceedings of the sixth Berkeley symposium on mathematical statistics and probability* 4: 137–41. Berkeley, Calif.: University of California Press.

SEASHORE, M. J. 1968. The formation of performance expectations for self and other in an incongruent status situation. Unpublished Ph. D. dissertation, Department of Sociology, Stanford University.

SHELLEY, R. K. 1972. Interpersonal influence and decision-making: monetary vs. non-monetary rewards. Unpublished Ph. D. dissertation, Department of Sociology, Michigan State University.

SOBIESZEK, B. I. 1970. Multiple sources and the formation of performance expectations. Unpublished Ph. D. dissertation, Department of Sociology, Stanford University.

―――. 1971. Alternative bases of source selection, *Canadian review of sociology and anthropology* 8.

―――. 1972. Multiple sources and the formation of performance expectations. *Pacific sociological review* 15 (January): 103–22.

SOBIESZEK, B. I., and M. Webster. 1972. Multiple sources and the absence of sources: a comparison and reformulation. Mimeograph. Department of Sociology, University of Rochester.

TRESS, P. H. 1971. Inconsistent status characteristics and influence processes: a replication and reformulation. *Technical report no. 6.* Department of Sociology, Michigan State University.

TRETTEN, R. W. 1970. Changing status space in Negro teacher-pupil interaction. Unpublished Ph. D. dissertation, Research and Development Center, Stanford University.

WEBSTER, M. A. 1967. The interaction control machines at the Laboratory for Social Research. Unpublished paper presented at the Small Group Session, Pacific Sociological Association meetings, April.

―――. 1969. Sources of evaluations and expectations for performances. *Sociometry* 32 (June): 243–58.

―――. 1970. Status characteristics and sources of expectations. *Report no. 82,* Center for Social Organization of Schools, The Johns Hopkins University.

WEBSTER, M. A., L. ROBERTS, and B. I. SOBIESZEK. 1972. Accepting "significant others": six models. *American journal of sociology* 78 (November): 576–98.

WEBSTER, M. A., and B. I. SOBIESZEK. 1973. *Sources of self-evaluation.* New York: Wiley-Interscience.

ZELDITCH, M., JR. 1969. Can you really study an army in the laboratory? In *Complex organizations,* 2d ed., ed. A. Etzioni, pp. 484–513. New York: Holt, Rinehart and Winston.

―――. 1972. Authority and performance expectations in bureaucratic organizations. In *Experimental social psychology,* ed. C. G. McClintock, pp. 484–513. New York: Holt, Rinehart and Winston.